Global capitalism
Theories of societal development

The global capitalism of today demands a re-examination of societal development. In *Global Capitalism*, Richard Peet surveys the various approaches made by social theory towards seeing history in terms of its regional dynamics. He reviews environmental determinism, and modernization, dependency and world systems theories, and argues that the most capacious and dynamic model continues to be historical materialism.

The book presents a broad outline of global development through time, analysing primitive communism, lineage societies and the various kinds of tributary modes, and providing a closer examination of capitalism in terms of the phases and forms of its past and present. The author defends the centrality of structural Marxism to theories of global development, and argues that its ideas can be furthered by the partial synthesis of other perspectives, such as the feminist critique.

This book assumes no previous knowledge of the theories surveyed. It introduces complex material in an understandable form, and will be valuable both to development professionals and to anyone interested in societal change.

Richard Peet is Professor in the Graduate School of Geography at Clark University, Massachusetts. He was editor of *Antipode: A Radical Journal of Geography* for fifteen years, and has worked and lived in England, the United States, Australia, the Pacific Region, southern Africa and the Caribbean.

Global capitalism /
Theories of societal development

Richard Peet

London and New York

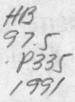
First published 1991 by Routledge
11 New Fetter Lane, London EC4P 4EE

Simultaneously published in the USA and Canada
by Routledge
a division of Routledge, Chapman and Hall, Inc.
29 West 35th Street, New York, NY 10001

Typeset by Pat and Anne Murphy, Highcliffe-on-Sea, Dorset
Printed and bound in Great Britain by
Biddles Ltd, Guildford and King's Lynn

British Library Cataloguing in Publication Data

Peet, Richard *1940–*
    Global capitalism: theories of societal development.
    1. Capitalism. Socioeconomic aspects
    I. Title
    330.122

    ISBN 0–415–01314–3
    ISBN 0–415–01315–1 pbk

Library of Congress Cataloging-in-Publication Data

applied for

For Kathy Jo Olsen

Contents

Tables

Figures

Acknowledgements

The origins of this book lie in a joint course I taught with Kirsten Johnson at Clark University. Its main ideas were discussed, criticized and strengthened by several generations of students in courses which developed subsequently. In particular I have benefited from conversations with a fine group of graduate students, of whom Brooks Bitterman, Tom Estabrook, Elaine Hartwick, Sheila Landsverk, Ann Oberhauser, Patricia Meono Picado, Jennifer Santer and Danny Weiner stand out. The 'Antipode group' were generally supportive even when we disagreed. Anne Gibson was more than helpful in drawing the maps and figures. Eddy the Cat was a good companion during long afternoons of otherwise solitary writing. But most important, in finishing the manuscript and enjoying doing so, was the loving friendship of Kathy Jo Olsen, to whom this book is dedicated as a token of appreciation.

Preface

The purpose of this book is simple indeed. It is intended as an introduction to theories of the development of global society giving particular attention to Marxist and neo-Marxist theories. The first chapters of the book discuss the claims and counter-claims made for theories of various political persuasion, while the latter chapters put radical theories into use by examining the broad outline of global development through time. The aim is to say a lot, in a short amount of space, about some significant aspects of societal development. An attempt is made to tell the tale in language comprehensible to the novice but still interesting for the specialist. Even so, this is a book to be perused slowly and thought about – skimmed quickly it will only give the reader a headache! Above all, the book is intended to be useful for popular self-understanding in the First and Third Worlds, the very point of explanation being an expansion of knowledge for guiding social change.

Writing a book on a broad topic like global development involves constantly choosing what to say and what to leave out. An author chooses to stress those things which seem significant – and significance depends on his or her beliefs and purposes. We humans have an inherent fascination with the nature of our being, with its change over time and variation through space. An essential part of being human is that we, for the first time in evolutionary history, are capable of controlling at least some of the main contours of our own development. The obstacles remaining in our path are no longer technological in form, but sociological and socio-geographical in content and shape. At the present time the main objectives of a politicized theorization are to extend the frontiers of democracy into every aspect of human existence, but especially into the factory and the family, to promote equality for all the people of the globe, especially those of the Third World, and to achieve harmonious relations between people and earth. These objectives require theories that are both deeply explanatory and liberative in intent. Indeed the needs which press from a world in crisis make anything less than a fundamental explanation ridiculously irrelevant.

Crises in social thought, such as those experienced in the 1980s, demand that we examine carefully some of the great ideas of the past, the validity of criticisms and claims for improvement and the potential for furthering certain lines deemed worthy of future interest. This author is disturbed by a tendency observable over the last decade for radical theories of great value to be criticized so much that they are virtually withdrawn from intelligent discourse. This particularly applies to structural Marxist ideas but extends to neo-Marxist notions like dependency theory. As part of the re-orientation of critical theory, the various aspects of human existence are conceptualized as separate and autonomous rather than interrelated and determined. This is convenient politically, for it allows a strategy willing partial change but with a general accommodation to the existing social order. It is part of a counter-current in 'radical' social thought which basically accepts what is and no longer dreams of what could be. This makes it strange indeed that structural Marxist and similar ideas have not been more vigorously defended, indeed furthered by incorporating the good arguments raised against them – the possibility of theoretical transcendence has been lost in the scrambling pragmatics of capitulation. This tendency is made especially tragic in that Marxist theories continue to demonstrate an ability to explain societal development which exceeds all previous systems of thought. It is time to counter this tendency by re-stating some of the themes of Marxist development theory, pointing again to the truths they contain, the events and characteristics they explain, and positing once more their potential for further elaboration. This project is made practically urgent by the continued poverty of the masses of people in the world, indeed by the intensification of impoverishment for hundreds of millions of people during recent supposedly beneficial changes in the Third World, such as the green revolution and the new industrialization. This is a time for reviewing what has been said about development, the changes suggested by valid criticisms, and where global development theory might go in the future. This book is intended as a small contribution to such a project.

Chapter one

Introduction

Social science tries to understand human life as it occurs in society. This entails looking at the human as an individual and the society as a collective entity, and at the relations between individuals and collective entities. Societies and human individuals vary greatly from one time and place to another. The causes of these variations are explored in this book.

This theme is examined from the point of view of geography. Even in Marxism, which claims to be a science of all human existence, there is a need to dwell on certain aspects of the whole life experience. Specialization has its rewards in allowing things to be seen from a particular vantage point and so allowing the more rapid advance of a part of knowledge. Geography actually looks at two aspects of life, which it claims are interrelated: the natural origins and relations of human existence and variations in the conditions of existence over earth space. The connection between the two is that spatial variations in social form are essentially different ways of transforming nature in the quest for human existence.

However, the problem with such academic specializations lies in relating fragmentary or aspect-biased disciplinary themes to an emerging whole system of understanding. A philosophy of social science can help with the linkages between themes derived from specializations. This eventually involves a structural understanding of the essential nature of life, its main activities, even life's 'purpose', if that term has not been hopelessly confused by religion. What essential activities must people engage in? Humans are natural beings who must, like all forms of organic life, reproduce their existence through fundamental activities like sex and labour. In particular, people act consciously and collectively to transform the environment into useful things needed in the material reproduction of existence. This essential activity provides a guide to the structural relations between the many activities and myriad

1

aspects of human existence. Knowledge of these aspects can then be integrated into an orderly synthetic science.

The mode of the production of existence (the character of its main forces, relations, institutions and thought patterns) varies over space. Most significantly, the degree of material development, particularly the standard of living, is completely different in one place and society from that in another. This entails different life-styles and life chances for individuals born at different locations on the earth's surface. Life is experienced as having some fundamental similarities with all other people, indeed with other organisms, but is also a definite version, or in the case of geography a place-bound version, of this entire existence. Real differences in the mode of life are what geography tries to understand as its specialization in social science.

Before this is pursued further perhaps we should also ask: what is science for? Why is it important that specialization yields insights? The reason could simply be to understand life better. But the answer given to the previous question of what activities are important suggests another answer here: the purpose of under-standing is to change the activities which make life impossible, or rather to improve them. Human beings are differentiated from the rest of nature mainly by consciousness and its application in guiding the reproductive process in a beneficial way. Humans thus have the potential to live well. But as we argued previously this potential is realized to differing degrees and in different ways, depending in part on the place in which life is conducted. The purpose of a geography of development thus becomes looking at the causes of material differences in order to change them, enabling more of the human potential to be realized, especially for people whose life chances are highly restricted (even eliminated) by scarcity. This is merely a more precise version of the purpose of science in general, that is to make the world a better place.

Relations between people and with nature are essential moments of the production of life. Unless we have been reduced to brutes by totally negative environment, we cannot avoid caring for, and feeling empathy towards, these essential conditions. The hard, practical edge is that if care is not taken of these original, essential parts of life – the natural environment and other people – problems arise which threaten the continuation of existence. The radical version of this sentiment involves realizing that material abundance for some derives from the destruction of nature and the deprivation of others. The central tenet of Marxism is that class systems essen-tially involve the exploitation of labour, so that many people work hard and long to support the high life-styles of a minority. And the main insight of underdevelopment theory is that rich people at one place live at the expense of environments and people in other places. With this realization, theory is driven by the search for social and spatial justice, an environmental ethic, and a moral desire to right practices which are obviously wrong. The geographic theory of development thus takes on political intent: in academia it becomes difficult for lecturers to retain their nuanced impartiality when speaking of regional differences, while students soon realize they are studying more than mere facts; in society at large understanding development becomes a source of self-criticism for the over-privileged, while for the oppressed majority, knowing the real causes of underdevelopment can be the mainspring of liberation.

Measuring the geography of development

The term 'development' refers to change in a complex of related features of social existence – economic, cultural and political. Change is in a positive direction, advance occurs, things are getting better over time. All these features need not change at the same time, nor even in the same direction – economic development can occur with cultural impoverishment – but the general direction has to be one of positive improvement for development to be said to occur. How is one change related to the others? Systems theory would say that the various aspects of change are related through feedback effects. Structural theory argues that change in one dimension determines the kind and degree of change in the others, so that total change occurs in an orderly way. Marxist structural theory takes the position that societal change is driven most essentially by the dynamics of the material production process, that is, by changes in the social relations and productive forces involved in the material transformation of nature. Economic development signifies a greater control over nature, gives a greater sense of controlling destiny, provides greater material inputs for supporting political power, enables cultural production at a higher level of material affluence, provides the space and time for intellectual activities, and in myriad other ways promotes socio-cultural change. All these features of a more advanced existence feed back positively on economic development – scientific thought, for example, promotes technological change – but structural Marxism maintains still that economic life continues to play the fundamental determining role.

Economic development in capitalist societies is conventionally measured as the size and rate of growth of the gross domestic product – that is the volume of the 'total final output of goods and services produced by an economy' (World Bank, 1989: 291); generally the higher the GDP per capita the more developed a country is assumed to be, and the higher the annual growth of GDP per capita the more rapidly a country is thought to be developing. In the late 1980s, the World Bank (1989: 159, 164–5) called forty-two countries 'low-income' because GDP per capita ('per capita income') is lower than $480, fifty-three countries are called 'middle-income' with GDP per capita in the $481–$5,999 range and twenty-five countries high-income ($6,000–$21,330). As shown by Table 1.1, 3,861 million people live in low- and middle-income countries (the 'Third World') where GDP per capital averages $700 a year (cf. Buchanon, 1980). By comparison 777 million people live in high-income countries (the 'First World') where GDP per capita averages $14,430. Furthermore, low- and middle-income countries have, for the last quarter-century, had a GDP per capita growth rate slightly higher (2.7 per cent a year) than the high-income countries (2.3 per cent a year). But this faster growth rate is attributable almost entirely to China's rapid growth (5.2 per cent) and to rapid growth (4–8 per cent) in a few industrializing and oil-exporting economies. Outside these growth centres, Third World economies are growing slowly (1.5–2.5 per cent a year) in terms of the products and services potentially available to each person. The table also shows other data frequently used to measure standards of living – life expectancy, calorie intake, infant mortality, population per physician, secondary education and use of commercial primary energy and electricity. The data confirm what is apparent from a superficial knowledge of the world: people living in different kinds of place live at entirely dissimilar material levels.

We should immediately note some problems with using this kind of official data. Not only do the data vary greatly in reliability from country to country, but their accuracy in measuring things like production, income, education or the use of energy is subject to suspicion. National and international agencies report only what can be measured using conventional accounting procedures. Whose 'convention' is conventional? – that of the First World market (capitalist) countries. Thus 'gross domestic product' (GDP) emphasizes that part of production which is sold for a price in a formal market, underestimating non-market production (i.e. products consumed within the family, or exchanged 'informally' – a major part of the economic activity ignored or underestimated is women's work (Rogers, 1980: 61)); education is measured in terms of enrolment in a 'school' and excludes informal educational institutions; energy consumption excludes 'traditional fuels' like firewood and dried animal excrement; and so on. Changes in GDP per

Table 1.1 Statistical indicators of economic development

	Population (millions) mid-1987	GDP per capita		Life expectancy at birth (years) 1987	Daily calorie supply 1986	Infant mortality (per 1,000 live births) 1987	Population per physician 1984	Percentage of age group enrolled in secondary education 1986	Energy consumption per capita (kilograms of oil equivalent) 1987
		Dollars 1987	Average annual growth rate 1965–87						
Low-income economies	2,822.9	290	3.1	61	2,384	76	5,410	35	297
China and India	1,866.1	300	3.9	65	2,463	62	1,640	39	390
Other low-income	965.9	280	1.5	54	2,227	103	13,550	25	116
Middle-income economies	1,038.5	1,810	2.5	65	2,855	56	2,390	54	1,077
Lower middle-income	609.6	1,200	2.2	64	2,777	61	3,330	51	867
Upper middle-income	432.5	2,710	2.9	67	2,970	50	1,170	59	1,392
Low- and mid-income economies	3,861.4	700	2.7	62	2,509	71	4,630	40	503
South Asia	1,080.9	290	1.8	57	2,228	102	3,570	32	183
Sub-Saharan Africa	441.7	330	0.6	51	2,101	115	23,760	16	82
East Asia	1,512.7	470	5.1	68	2,594	40	2,400	45	477
Latin America and Caribbean	403.5	1,790	2.1	66	2,701	56	1,230	48	1,071
Europe, Middle East and North Africa	389.6	1,940	2.5	64	3,177	65	2,440	56	1,204
High-income economies	777.2	14,430	2.3	76	3,375	10	470	92	4,953

Source: World Bank, *World Development Report 1989*: 164–227

capita, energy use, or education may merely reflect an increase in
the proportion of activity occurring in the market sector of an
economy rather than in the family or informal sector. Also GDP
measures quantitative change in market production but is a gross
indicator when it comes to the quality of 'development'. Finally,
and most significantly, average figures like GDP per capita, or
people per physician, hide great differences in distribution between
groups within countries, such as between classes, or between rural
and urban populations. Generally, Third World countries have
more unequal income distributions than First World countries in
terms of class and space. The poorest fifth of families receive 4.6
per cent of national income in the twenty-six low- and middle-
income countries for which data are available, while the poorest
fifth receive 6.5 per cent in twenty high-income countries (World
Bank, 1989: 222–3). The difference at the other end of the class
spectrum is even wider, with the richest fifth of families receiving
56.3 per cent of income in low- and middle-income countries and
40.4 per cent in high-income countries. Looking at another key
social indicator, the number of people per physician is 5,410 for all
low-income countries, but 77,360 for Ethiopia where, in addition,
most physicians practise in cities and towns – hence formally
trained physicians are effectively unavailable in rural Ethiopia. In
summary, the available data give only a poor and sometimes misleading indication of the level and movement of economic development if by this term we mean the material standard of living of an
entire people. However it remains the case that differences in living
standards between peoples with $700 a year and those with $14,000
are so profound, no matter how much the data are biased, that we
can proceed to theorize about entirely different regional levels of
development.

Accepting that the available statistical data give a poor repre-
sentation of reality we can proceed, with some trepidation, to look
at the broad patterns of development distributed across earth space.
Figure 1.1 shows countries (with highly simplified outlines) in
proportion to their populations and shaded according to the rate of
population increase. Figure 1.2 shows countries in proportion to the
size of GDP and shaded according to GDP per capita. Comparing
the two we can make a simple statement: the geographic distribution
of income across societies is more uneven than the most inegalitarian class structure in any one society. The high-income people of
the First World, constituting 15 per cent of global population, have
75 per cent of the world's income; the low-income countries of the
Third World, with 56 per cent of the global population, have less
than 5 per cent of the world's income; the remaining people and

Figure 1.1 The world according to population

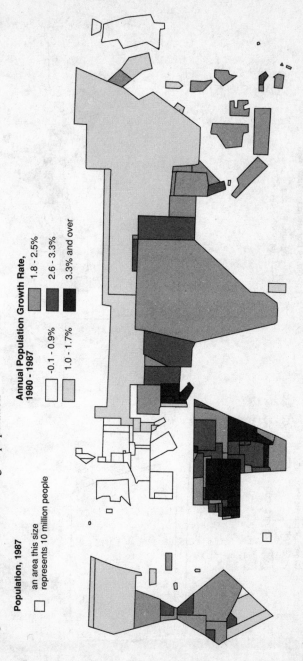

Population, 1987

☐ an area this size represents 10 million people

Annual Population Growth Rate, 1980 - 1987

☐ -0.1 - 0.9%

◻ 1.0 - 1.7%

▨ 1.8 - 2.5%

▨ 2.6 - 3.3%

■ 3.3% and over

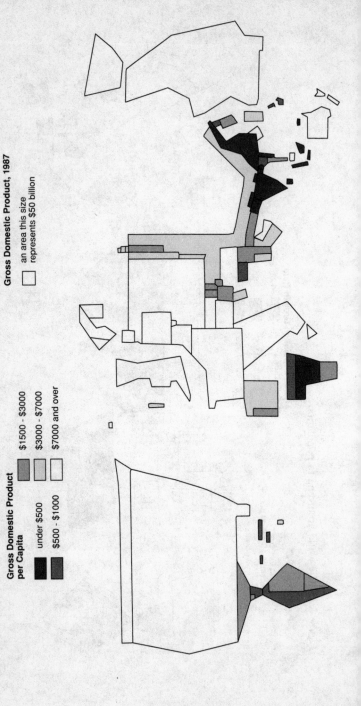

Figure 1.2 The world according to production and income

income are in the socialist Second World. This analogy with class in the distribution of income is not accidental: class processes yield dissimilar income levels within and between national populations; but at the global scale other 'geographic' processes further concentrate income in certain places – explaining the small size of Latin America, Africa, India and China in the GDP cartogram is impossible except in relation to the large size of western Europe and North America. Drawing these inferences together, an effective analysis of the global system of development has to involve a critical synthesis of class-type processes internal to societies and the spatial relations between societies.

The argument

This book tries to provide such an analysis by surveying some of the leading theories of societal development. The pattern of affluence and poverty which characterizes the contemporary geography of the globe was already obvious in the nineteenth century, and immediately stimulated intense social scientific interest. However, scientific interest is hardly separable from the desire for social legitimation (Peet, 1985a). A good theorist always intends rationality, logic and and the pursuit of truth. But the theorist's logical capability is not located in a sphere separate from an empathy for others, a desire for self-justification, or a wish to be of service to the dominant social order. The connections between science and values are especially evident when issues like the development of some people at the expense of others arise in the imagination. Theory easily diverts into ideology when the mind tries to comprehend scarcely comprehensible things like racism, imperialism, sexism and exploitation.

With such notions of ideology as partial and biased 'truth' in mind, we first survey two system-supporting theories of uneven development. Chapter 2 discusses how the first modern (late nineteenth-century) theories of societal development drew on evolutionary biology for explanatory power, essentially arguing that geographic differences in human achievement were the inevitable consequences of prior variations in natural environments. There were two versions of this idea: the strong (deterministic) thesis that nature creates people with unequal potentials of consciousness and effective action; and the weak (possibilistic) thesis that nature provides superior resource environments which permit easier or quicker development in some places. In concluding that the natural environment determines levels of development, both versions of the theory say that nature chooses who should be successful, while by arguing that the strong have to exploit the weak in order to survive, social Darwinism legitimated European imperialism as the inevitable consequence of natural history.

As all the world's people came to live in colonies or spheres of dominant Euro-American and Japanese influence, the urgency of a theory of natural inevitability declined. Social Darwinism dropped out of scientific favour (to be rejuvenated later as socio-biology), while environmental determinism was exposed as having no theory of society mediating the relation between nature, consciousness and action. Chapter 3 argues that structural functionalism, which became a leading theory of society in the 1940s and 1950s, also drew on Darwinian biology: the main functions carried out by all organisms are replicated by the sub-systems of society. Hence this theory postulates more complex social mediations between nature and human behaviour. Modernization theory applied this formulation to societal evolution, saying that modern forms of behaviour first appeared in the fifteenth and sixteenth centuries, and that subsequent development took the form of the growth and spread of modernism. Modernization geography thus explains regional variations in development in terms of the diffusion of modern institutions from originating cores. These originating cores 'just happened' (in Rostow's terminology) to lie in Euro-America. Modernization theory can thus be seen as continuing the ideological tradition of environmental determinism, this time justifying the post-war global hegemony of the United States. The events of the 1960s and early 1970s upset this political and ideological order. Thus structural functionalism was shown to lack an adequate connection between societal necessity and the choice of human action, while modernization theory was criticized and eventually rejected for claiming that only Europeans and North Americans are capable of initiating the development process.

From this point we concentrate on radical theories of societal development. The most powerful critique of modernization came from theorists schooled in a new dependency perspective emerging from the periphery. Dependency theory argues, on a neo-Marxist basis, that contact with the Europeans may indeed bring 'modern' elements to the societies of the Third World, but has also connected them to an exploitative social order. Modernism in the centre countries was achieved via class forms of exploitation leading to the concentration of wealth in the hands of a few; likewise the spread of 'civilization' to the periphery was accompanied by the extraction of social surplus. Instead of being developed ('modernized') in relation to their degree of connection with the centre of the global capitalist order, peripheral societies were underdeveloped in exactly that same degree. But dependency theory, and its elaboration as world systems theory, were in turn criticized. This time the main criticism, usually constructive, came from the left. Dependency theory, the critics said, focuses too exclusively on the external relations between societies without considering their internal class relations. This means that dependency can be made to serve the ideological function of justifying a change in external relations, like increased regional autonomy, without fundamentally changing internal social relations of exploitation. This is discussed futher in Chapter 4.

We turn next to structural Marxism, which also developed in the 1960s as a total critique of the entire capitalist system – class, spatial structure, culture and all. Marxism is a materialist understanding of societal structure which sees humans as active agents transforming nature through the labour process and achieving development through building the productive forces. However, the progress that has occurred takes place in class-divided societies, so that the material benefits of development are unequally distributed and class struggle forms the basis of the societal dynamic. Hence Marxism has a dialectical understanding of history, in which change stems from contradictions between human groups and between society and the natural world. Marxist structuralism sees new modes of production emerging from the contradictions in the old, maturing and spreading in space, bringing different types and levels of development. The idea of articulations (interpenetrations, combinations) between modes of production is therefore proposed as a way of understanding intersocietal contact which yields a richer version of the theory of underdevelopment than dependency theory. But in emphasizing class, Marxism has ignored gender relations. By listening to the feminist critique and changing, structural Marxism remains capable of providing the most coherent, insightful critical theory of societal structures and dynamics available at the present time. This is discussed at length in Chapter 5.

We could argue on epistemological grounds forever without resolving very much. So the following chapters explore the claims made for structural Marxism in the only really believable way – using its ideas in the interpretation of the history and contemporary geography of capitalism. The analysis is pursued at various levels starting at the most general and abstract and becoming more particular and empirical as the contemporary world is approached. Dialectical materialist knowledge knows no limits of history, for it sees things in terms of their origins, no matter how distant in time, and their subsequent interactive development, no matter how widely in space. Thus we cannot understand capitalism without knowing where, when and under what conditions there emerged social characteristics like class, gender inequalities and the state. Likewise we cannot understand capitalist development without contrasting it with the many forms of pre-capitalist development. Chapter 6 explores such issues by surveying Marxist, feminist and other critical theories of the pre-capitalist world.

More specifically, how did capitalism emerge and where did its main elements come from? Even Marxist theories are divided, between those stressing the originating power of external spatial relations and those stressing internal processes of change in social relations. The two dimensions of analysis are hardly separate – stressing class does not have to mean ignoring space. However, we follow Brenner (1977) in arguing that Europe developed because of the emergence of a new class system which necessitated efficiency and innovation. This argument is so convincing that we feel it has to be accepted as the basis of socio-spatial synthesis. This is discussed further in Chapter 7.

The growth of capitalism in Europe, and its subsequent spread to North America, Japan and beyond, can then be seen in terms of a series of contacts or articulations with the non-capitalist world. Capitalism is a self-expanding system, in terms of economic and technical growth, but also in the sense of geographical extension. Focusing on four great regions of pre-capitalist civilization, we follow the diverse history of capitalist spatial relations and articulations which, however, yield a common outcome – underdevelopment for the majority, development for the minority of the world's people. The several ways in which this common outcome emerged are discussed in Chapter 8.

Even a survey of theories, such as this, cannot encompass the variety of tendencies and events in the contemporary geography of global capitalism. A choice has to be made of what to pursue in any detail. At the expense of ignoring whole economic activities, like agriculture, and scarcely mentioning social dimensions, like culture, we focus on the leading question of the present day – can industrialization transform the Third World as it did the First? A review of Marxist theories and debates, especially of the neo-structuralist French regulation school, suggests a negative answer under the existing relations of production, but a possibly positive answer under different social relations. See Chapter 9 for the details.

Having used structural Marxist ideas to explain the origins, development and transformative potential of global capitalism, we return to questions of theoretical adequacy raised in Chapter 5. Marxism in general, and structural Marxism in particular, were widely criticized in the 1980s as theories of human society and as theories of unequal development. Post-structuralist notions stress contingency at the expense of structural determinancy; theories of modernism and post-modernism revive modernization theory in various new guises; the role of critical theory in making historical change is challenged by claims for a 'post-historical' world, one in which societal perfection has been reached in the form of liberal democracy. Notions such as these have to be seen for what they are, ideas with insight and some good intent, but serving the ideological role of disguising the continuation of an unequal capitalist development which starves people in Africa, uses women as expendable, cheap labour in East Asia, and plunges Latin American societies into debt which cannot be repaid. We find a continued need for a structural understanding of global capitalism, think that the critique of structural Marxism was really a critique of its rationalist excess, and conclude that rumours of the death of Marxism are premature. Mode of production analysis remains the most insightful critical theory of the historical process of development, and democratic socialism remains the best hope for a form of development which will meet human needs in the future. Structural Marxism should not ignore its critics and should incorporate their insights, so Chapter 10 expands the analytical category mode of production in the direction of the concept of of a mode of *re*production which includes gender and natural relations as essential components of societal structure and dynamics. Such a concept, we conclude, continues the progress already achieved towards making a science of society.

Finally the author's belief that theory is not made from the exercise of logic alone, but reflects the theorist's moral reaction to the world, emerges in a brief epilogue on the ethics of societal development. Readers who think that Marxism is the dismal science of political dinasaurs might glance at this last chapter first.

Chapter two

Environmental determinism

Profound differences in material standards of living and levels of development between regions point to basic characteristics of nature, people, society or historical process as essential causes. The task of critical analysis is to find and examine these causal characteristics. Pragmatic reasons of effective policy formation demand an accurate understanding of development. Perhaps an even more important reason, giving urgency to this task, is the frequently asserted association between the level of material existence and human worth, particularly when racial or ethnic characteristics are associated with levels of economic development – for example, when skin colour and poverty are correlated. Even the victims of poverty may begin to accept that their personal characteristics are the underlying cause of the material quality of their lives. Finding the true causes of underdevelopment is thus necessary for correcting arrogance and aiding the achievement of human dignity.

What does this imply for a critique of the existing theories of development? The only theories worth examining in detail are those linking development with fundamental characteristics of nature, people or society. These theories must be examined critically in a way that reveals their underlying politics and biases as well as their logical consistency and empirical validity. Also, as fundamental theories, they should be ransacked for the good ideas or true insights they contain. Theories that linger probably confirm people's prejudices; but they also probably contain some truth, or at least have a viewpoint that has merit. We should try to find these truths and combine them into a science of development.

For most people in the past, and for many people today, the causes of differences in level of development are unproblematic. God makes 'men' with different qualities which they display in their works. The different 'works' (i.e. material accomplishments) confirm God's intent. This tautology remained sufficient until the idea that 'God makes man' was challenged by Charles Darwin's (1859) theory of natural selection in the mid-nineteenth century. Darwin made human advancement contingent on competitive success and natural advantage. The question remained, however, what were the origins of competitive advantage? 'God' was no longer sufficient in a Victorian age characterized by materialism and scientific rationality, although the idea that God was the original maker of the earth left open the possibility that 'He' may have implanted advantages in its natural structure.

Organismic theory

A solution was proposed by the English philosopher Herbert Spencer. By analogy, he argued, the biological principles of organismic evolution apply also to the development of the 'social organism'. Just as animals derive advantages from their relationship with nature, so societies occupying different natural environments are differently endowed in the struggle for survival. Rich natural environments enable high population densities, increased specialization and division of labour, greater political size and armed might – what he calls 'superorganic' evolution – and in turn the attainment of civilization. Societies go through life cycles, the young conquering the old, with the whole process of survival of the fittest leading towards an eventual utopian paradise characterized by high levels of development and the pursuit of culture (Spencer, 1882).

Spencer's ideas were extremely significant in middle to late nineteenth-century social thought, especially in the United States (Hofstadter, 1955). Environmental determinism, the leading school of geography in the late nineteenth and early twentieth centuries, was profoundly influenced by Spencer's ideas. In the work of Ellen Churchill Semple, for example, the natural environment determined people's racial qualities, their consciousness, productivity and level of economic development (Semple, 1911). Like Spencer she believed that Europe's physically articulated yet protected regions were environments conducive to high population densities and the growth of civilization. But as a North American she also believed that frontier conditions have a stimulating effect on the 'Anglo-Saxon race', fostering democracy and entrepreneurship. Like most environmental determinists, she fully supported imperial conquest and economic domination by powerful nations (Semple, 1903).

Figure 2.1 Huntington's map of the distribution of human energy

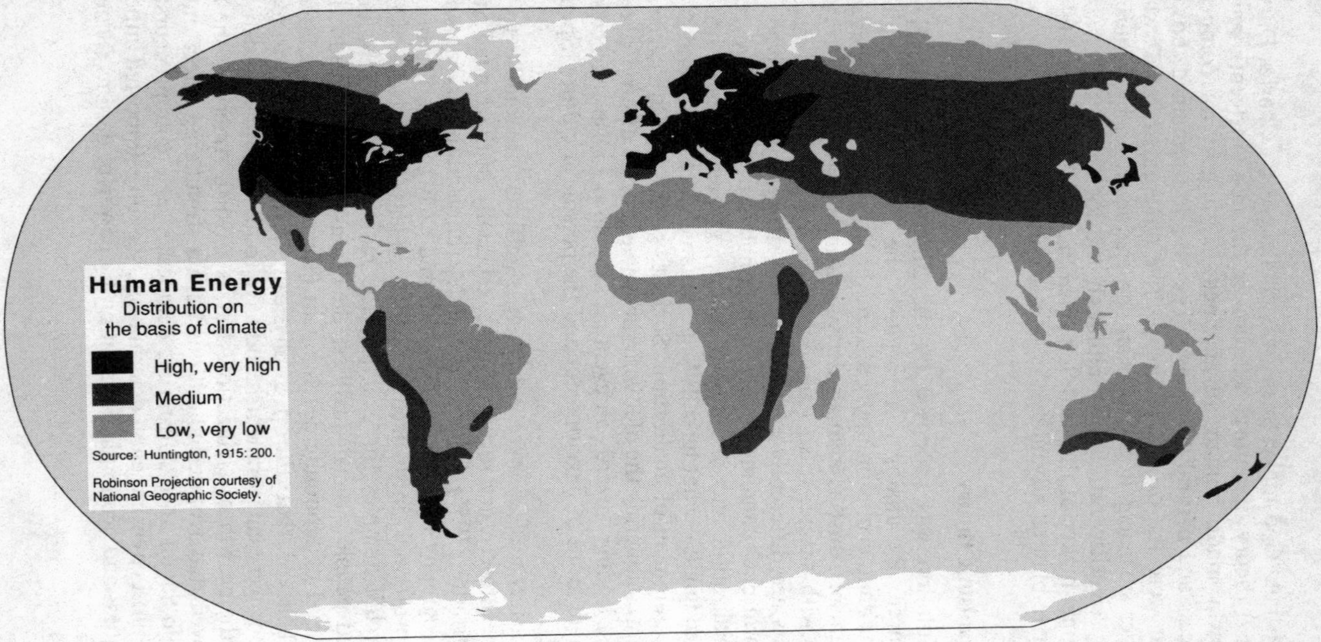

Human Energy
Distribution on
the basis of climate

High, very high
Medium
Low, very low

Source: Huntington, 1915: 200.
Robinson Projection courtesy of
National Geographic Society.

Figure 2.2 Huntington's map of the distribution of civilization

Distribution of Civilization

High, very high
Medium
Low, very low

Source: Huntington, 1915: 200.
Robinson Projection courtesy of National Geographic Society.

Climate and civilization

Ellsworth Huntington (1915) similarly believed that race and environment were the sources of the growth of civilization, but placed causal emphasis on the stimulating or depressing effects of climate, especially temperature. After testing factory operatives and students in the United States, Huntington concluded that people are most physically active when temperatures average 60–65 °F, mentally active when nights are cool, and work well when temperatures change moderately. From data like this he constructed a map of human energy (Figure 2.1) on the basis of climate which he correlated with subjective impressions of the 'level of civilization' (Figure 2.2). The problem that civilizations in the past arose in areas with non-optimal climates was dealt with by theorizing that climatic belts shift over time (his 'pulsatory hypothesis'). This allows the conclusion that 'a certain peculiar type of climate . . . seems to be a necessary condition of great progress' or negatively 'the climate of many countries seems to be one of the great reasons why idleness, dishonesty, immorality, stupidity, and weakness of will prevail' (Huntington, 1915: 9, 294).

Semple's and Huntington's ideas continued to influence geographic thought long after they had been subjected to criticism and dropped from polite intellectual conversation. Even today many conventional geography textbooks begin with the physical environment and work their way through population to culture and economy, the implication being that nature determines social characteristics. And the idea that environment stimulates certain peoples to economic success is hardly restricted to academic geography. It is still probably the most pervasive theory of development, a disguised kind of natural racism which underlies many popular beliefs and resounds through millions of prejudiced statements made every day.

Critique

A critical appreciation of this set of environmentalist ideas might begin with their ideological basis. Simply put, ideology is a partial or biased account directly or indirectly constructed on behalf of a certain class, national or ethnic interest. Ideologies directly propagating a political position are easily recognizable as propaganda – witness newsreels from the Second World War or the McCarthy period in the United States, or television advertisements in the present day. Less obvious are ideologies constructed as part of a search for truth by scientists imbued with the values of their society and sharing its myths. In this latter sense, environmental determinism was an attempt to borrow (by analogy) the principles developed by the more advanced biology as part of a search for a higher level of theoretical understanding in a new, 'modern' social science. This, however, was not a neutral process, for the scientists of the nineteenth century were prisoners of their times, as we are of ours. Thus Huntington's map of civilization was merely the average prejudices of a list of fifty-four eminent geographers, anthropologists, missionaries, statesmen and administrators dominated by North Americans, Britains and 'Teutons'. Certainly these wise scholars accurately gave their scientific opinions based on the best information of the time; but they just as accurately displayed their racial prejudice, for 'civilization' exactly corresponds with the distribution of Western Europeans in the world.

Why this mixing of science and ideology? During the nineteenth century, the European peoples increased their share of direct control over the world space from 35 per cent in 1800 to 85 per cent in 1914 (Fieldhouse, 1973: 3). The end of the nineteenth century saw a particularly severe struggle for global space. This process of struggle and expansion involved the elimination of whole ethnic groups (the Aborigines of Tasmania and Indian tribes in the United States), the destruction of ancient civilizations (China), and the usurpation of European control over entire continents (Africa). There was a desperate need for European and North American intellectuals to legitimate what often had to be morally inexcusable actions by their societies.

This need was met by environmental determinism. The Euro-Americans explained their 'superiority' as a gift of nature, perhaps emanating originally from God. They explained conquest as part of a struggle for survival, part of the natural (and therefore unavoidable) course of history. Borrowing from Spencer's vague utopianism they even claimed they were spreading civilization, 'sacrificing' in order to attain a higher order of existence for everyone. The analogy between biology and social science persisted, therefore, because it served to legitimate European domination. Yet there are great differences between humans and other natural organisms. Humans are self-conscious, aware of what they are doing, able to choose different courses of action within limits. They can plan their actions and guide their reactions to nature. They interpose complex forces of production between themselves and nature: for example technologies so powerful that nature can now be destroyed by nuclear catastrophe. All this influences the relation between society and nature so much that the organismic analogy and socio-biological conceptions of causation have to be rejected as ideological diversions from a more essential truth (Peet, 1985a).

Environmental determinism was not simply propaganda, however. It recognized the essential link between human existence and the rest of nature. This can lead to the realization that production is the social transformation of nature, and suggest that development is the ability to transform greater amounts of nature into more products to support life at a higher material level. Environmental awareness can point the way to a model of development compatible with nature. We can learn from the environmental school the need to include relations with nature as a basic tenet of the theory of development, even while we reject the simple idea that nature creates the human being in all its manifestations.

Chapter three

Structural functionalism and modernization theory

Conceptions of the determination of human development by the natural environment did not disappear merely because they were revealed to be ideologically biased. Environmental determinism continued in a pure form (as climatic determinism) in several popular books written by Ellsworth Huntington in the 1920s, 1930s and 1940s (e.g. Huntington, 1965) and also, in a modified form, in the writings of the illustrious historian Arnold Toynbee (1976). Natural explanations of social phenomena have more recently been revived as socio-biology which sees, in Ardrey's words, humans acting 'for reasons of our evolutionary past, not our cultural present' (Ardrey, 1970: 5). But the analogy between social and biological processes is present also in structural functionalism, the leading post-Second World War theory in sociology and, more indirectly, in its offspring modernization theory, the leading conventional theory of development between the 1950s and the 1970s.

We should not find the persistence of biological analogies in social science surprising – humans are natural beings, and social systems share similar characteristics with natural systems. In line with the brief discussion of theory as ideology in the previous chapter, the remarkable thing about the persistence of naturalism is its prevailing use as a moral and conceptual underpinning of conservative, often nationalistic opinion. Yet naturalistic theories are not inherently conservative. The geographer Peter Kropotkin, for example, argued that the struggle for existence was carried out by co-operative groups, leading him to reaffirm the predominance of a natural, inherent tendency towards mutual aid within species in the quest for survival and advance of civilization (Breitbart, 1981). Naturalism can therefore form the basis of a critique of competitive social systems. The interpretation placed on naturalistic explanation thus depends on the position of theory in an ideological complex, and the interpreter's response to the political demands made on theory. Powerful social and political interests pressure the making of naturalistic theory to legitimize what exists, rather than to justify what could be.

Structural functionalism

The idea of rooting social evolution in biology was revived after the Second World War in the form of structural functionalist sociology. Advances in the biological sciences were thought to have generated a new level of understanding of the fundamental continuity between organic and socio-cultural evolution. In the mind of Parsons (1966: 109–10), a leading theorist, the development of evolutionary theory enabled the construction of a more sophisticated evolutionary scheme than had been possible in Spencer's time, one in which there was considerable variability and branching among developmental lines. As the structural functionalist ideas of Parsons developed, the reference to biological systems theory increased. So for Parsons (1966: 2), the study of societies is guided by an evolutionary perspective, with humans being integral parts of the organic world, and human culture analysable in the general framework of the life process. Basic concepts of organic evolution, like variation, selection, adaptation, differentiation and integration can be adjusted to social and cultural subject matters and used as central components of analysis. Thus social development, like organic evolution, has proceeded by variation and differentiation from simple to progressively more complex forms. Drawing explicitly on biology, Parsons derives a general paradigm which analyses any system in terms of four functional categories: (1) the maintenance of the highest 'governing' or controlling patterns of the system; (2) the internal integration of the system; (3) its orientation to the attainment of goals; (4) its more generalized adaptation to the broad conditions of the environment. In human action systems, cultural systems are specialized around the function of maintaining symbolically organized cultural patterns; social systems around the integration of acting units (human personalities engaged in roles); personality systems around goal attainment; and the behavioural organism around adaptation. A hierarchy of controls organizes the interrelations of these systems – this includes the cybernetic aspect, by which systems high in information but low in energy (culture), regulate other systems higher in energy but lower in information (organism). The physical environment is ultimately conditional – if physical factors are not controllable by cybernetically higher order systems, they must be adapted to or human life will disappear. Technology is the socially organized capacity for controlling and altering the physical environment in the interest of

Table 3.1 The societal community and its environments

Functions in general action systems	Extra-social environments of societal community	Intra-social environments of societal community	Environments of action	Cybernetic relations
				High information (controls) → Hierarchy of controlling factors →
				← Hierarchy of conditioning factors ←
Pattern maintenance	Culture system	Maintenance of institutionalized cultural patterns	'Ultimate reality'	
Integration	Social system	Societal community		
Goal attainment	Personality system	Polity		
Adaptation	Behavioural system	Economy	Physical-organic environment	High energy (conditions)

Source: Parsons, 1966: 28–9

human need, while economy provides linkage with the societal community (Table 3.1).

Society is constituted by a normative system of order and by (varying) statuses, rights and obligations pertaining to membership. To survive and develop, a social community must maintain the integrity of its cultural orientation, which is the basis of its identity, and meet conditional exigencies regarding the integration of its members. Hence the central functional exigency of the cultural system is the legitimation of the society's normative order – the mode of legitimation is grounded in religious orientations, but with differentiation other cultural structures, particularly the arts and science, assume increasing independent importance in legitimation. The major functional problem of the personality system involves maintaining adequate motivation for participating in socially valued and controlled patterns of action. Successful socialization requires that social and cultural learning be motivated through the pleasure mechanism of the organism. Individuals perform services in some collective organization and receive satisfaction and rewards. Political structures organize collective action for the attainment of collectively significant goals. Interlocking economic and political interests reinforce socialization (the internalization of society's values and norms by its members). The whole emphasis in Parsons' work (1966: 14) is the maintenance of social stability in the face of exigencies and strains – the ultimate preventative of disruptive action being the use of physical force.

How then does change (or, rather, evolution) occur in the social system? The most important change process in an evolutionary perspective is the enhancement of adaptive capacity, either within the society (originating a new type of structure) or through cultural diffusion and the importation of new factors. Change involves differentiation, as sub-systems specialize and divide. The other main component of the change process involves the value system, characterized by a particular pattern which, when institutionalized, establishes the desirability of a general type of social system. Through specification the implications of the general valuation are spelled out for the various differentiated sub-systems. New, more generalized value patterns are resisted by fundamentalist commitments to lower orders of generality – severe conflicts often crystallize about such issues. The state of any society or system of ordered societies is a complex resultant of progressive cycles involving these (and other) processes of change, while at any stage there is a fan-like spectrum of societal types. Some variants favour additional evolutionary steps more than others; other variants are so beset with internal conflicts they can hardly maintain themselves, or even deteriorate. Somewhere in the variegated population of societies, there emerges a developmental breakthrough, which endows a society with a new level of adaptive capacity, changing its competitive relations with other societies in the system. The others can destroy this innovation, adopt the innovation (the present drive to modernization among underdeveloped societies being a case in point), confine it to an insulated niche, or lose their social identity through disintegration or absorption by a larger societal system (Parsons, 1966: 24).

In explaining the evolution of modern society, Parsons (1971) traces cultural innovation to the small 'seedbed' societies of ancient Israel and Greece. Elements derived from these sources, after undergoing development and combination, comprised some of the main cultural components of modern society. Christianity proved able to absorb major components of the cultures of antiquity and to form a matrix from which a new secular culture could differentiate. The Roman empire was the principal social environment in which Christianity developed and itself provided institutions incorporated into the foundations of the modern world. Feudalism then represented a drastic regression toward archaic forms. However, once the point of maximum regression had been reached, recovery and dynamic advance were rapid through cultural innovations like the Renaissance and the Reformation. Modern society dates from seventeenth-century developments in the societal community – the main process being described as continuing the internal process of functional differentiation already present in feudal times in the context of processes of integration:

> the division between predominantly Roman Catholic and Protestant areas among ethnically and linguistically distinctive 'nations' and politically independent states. . . . Such differentiation was a major contribution to the capacity of the system not only to initiate but also to create the conditions for institutionalization of significant evolutionary change. . . . Despite fragmentation 'the West' was, throughout the period of concern, an area with a common culture.
>
> (Parsons, 1971: 139–40)

Counter-Reformation societies (archetypically the Italian states and Spain) then tended to freeze the process of differentiation, opposing many modernizing trends, primarily because of relations between their political regimes and a defensive church. By comparison in north-west Europe the industrial revolution was a source of new orders of productive differentiation and increased organic solidarity, in this case through the democratic revolution which justified inequalities of wealth and privilege. The emergence of full modernity further weakened the ascriptive framework of monarchy, aristocracy, established church and an economy circumscribed by kinship and localism, while certain modern components became increasingly important, like a universalistic legal system and the secular culture diffused through Western society by means of the Enlightenment. A second phase of modernity combining industrial revolution and democracy more intimately, and initiating further structural innovations, grew in the fertile soils of the United States. Japan first selectively adopted a modernizing pattern closer to that of the eastern wing of the European system (i.e. imperial Germany), one which emphasized hierarchy and collective goal attainment, and then turned to a more liberal adaptive-integration pattern after 1945. Finally the trend towards modernization has now become world-wide, the elites of most non-modern societies accept crucial aspects of modernity, especially economic development, education and some form of democracy, but the institutionalization of these values remains uneven and fraught with conflict. A clear outcome from the post-imperial period of ferment cannot be forecasted, but Parsons (1971: 137) expects the general trend towards modernization to continue in the non-Western world (see also Parsons, 1948, 1960, 1961; Parsons and Shils, 1951; Parsons and Smelser, 1956; Roches, 1975).

Parsons' theory, set in the context of a quasi-biological understanding of societies as living, evolving systems, combines the sociology of Durkheim and Weber with systems theory from biology and input–output models from economics. This modern synthesis, originally 'progressive' but rapidly becoming conventional, profoundly influenced the conception of development as academic and governmental interest turned to the Third World in the 1950s and 1960s.

Sociological modernization theory

According to S.N. Eisenstadt (1973b: 12–15), a leading exponent, modernization theory is interested in elaborating the differences between traditional and modern societies in terms of their positions on various indices of modernity or development, and to the extent to which they approximate the model of modern industrial society. Modernization theory asks: what impedes advance and what are the conditions and mechanisms of social transition, from traditional to modern? Traditional societies are viewed as restrictive and limited in the environments they can master, whereas modern societies are expansive, able to cope with a wider range of environments and problems. The more the characteristics of structural specialization can be found in a society, the higher it is on an index of modernization. And the more thorough the disintegration of traditional elements, the more society can absorb change and develop such qualitative characteristics of modern societies as rationality, efficiency and a predilection to liberty.

A key concept in modernization theory is derived from Karl Deutsch's (1961) term 'social mobilization' defined as 'the process in which major clusters of old social, economic, and psychological commitments are eroded and broken and people become available for new patterns of socialization and behaviour' – this in turn depends on things like exposure to modern life, the media, urbanization, literacy and so on. The main structural characteristics of modernization are then identified as:

> the development of a high degree of differentiation, of free resources which are not committed to any fixed, ascriptive (kinship, territorial, etc.) groups, the development of specialized and diversified types of social organization, the development of wide nontraditional, 'national', or even super-national group identifications. This requires also the concomitant development, in all major institutional spheres, of specialized roles and of special wider regulative and allocative procedures and organizations – such as market mechanisms in economic life, voting and party activities in politics, and diverse bureaucratic organizations in most institutional spheres.
>
> (Eisenstadt, 1973b: 21–2)

More specifically in the economic sphere this means specialization of economic activities and occupational roles and the growth of markets; in terms of socio-spatial organization it means urbanization, mobility, flexibility and the spread of education; in the political sphere, it means the spread of democracy and the weakening of traditional elites; in the cultural sphere, growing differentiation between cultural and value systems (e.g. between religion and philosophy), secularization and the emergence of new intelligentsia. These developments are closely related to the expansion of modern communications media and the 'consumption' of culture created by centrally-placed elites, this being manifested as changes in attitudes, especially the emergence of an outlook that stresses self-advancement. In general, modern societies become able to absorb change and assure their own continuous growth.

Parsons' (1951) theory of social action was also used to reformulate economic theory. For Parsons, humans are goal-seeking beings, active in creating their own lives. Action guided by values is necessarily a matter of choice, each conceptualized as a dilemma between two polar opposites. Parsons (1951: 58–67) believed it possible to categorize these as 'pattern variables': (1) a social actor may judge a physical or social object according to criteria applicable to a range of objects (universalism), or by criteria peculiar to the object (particularism); (2) an actor can judge an object by what it does (performance), or in itself (quality) – this is also described as the difference between achievement and ascription; (3) an actor can set feelings aside in making judgements (affective neutrality), or can directly express feelings in relation to objects (affectivity); (4) actors may be in contact with each other in specific ways (specificity), or be related through multiple ties (diffuseness); (5) actors can aim at achieving their own interest (self-orientation), or the aims of the community (collectivity orientation). Bert Hoselitz (1960) found four of Parsons' pattern variables applicable to the differences between modern and traditional societies. He argues that in traditional societies (i.e. undeveloped economies) particularism prevails in the distribution of economic roles whereas, in more complex societies (i.e. developed economies), universalism underlies a more efficient allocation of labour and resources. Traditional societies usually exhibit a lack of reliance on individual achievement, emphasizing instead ascription (e.g. kinship relations) as the basis for distributing economic goods. In traditional societies the performance of economic tasks is typically diffuse, whereas advanced societies are characterized by specificity of roles. And finally in undeveloped societies the elite is self-oriented whereas elites in the advanced countries exhibit collectivity-oriented attitudes. These positions are summarized in Table 3.2.

Hoselitz then applies these differences to an analysis of the development process under the assumption, drawn from Adam Smith, that increasing productivity is associated with an increasing social division of labour. In more detail:

A society on a low level of economic development is, therefore, one in which productivity is low because division of labor is little developed, in which the objectives of economic activity are more commonly the maintenance or strengthening of status relations, in which social and geographical mobility is low, and in which the hard cake of custom determines the manner, and often the effects, of economic performance. An economically highly developed society, in contrast, is characterized by a complex division of social labor, a relatively open social structure in which caste barriers are absent and class barriers are surmountable, in which social roles and gains from economic activity are

Table 3.2 Hoselitz's ideal-type societies using Parsons' pattern variables

Parsons' pattern variables (dilemmas)	Hoselitz's ideal-type societies	
	Underdeveloped or 'backward' societies	*Developed or 'modern' societies*
I Choice between types of value-orientation: universalism versus particularism	Particularistic norms	Universalistic norms
II Choice between modalities of the social object: performance versus quality	Quality (ascription)	Performance (achievement)
III Gratification–discipline dilemma: affectivity versus affective neutrality	Not relevant	Not relevant
IV Definition of scope of interest in the object: specificity versus diffuseness	Functional diffuseness	Functional specificity
V Private versus collective interest: self orientation versus collectivity orientation	Self-orientation	Collectivity orientation

Source: Parsons, 1951: 67; Hoselitz, 1960: 41–2

distributed essentially on the basis of achievement, and in which, therefore, innovation, the search for and exploitation of profitable market situations, and the ruthless pursuit of self-interest without regard to the welfare of others is fully sanctioned.

(Hoselitz, 1960: 60)

As a consequence, the main problem for a theory of economic growth is to determine the mechanisms by which the social structure of an underdeveloped country can be modernized – that is, altered to take on the features of an economically advanced country. Hoselitz's answer is based in the 'theory of social deviance': the capitalist entrepreneur of late medieval and early modern Europe was the prototype of a socially or culturally marginal individual who originates important new forms of economic activity. By extension, entrepreneurs or bureaucrats imbued with modern ideas can do the same for underdeveloped countries today. In terms of the geographic place of 'deviant' behaviour, Hoselitz argues that the city is now the focal point for the introduction of innovative ideas and new social and economic practices. In underdeveloped countries, cities modelled after the urban centres of the West exhibit a spirit of difference from the traditionalism of the countryside. In terms of policy, therefore, Hoselitz favours a shift in political power to promote the economic leadership of the urban modernizers in undeveloped countries (see also Barnett, 1989).

Socio-psychological theories of modernization

A group of theorists turned their attention more exactly to the psychological and behavioural dimensions of modernization. Everett Hagen (1962) links differences in human personality to technological progress and more generally to social change in an attempt at reformulating purely economic theories of growth. People's images of the world in traditional societies include the perception that uncontrollable forces restrict and dominate their lives. Traditional people, fearing the world and its problems, are uncreative and authoritarian. But the authoritarian personality can change if groups of people experience a reduction in respect, for example through domestic or external conquest or migration, and then search for a satisfactory new identity through withdrawal and social deviancy. As retreat deepens through successive generations, the circumstances of home life and social environment eventually become conducive to the development of an innovative personality, for example through a high need to achieve. Under certain cultural circumstances, creative individuals see technological prowess as a path to the satisfaction of their needs. The values of a new generation may turn in the direction of innovations in production, institutional reform and economic growth. The deviant group then leads the society towards modernization.

A similar, if more extreme, position is taken by the psychologist David McClelland. For McClelland (1961) part of the push for economic development comes from a psychological characteristic *n* Achievement, or the need for achievement, which suits particular individuals for entrepreneurial roles. Societies with high levels of need for achievement produce energetic entrepreneurs who, in turn, lead rapid economic development. The amount of *n* Achievement can be enhanced through 'achievement motivation training', which McClelland recommends as a low-cost way of stimulating economic development in low achievement countries (McClelland and Winter, 1971).

In brief, economic development originates in the development of a modern personality, with a high need to achieve satisfied through innovative behaviour. Faced with the problem of explaining how this new personality type arises from traditional society, modernization theory must turn either to inherent differences in societies, which leads back in the direction of environmental determinism, even to racism, or to the rise of behavioural types which deviate from traditional norms, in which case the argument becomes convoluted (withdrawal–deviancy–innovation or changes in 'need for achievement').

Historical stages of modernization

A more plausible resolution of essentially the same dilemma is provided by historical theories of the growth stages intervening between traditionalism and modernity. Here also the politics of the whole modernization approach, hinted at when social-psychological theories stress the role of the entrepreneur, become more apparent – thus W.W. Rostow's (1960) *Stages of Economic Growth* was proposed as an alternative to Karl Marx's theory of history. Rostow argues that in their economic dimensions, all societies lie within one of five categories:

1 *Traditional societies* have limited 'production functions' based in pre-Newtonian science; primitive technologies; and spiritual attitudes towards the physical world. These place a ceiling on productivity and limit economies to the agricultural level. A hierarchical social structure, in which political power is held by

landowners, gives little scope for social mobility. The value system is derived from long-run fatalism. Rostow admits that placing infinitely various, changing societies in a single category says very little about them, but justifies such an historical conflation as necessary for 'clearing the way to get at the subject of this book; that is, the post-traditional societies, in which each of the major characteristics of the traditional society was altered in such ways as to permit regular growth' (Rostow, 1960: 6).

2 The second universal stage is the development of a set of *preconditions for economic take-off*. These occur in western Europe in the late seventeenth and early eighteenth centuries as the insights of modern science are translated into new production functions in agricultural and industry in a setting given dynamism by international expansion. Favoured by geography, trading possibilities, and social and political structure, Britain was first to develop these preconditions. Elsewhere they arise not endogenously, but exogenously from intrusions originating in more advanced societies. These external influences shake traditional society and begin, or hasten, its undoing. Essentially this involves the spread of the idea of progress, not just as a possibility, but also as a necessary condition for some other purpose judged to be good – like national dignity or private profit. Education spreads, new people come forward, banks appear, investment increases, the scope of commerce broadens, and some manufacturing plants spring up, all however within societies still characterized predominantly by traditional methods, structures and values.

3 *Take-off* is the great watershed in the life of modern societies, when blocks and resistances to steady growth are finally overcome. In Britain and the 'well-endowed parts of the world populated substantially from Britain' the proximate stimulus for take-off was mainly technological, but elsewhere a political context favourable to modernization is also necessary. During take-off the rate of effective investment rises from 5 per cent of national income to 10 per cent or more, new industries expand, profits are ploughed back, urban-industrial employment increases, and the new class of entrepreneurs expands. New techniques spread to agriculture and, in a decade or two, the economy and the social and political structure of society are transformed so that steady economic growth can be sustained.

A question immediately arises: if the break-up of traditional societies comes exogenously, from demonstration effects from other societies, how can we account for the first take-off in Britain? Rowstow's answer (1960: 31) is that a 'combination of necessary and sufficient conditions for take-off in Britain was the result of the convergence of a number of quite independent circumstances, a kind of statistical accident of history which, once having occurred, was irreversible, like the loss of innocence.' The more exact answer to the question unfolds as two features of post-medieval Europe – external discoveries and the internal development of modern science. Rostow also finds crucially significant Britain's toleration of religious non-conformists (i.e. Hoselitz's 'social deviants'), the relatively open social structure, and the early achievement of a national consciousness in response to threats from abroad – this last, he says, places the first instance back into the general case of societies modernizing in response to intrusions from abroad.

4 Following 'take-off' a society *drives toward maturity* over a long interval of time as modern technology spreads over the whole front of its economic activity, 10–20 per cent of the national income is invested, and growth outstrips any increase in population. Some sixty years after take-off a society attains maturity, that is a state in which there are sufficient entrepreneurial and technical skills to produce anything it chooses – machine tools, chemicals and electrical equipment industries are examples.

5 This leads eventually to the final stage of *high mass consumption*, where the leading industrial sectors become durable consumer goods and services. Real income rises to a level permitting a large number of people to consume at levels far in excess of needs, and the structure of the work force changes towards the urban-skilled and office types of employment. Western societies at this level choose to allocate increased resources to social welfare and security. Stage 5 was reached by the United States in the 1920s and, more fully, in the immediate post-war decade; western Europe and Japan entered the stage in the 1950s; the Soviet Union has the technical capacity to enter should its 'Communist Leaders' allow (Rostow, 1960: 12).

Such are the universal stages of growth lying between traditional and modern, undevelopment and development. The policy implications of this theory are clear – societies wishing to develop need only copy an already-proven example. In geographical terms, given the development of modernity in the restricted space of Euro-America (and Japan), backward countries should encourage the diffusion of innovation from the centre, should adopt capitalism as the mode of social integration and should welcome United States aid and direction.

Modernization geography

Several kinds of interest also emerged in the *spatial* aspects of modernization. Many of the theorists discussed thus far implicitly recognize the uneven development of modernization processes in space – for example Rostow's ideas on the origins of modern society in Britain and its subsequent movement to nearby, highly connected regions in western Europe and North America. The spatial implications of modernization theory are more explicitly drawn out by geographers. The Swedish geographer Torsten Hagerstrand (1952) pioneered work on the diffusion of innovations, seeing these as waves of change moving across space which gradually lose power due to the friction of distance. Peter Gould (1964) stresses that innovations diffuse over space in patterns because people are persuaded to adopt new things through communication with each other. These geographical versions of diffusion theory were then synthesized with ideas from the main body of modernization theory to yield a hybrid 'geography of modernization'. In this view, Third World countries are isolated, parochial, technically primitive subsistence economies where disease, hunger and malnutrition are daily problems. Change shows as islands of progress in a sea of stagnation and transformation is viewed as a progressive spatial process:

> Unlike former days, when people moved to clear new fields, to conquer their neighbors, or to flee the invader, they act today in response to the new foci of change, the towns and the cities. Modern transport systems extend the length and breadth of the country [Sierra Leone], bringing new ideas, new methods, and new people even to the most remote corners. . . . These changes, which affect all spheres of life – political, social, economic, and psychological – constitue the modernization process.
>
> (Riddell, 1970: 43–4)

Modernization is seen as a spatial diffusion process, originating in contact situations, such as port cities or colonial administrative centres, with patterns of change moving across the map, cascading down urban hierarchies, and funnelling along transport systems. This process can be measured by the spread of institutions like schools or medical facilities and mapped as a modernization surface (Figure 3.1). In keeping with the strongly quantitative tenor of the time, the objective was to devise statistical indices to measure real variations in modernization, like: (1) the development of transport networks; (2) the expansion of communication and information media; (3) the growth of an integrated urban system; (4) the

Figure 3.1 Levels of modernization in Sierra Leone

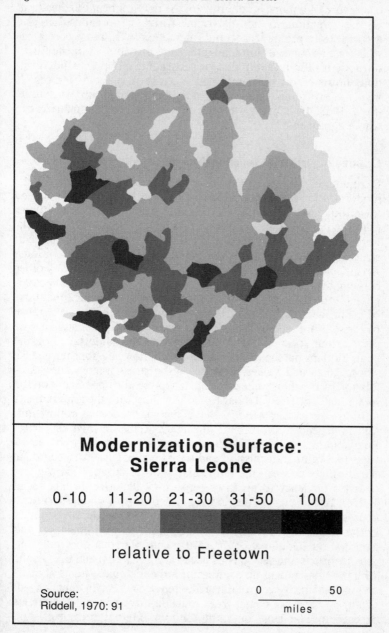

Modernization Surface: Sierra Leone

| 0-10 | 11-20 | 21-30 | 31-50 | 100 |

relative to Freetown

Source:
Riddell, 1970: 91

0   50
miles

breakdown of traditional ethnic compartmentalization; (5) the emergence of a money economy; (6) the development of education; (7) participation in non-parochial forms of organization and activity; (8) a proximity to, and interaction with, those core areas which act as concentrators, adapters and distributors of the forces of modernization; (9) physical or geographic mobility. Modernization, however, 'is not simply an increase in a set of indices. It involves profound changes in individual and group behaviour' (Soja, 1968: 4). In many ways this simple statement summarizes the whole approach.

Critique of structural functionalism and modernization theories

Beginning in the late 1950s, but especially from the middle 1960s, modernization theory was subjected to an intense criticism – indeed the critique was ferocious when coming from Third World sources (e.g. Frank, 1969a) or political leftists (e.g. Szentes, 1976). Attacks were launched on all aspects of the theory, from its original base in structural functionalism to the politics of its policy presciptions. Alvin Gouldner (1970: 168) says that Parsons 'more than any other contemporary social theorist has influenced . . . academic sociologists . . . throughout the world', through his own writings and those of his influential students. However, functional theories like those of Parsons are seen by Gouldner as devoted to the maintenance of the existing social order. While stressing the importance of the goals humans pursue, or the values they follow, Parsons never asks whose goals and values these are – the stress is on value transmission rather than value creation. Theoretical emphasis lies on the individual's plastic potential for conforming with the requirements of his or her social position – that is, people are seen as hollow containers dependent on training in social systems for their character. For Gouldner (1970: 218–19) the reason for stressing characteristics like value transmission and social malleability is to eliminate the conflicts between the individual and the group. This neglects people's tendency to avoid or resist total inclusion in any social system. In Parsons' system individuals conform with one another's expectations and exchange equal benefits. This neglects variability in the degree of mutuality of gratification, power imbalances and exploitation (Gouldner, 1970: 240). Thus Parsons does not conceive conflicts and tensions as necessary parts of social life. Along with this goes a focus on equilibrium, that is stable systems of interaction which, once established, tend to remain unchanged. Changes have to come from outside, overwhelming systemic defence mechanisms, or from random internal pressures. And change is cyclical or rhythmical rather than transformative. Differentiation is a way for systems to change in an 'orderly' manner – that is, in a manner not threatening to existing power centres. All of this contributes to a crisis in functional theory, and in academic sociology more generally (Gouldner 1970: 351–61). For our purposes, limited to the implications for development theory, we need only point out that Gouldner finds structural functionalism unsuitable as the basis for a theory of social dynamics because of its bias towards unidirectional and non-threatening types of evolutionary change.

Anthony Giddens (1977) traces modern functionalism (via Comte, Spencer and Durkheim) to advances in biology in the nineteenth century. Functionalism borrows biological principles (by analogy) to explicate the 'anatomy and psychology' of social life. Its appeal lies in a desire to demonstrate the logical unity between the natural and social sciences, in its ability to show the various forms of social organization as interdependent parts of integrated unities, in its teleology by which social needs are satisfied through the unintended consequences of social action, and in its inherent political conservatism – i.e. its rejection of radical politics in favour of a reconciliation of progress with social order (Giddens, 1977: 104–5). Giddens then 'decodifies' functional analysis in an attempt at encompassing its emphases within a different conceptual scheme which he calls 'structuration theory'. Like Gouldner, Giddens finds functionalism teleological, a theory which allows for only a limited and deficient explication of purposive human action. Giddens finds the concept 'function' usually to mean an effect, but also the cause, of an event. Homeostatic processes (in which change in one element causes change in another which causes re-adjustment in the first) have to be seen as fulfilling some systemic need to be the basis of 'causal' functional theories. In functionalist social theory this turns out to be a social system's 'needs'. For Giddens, by comparison, social systems are unlike organisms in that they do not have needs; rather social actors have wants. Giddens also finds that structural functionalism mistakenly assimilates the notions of structure and system – structure is like anatomy, while system includes how the anatomy functions. In social life, structures (patterns) only exist in so far as they are constantly produced and reproduced in human action, so there is no place for the two terms as used in structural functionalism. Furthermore purposiveness in human affairs cannot be grasped as a homeostatic process involving merely cybernetic control through feedbacks of information – rather human action involves not just self-regulation, but self-consciousness or reflexivity:

> 'Purpose' in relation to human affairs is related in an integral
> way to the possessing of reasons for action, or to the rationaliza-
> tion of action in processes of self-reflection. In this respect, it is
> quite different from whatever teleology is involved in self-
> regulating processes in nature.
>
> (Giddens, 1977: 116)

This leads Giddens (1977: 118) to his concept of structuration –
that is the modes whereby systems, through the application of
generative rules and resources, are produced and reproduced in
social interaction.

Finally, Giddens turns to the functionalist conception of change,
that is the theory of social evolution through the adaptation of
societies to environments. Here the sources of the stimulus to
change are exogeneous rather than internally generated, through
class struggle for example; evolution in the animal world operates
blindly, whereas there is an attempt to consciously control human
development; and the relation of human society to its material
environment is ill-conceived as one of mere adaptation – as Marx
points out, humans actively *transform* nature (Giddens, 1977:
118–21).

Structural-functionalist modernization theory has also been criticized for its concept of history, or more exactly for its ahistoricism,
with critical attention focused on Rostow's concept of the
universality of the process of modernization (i.e. change does not
change but is the same everywhere at all times), his notion of a
single, fixed end-stage of development and his ethnocentrism.
Frank (1969a) is particularly effective in exposing the politics of
Rostow's 'theory of history'. First, Rostow describes all 'backward' societies in terms of a uniform traditionalism which, for
example, equates ancient China, Aboriginal Australia, Mayan
Central America and the civilizations of southern Africa with
feudal Europe. This denies the specific pre-capitalist histories of
Third World societies, reducing them to a common backwardness
(whereas in fact many were more developed than Europe), the more
to disguise the (*under*developing) effects contact with European
capitalism had on the world's civilizations. Second, the developmental history of Euro-America is generalized into a sequence of
stages of economic growth which all societies must follow. But how
can history repeat itself when Europe's development has already
altered the context in which historical events occur? Specifically the
development of capitalism has already created a centre of power
and a dependent periphery so that progress in the underdeveloped
world must now contend with a global structure inimical to such

progress. Third, 'high mass consumption' of the North American type is propagated as the end point for all development, yet many would wish to live well without the social and environmental problems associated with over-consuming societies. Rostow subverts the dreams of a better future and converts them to the worship of the almighty dollar. In brief, Frank (1969a: 40) finds this entire approach to economic and cultural change attributing a history to the developed countries but denying history to the underdeveloped countries. An economic policy for the underdeveloped societies has to be based on *their* experience – specifically, for Frank, their active underdevelopment through contact with developed societies.

The criticism of Eurocentrism can also be levelled at structural functionalism in general. As we have seen, Parsons traces the origins of European modernization to development in classical antiquity. In doing so he fails to see that classical Greece was not the cradle of a distinctively Western civilization, but was itself derived from African and Asian sources. As Bernal (1987) argues, this 'ancient model' of the Afro-Asian origins of Western civilization was down-played in the nineteenth century in favour of an 'Aryan model' which conformed better with the racialism and imperialism of the period. The earlier model casts an entirely different light on the origins of modernization.

There were many more particular criticisms of the exact contents of modernization theory. To use a self-critical summary provided by Eisenstadt (1973a: 98–112), the dichotomy of traditional versus modern was attacked on the grounds of its generalizations 'traditional' (there are many differences between traditional societies) and 'modern' (there are many traditional elements in modern societies), its limiting of the agency of development to progressive modern elites (traditional groups can reorganize themselves in modern settings) and its concept of the unidirectionality of the modernization process (traditional models can re-assert themselves after the initial phases of modernization). Elsewhere, Hoselitz's application of Parsons' pattern variables to traditional and modern societies comes in for particularly sharp criticism. Frank (1969a: 26) argues that the 'universalist flag' displayed by developed countries 'is little more than the cover for unsavoury particularist private interests'. Economic roles in countries like the United States are based on ascription at the highest levels of business management and at the bottom of the social order (e.g. for blacks), while 'functionally specific' positions are interchanged readily between members of the ruling class. Likewise, underdeveloped countries may be just as universalistic, achievement-oriented and functionally specific as developed countries. Hoselitz's 'ideal types' thus present a distorted conception of social reality in both developed and underdeveloped countries. Szentes also criticizes modernization's concepts of behaviour motivation, personality types, ideas, etc. – these can be found in many different historical and social contexts, and while effective for achieving development in one, may not be in another:

> In other words, apart from cases bordering on the absurd, there are not *generally* favorable and generally unfavorable behaviors, development-promoting or -hampering ideas, customs, individual qualities and modification . . . the ideas, customs and individual qualities of the members of society develop and change under the impact of the social relations of production.
>
> (Szentes, 1976: 71)

Values, institutions or technologies developed in one society often do not fit other cultures and may actually be dysfunctional for development – it would be better for Third World countries to modify or re-create their own institutions rather than imitate those of the West (see also Whyte, 1968; Slater, 1973). Likewise, in terms of the geography of modernization, diffusion is not merely a case of communications (e.g. hearing of an innovation) but also the ability to *use* information – especially economic ability, control over resources and other class-based characteristics (Yapa, 1977). Modernization surfaces are only the spread of capitalism in disguise. And economic development can be initiated by local effort aimed at satisfying people's needs rather than opening a society to the global division of labour and meeting the centre countries' requirements.

We could go on with the criticisms, but modernization theory was declared moribund in 1976 (Wallerstein, 1979: ch. 7). This declaration was perhaps premature. Parsonian theory continues often in combination with Marxian and Weberian notions (Gould, 1987; Munch, 1987). And theories very similar to modernization continue to direct policy in governmental and international aid agencies (such as the World Bank), but theoretical justification tends to be sought more in neo-classical economics than developmental sociology.

We might illustrate one strand of the continuation of modernization theory by briefly following the theoretical career-path of a prominent theorist. Eisenstadt (1987: 5) admits that the initial modernization model 'disintegrated' in the 1970s. He finds, however, a new perspective beginning to develop drawing on classical modernization theory, but also on Marx, Gramsci and Weber, which recognizes the uniqueness of modernity and the great variety of symbolic, ideological and institutional responses to it. Instead of looking at European-style modernization as the ultimate end-point latent in all societies, modernity is now viewed as a specific type of civilization, originating in Europe, and spreading over the world to encompass most of it. Modernity challenges the symbolic and institutional premisses of the incorporated societies, calling for responses, out of which develop a variety of modernizing societies, sharing many common characteristics, yet evincing great differences (Eisenstadt, 1987: 6). This leads Eisenstadt to an analysis of the basic characteristics of the new, modern (Western) civilization, under what is now called a 'civilizational approach', emphasizing the cultural visions of elites (especially their political beliefs), their institutionalization and reactions to them. Stress is laid on revolutions in consciousness, such as the transcendental vision which emerged in several ('Axial Age') civilizations in the first millennium before Christ (Eisenstadt, 1986). We conclude that this is merely a restatement of modernization theory which replaces the earlier emphasis on social behaviour and practices with an emphasis on leaps in consciousness. Modernization theory has thus proven to be a particularly tenacious perspective on the question of societal development.

Conclusion

Structural functionalism continues, in a far more sophisticated form, the biologically-based analysis of environmental determinism. Rather than naturally-based racial characteristics determining human behaviour, structural functionalism conceives people as the products of socialization and enculturation. What determines the direction and content of the socialization process? Structural functionalism, as outlined by Parsons, argues that societies have structures similar to those of all organisms, that there are imperatives which the functional order must pursue, and that culture and socialization respond quite automatically to these needs: people are what their society needs them to be. In the structural functionalist conception, development is one more instance of the natural process of differentiation, in this case of the component parts of society, or the various aspects of an economy. This passes easily into the essential idea of modernization, that there is a single (universal) process of the evolution of civilization, with Euro-America occupying the eventual position towards which all societies are tending. Development for the periphery is reduced to a process of spatial diffusion of innovation from the global centre of civilization. The policy conclusion is that societies wishing to develop should open their borders and let change in, should become part of the existing global system, and should welcome and indeed encourage multinational corporations, advanced technology, and export-oriented agriculture.

This line of argument is criticized on several grounds. Its base in structural functionalism is criticized in terms of the crude application of biologically deterministic notions to societies and human personalities. Modernization theory is criticized as producing a conception of development which takes unilinearity to the extreme of tunnel vision. Rostovian economic history denies historical specificity to the many different peoples of the Third World, and the whole enterprise is seen as a cold war attempt at legitimating United States domination of the global system.

Modernization theory persists in contemporary notions of modernism and post-modernism, and in the policies favoured by international development agencies. In part this is because of its legitimation function, in part because modernization does correspond, however inexactly, to certain empirical facts, and in part because the original idea of a structure of functions as the basic order of society retains some theoretical validity. We take up the last point in Chapter 5. Next, however, we look at theoretical developments which emerged as a reaction against the modernization viewpoint, especially against its Eurocentrism and ahistoricism. These critical developments take the general name of dependency theory.

Chapter four

Dependency and world systems theories

Modernization theory originated at the centre of the global capitalist system as the un-self-critical celebration in thought of Euro-American material accomplishment. Dependency theory, by comparison, originated in Latin America as a series of critical reflections on the historical experience of the peripheral peoples of the world. More exactly, dependency theory was a reaction against the failure of earlier theories to adequately explain economic backwardness in Latin America, or to offer a convincing model of the future development process. Early Latin American theories had either accepted backwardness as the inevitable consequence of the intrinsic qualities of the continent's people (laziness, arrogance, spiritualism, violence, etc.) or had naïvely blamed 'imperialist exploitation' as part of an anti-(North) American nationalism. Later explanations retained the latter sentiment, but theorized it in opposition to ideas stressing unicentred and unilinear growth emanating from Europe. This chapter traces such theorization from the beginnings of dependency theory in debates over development policy in the post-war period to the modern versions based in neo-Marxism and world systems theory.

The ECLA analysis

Early Latin American development strategies favoured an outward-oriented model in which the region provided primary goods to Euro-American markets. The depression of the 1930s revealed the weaknesses inherent in this, as international demand fell to such a degree that coffee exports were burnt as fuel on the Brazilian railroads. After the Second World War a coherent Latin American perspective on the development process began to be formulated by the United Nations Economic Commission for Latin America (ECLA). This argued that conventional economic theory favoured the central capitalist countries and was inadequate for understanding the

43

underdeveloped world. Instead an appreciation of the different historical contexts and national situations of these countries, their different social structures, types of behaviour and economies, required a new 'structuralist' perspective (the term structure being used somewhat differently than in Marxism). The main tenets of this theory were outlined by Raúl Prebisch, formerly head of the Central Bank of Argentina.

In conventional economic analysis, the theory of comparative advantage argues that the exchange of the centre countries' industrial goods for peripheral primary goods is to all countries' advantage. Technical progress in the centre would lead to lower prices for industrial exports, so that one unit of primary exports would eventually buy larger amounts of industrial imports – over the long term, progress would accrue to the periphery without industrialization. Opposing this view, Prebisch argued that Latin America's peripheral position and primary exports were causes of its lack of progress, specifically because of a long-term decline in the terms of trade of the periphery (i.e. the ratio between the value of exports and the value of imports) and a rise in those of the centre. Using British trade as a case study, Prebisch showed that the terms of trade for the centre countries had improved with industrialization, from which he concluded that the terms of trade of the periphery must have deteriorated. Thus technical advance benefited the centre countries rather than the entire world. This was not a temporary phenomenon, but a structural characteristic of the global system. Conventional economic theory failed to work because: (1) the factor and labour markets of the centre were characterized by imperfect competition so that price reductions could be avoided, while competition among many primary producers reduced the prices for their goods; and (2) the income elasticity of demand for industrial goods (i.e. degree to which demand changes with a given change in income) is higher than for primary goods, so that prices for peripheral goods tend to decline relative to those of centre goods. Latin America's underdevelopment was thus due to its emphasis on primary exports.

The solution lay in structural change. Prebisch and other Latin Americans of the post-war period favoured industrialization under an import substitution strategy (i.e. replacing industrial imports with domestic production under tariff protection), with income from primary exports being used to pay for imports of capital goods. In this model the state planned industrialization but, paradoxically, foreign companies were invited to help start local businesses. This approach was widely adopted in Latin America, as elsewhere in the Third World, at first with impressive results. Over time, however, import substitution was associated with high-cost, low-quality industrial output, the neglect of agriculture and entrenched positions for foreign capital. The remedy came to be seen as a cause of the economic illness (Blomstrom and Hettne, 1984; Chilcote, 1984; Harris, 1986).

Dependency theory

From the above summary, it can be seen that Prebisch used similar analytical terms to the neoclassical economic theories he was criticizing. The dependency school, which developed as a critical reaction against ECLA-type analysis, turned instead to Marxist and neo-Marxist ideas for analytical power. However, the official Marxism of the organized communist parties did not enjoy mass worker or intellectual support in Latin America, where anarchist ideas from Southern Europe often served as the basis of revolutionary thought (Liss, 1984). Che Guevara's ideas of the revolutionary peasantry were more in tune with Latin American reality than unionized worker models based in the European experience. The ideas of the Monthly Review school in the United States were also influential. Paul Baran's (1960) thesis that peripheral underdevelopment is caused by the loss of economic surplus to the centre, and his insistence that the underdeveloped countries were not following a universal evolutionary line towards capitalism and development, proved appealing. Hence, it was the 'neo-Marxism' of the New Left, rather than the official Marxism of the Old Left, which intersected with critical liberal ideas of the ECLA type, to create the innovation in developmental thought called 'dependency theory' (Blomstrom and Hettne, 1984: ch. 2).

The basic hypothesis of the dependency school is that development and underdevelopment are interdependent structures within the global economic system. The relationship between centre and periphery assumes, in Dos Santos's (1970) words, the form of a dependence in which some countries (the dominant) achieve self-sustaining growth while others (the dependent) can grow only as a reflection of the dominant countries. The incorporation of Latin America into the capitalist world economy, directly through colonial administration, and more subtly through foreign trade, ensured that the region's production was geared towards the demands of the centre. This economic position skewed the periphery's social structure so that local power was held by a small ruling class (who used the gains from exporting for luxury consumption rather than investment), while real power was wielded from external poles of command in dominant ('metropolitan') countries. Dependence continues into the present through international ownership of the region's most dynamic sectors, multinational corporate control over technology, and payments of royalties, interest and profits.

This position, pieced together by writers such as Sunkel (1972), Furtado (1963), Cardoso and Faletto (1979) and Dos Santos (1970), was popularized in the English-speaking world by the writings of André Gunder Frank. As we have seen, Frank took a leading role in the critique of modernization theory. This entailed a criticism of the 'dual society' thesis, which maintained that underdeveloped societies have a dual structure (modern and traditional), each with its own dynamic (Meier, 1970). For Frank, attributing underdevelopment to traditionalism (or feudalism) rather than capitalism is an historical and political mistake. World capitalism destroyed or transformed the earlier systems even as it came into existence and converted them into sources of its own further development (Frank, 1969a).

For Frank, the economic, political, social and cultural institutions and relations of the underdeveloped countries are results of the penetration of capitalism, rather than being original. Frank focused on the metropole–satellite (or centre–periphery) relations which he found typical in Latin America. Centre-capitalist underdevelopment of peripheral-capitalist regions and people, he said, is characterized by three 'contradictions': the contradiction of the monopolistic expropriation of economic surplus; the contradiction of metropole–satellite polarization; and the contradiction of continuity in change. Drawing on Marx's analysis of the class expropriation of surplus value, and Baran's (1977) version of Marx which emphasized the potential surplus which could be made available for investment, Frank argued that external monopoly has always resulted in the expropriation (and thus local unavailability) of a significant part of the economic surplus produced in Latin America. Using a case study of Chile, Frank describes the geographical pattern of surplus expropriation as follows:

> The monopoly capitalist structure and the surplus expropriation/ appropriation contradiction run through the entire Chilean economy, past and present. Indeed, it is this exploitative relation which in chain-like fashion extends the capitalist link between the capitalist world and national metropolises to the regional centers (part of whose surplus they appropriate), and from these to local centers, and so on to large landowners or merchants who expropriate surplus from small peasants or tenants, and sometimes even from these latter to landless laborers exploited by them in

turn. At each step along the way, the relatively few capitalists above exercise monopoly power over the many below, expropriating some or all of their economic surplus. . . . Thus at each point, the international, national, and local capitalist system generates economic development for the few and underdevelopment for the many.

(Frank 1969b: 7–8)

This idea of surplus transfer was further developed in Frank's discussion of the second contradiction, whereby centre and periphery become increasingly polarized as capitalism develops the one and underdevelops the other in a single historical process. In this perspective only a weaker or lesser degree of metropole–satellite relation may allow the possibility of local development. These two contradictions suggest a third to Frank – the continuity and ubiquity of structural underdevelopment throughout the expansion of the capitalist system.

From this perspective on underdevelopment, Frank generates more specific hypotheses which can be used to guide development theory and policy. In contrast to the world's metropole, which is satellite to no other region, the development of national and regional metropoles is limited by their satellite status – for example, local metropoles such as São Paulo, Brazil, and Buenos Aires, Argentina, can only achieve a *dependent* form of industrialization. Similarly in an hypothesis directly opposed to the finding of modernization theory that development is diffused through contact with the metropole, Frank hypothesizes that the satellites experience their greatest development when ties to the metropole are weakest, historically during wars and geographically in terms of isolated regions. By extension, regions which are most underdeveloped today had the closest ties to the metropole in the past – Frank finds this confirmed by the 'ultra-underdevelopment' of the sugar-exporting and mining regions of Latin America. In summary, underdevelopment in Frank's theory is not an original condition, nor does it result from archaic institutions surviving in isolated regions. Rather it is generated by the same process which develops the centre; in particular, underdevelopment in the periphery results from the loss of surplus which is expropriated for investment in the centre (Frank 1969b: 3–14).

An immediate weakness in Frank's theory resides in his failure to specify the surplus-extraction mechanisms. In some cases, these are obvious – for example when centre corporations own land or productive facilities in the periphery and withdraw surplus as rent or profit, or when centre banks loan capital to peripheral states and enterprises and withdraw surplus as interest. But what of peasant producers owning their own land and producing cash crops for centre markets, a situation typical of much of the periphery in the nineteenth and twentieth centuries? Here the beginning of an answer is provided by Emmanuel (1972; see also deJanvry, 1981: 15) in the theory of unequal exchange. Emmanuel argues against the classical economic theory of trade which posits that the existing international division of labour and system of trade has advantages for all participants. Instead Emmanuel argues that trade makes poor countries poorer and rich countries wealthier. Emmanuel assumes the perfect international mobility of capital but the immobility of labour between countries – hence wage rates persistently differ greatly between the two types of country. Peripheral countries export (agricultural) products that embody large quantities of their cheap labour and import (industrial) products embodying small amounts of expensive centre labour. This leads to terms of trade favouring the higher-cost products of the centre, while devaluing the exports of the periphery. Unequal exchange in trade is thus a hidden mechanism of surplus extraction and economic stagnation in the periphery. Samir Amin (1976: 143–4) estimates the amount of surplus transferred from poor to rich countries via unequal exchange to be 1.5 per cent of the product of the rich countries, but 15 per cent of that of the poor countries, an amount which Amin says is 'sufficient to account for the blocking of the growth of the periphery'. Putting the matter bluntly, it is exactly this expropriated surplus which the peripheral countries have had to borrow back to finance 'development schemes'.

As Blomstrom and Hettne (1984: 69–76) argue, dependency theory is holistic in that it attempts to place a country into the larger (global) system. It stresses the external causes of underdevelopment rather than those internal to a peripheral society. A strong emphasis is also placed on economic rather than social interactions, while in Frank's version the accent is on regional or spatial aspects, rather than class contradictions. For most theorists, dependency and underdevelopment are synonymous, although Cardoso, for example, thinks a dependent form of capitalist development can be achieved. And finally, dependency is politically radical, with most adherents proclaiming the need for some kind of socialist revolution, although a purely nationalist politics (merely cutting a peripheral country off from the world capitalist system) can also emerge from spatial versions of the dependency perspective.

World systems theory

World systems theory draws on the dependency school but also has antecedents in a version of history named after *Annales: économies, sociétiés, civilisations*, a French journal founded in 1929 by Lucian Febvre and Marc Bloch. Dissatisfied with conventional history because it was isolated and unrealistic, the founders of the *Annales* school aimed at remaking the discipline. Their intention was to use the comparative method over long sweeps of time to examine differences and similarities between societies. The geographer Vidal de la Blache, who believed that *genre de vie*, or way of life, mediated between people and environment, deciding which of nature's possibilities is used, was an ally of the school, which has always had a strong geographical component in its regional histories, geo-histories, studies of transportation, etc. The *Annales* school's themes are history as social history, especially of the material conditions of the masses, an emphasis on structural factors or relative constants, the 'long term' as a common language for the social sciences and, while this is not a Marxist school of thought, a concern with the relations among economy, society and civilization. Ferdinand Braudel (1972; 1973), the most famous of the school's second generation scholars, has particularly been interested in structural limitations on material and economic life, the great slopes of historical change over centuries, regional histories and the sudden break-up of ancient ways in the nineteenth century. This kind of view is suited to the study of the long-term history of the peoples of the Third World and the sudden changes thrust upon them through inter-societal contact.

A more obvious connection with development theory is forged by a leading English-speaking representative of the *Annales* school, the sociologist Immanuel Wallerstein. The broad spatial scale and long historical time span of *Annales* history is retained by treating world history as the development of a single system. By 'system' Wallerstein means a social entity with a single division of labour so that all sectors or areas are dependent on economic interchanges. The past is characterized by mini-systems, small entities with a complete division of labour and a single cultural framework, as in simple agricultural or hunting and gathering societies. But the recent integration of the hill tribes of Papua New Guinea and the bushmen of the Kalahari into the capitalist world system means that mini-systems no longer exist. World systems, characterized by a single division of labour and multicultural systems, are now long dominant. The outstanding example is the capitalist world economy, in which production is for profit and products sold on the market. In such a system production is constantly expanded, as long as profits can be made, and producers innovate to expand the profit margin – hence the secret of capitalist success is the pursuit of profit. In the past, 'world' economies were unstable and tended to degenerate into world empires, like China, Egypt and Rome, held together by a common political organization. The capitalist world economy has resisted various attempts to create a world empire (for example by Britain and the United States) and capitalism has therefore proven to be a lasting way of regulating and co-ordinating global production (Wallerstein, 1979).

For Wallerstein, the capitalist world economy originated in sixteenth-century Europe, in an era of increased agricultural production for growing urban markets. At the core of the developing world economy, in England, the Netherlands and northern France, a combination of pastural and arable production required high skill levels and favoured wage labour. The periphery of the system, in eastern Europe and increasingly the Americas, specialized in grains, cotton and sugar together with bullion from mines, all of which favoured the use of coerced labour (either a kind of serfdom which Wallerstein calls 'coerced cash crop labor' or pure slavery). In between lay a series of transitional regions, mainly former cores degenerating towards peripheral status, making high-cost industrial products, giving credit and dealing in specie, and using sharecropping in the agricultural arena (e.g. northern Italy). Whereas the interests of capitalist landowners and merchants coincided in the development of the absolute monarchy and strong, central state machineries in the core, ruling class interests diverged sharply in the periphery, leading to weak states. Unequal exchange in commerce was imposed by the strong core on the weak peripheries and the surplus of the world economy was thereby appropriated (Wallerstein, 1974: chs 2 and 3). From this geo-sociological perspective, Wallerstein outlines the main stages of the history of the world capitalist economy:

1 The European world economy emerged in the long 'sixteenth century' (1450–1640). The crisis of feudalism posed a series of dilemmas that could only be resolved through geographic expansion of the division of labour. By the end of the period, north-west Europe had established itself as core, Spain and the northern Italian cities declined into the semi-periphery, and northern Europe and Iberian America were the main peripheries of the system.

2 A mercantile struggle during the recession of 1650–1730 left England as the only surviving core state.

3 Industrial production and the demand for raw materials increased rapidly after 1760, leading to geographic expansion of the system, which now became truly a world system under British hegemony. Russia, an important external system, was incorporated into the semi-periphery, while the remaining areas of Latin America, and Asia and Africa were absorbed into the periphery. This expansion enabled former areas of the periphery (the United States and Germany) to become semi-peripheral and, eventually, core states. The core exchanged manufactured goods with the periphery's agricultural products. The mass of industry created an urban proletariat as an internal threat to the stability of the core of the capitalist system which the industrial bourgeoisie eventually had to 'buy off'. This also solved the problem of what to do with the burgeoning output of manufacturing.

4 The First World War marked the beginning of a new stage characterized by revolutionary turmoil (the Russian revolution ended the country's further decline towards peripheral status) and the consolidation of the capitalist world economy under the hegemony of the United States. After the Second World War, the urgent need was expanded markets, which the hegemonic power met by reconstructing western Europe, reserving Latin America for United States investment, and decolonizing southern Asia, the Middle East and Africa. Since the late 1960s a decline in US political hegemony has increased the freedom of action of capitalist enterprise, now in the form of multinational corporations. However, the present conjuncture has two fundamental contradictions: in the short run withdrawing surplus from the working class in the form of corporate profit conflicts with a long-run reliance on mass consumption by the same working class; and co-optation of oppositional movements by giving them a minor share of privileges may eliminate class opponents in the short run but ups the 'ante' in the next crisis of the world economy – the cost of co-optation rises ever higher while the benefits from it seem less worthwhile. Wallerstein believes that struggles will take place in all the areas of world capitalism over a long period of time resulting eventually in a socialist world government (Wallerstein, 1979: 35).

The world system thus has structural parts and evolving stages. Within such a framework, Wallerstein argues, we can make comparative analyses of the whole system and its regional parts. With such an analysis we can link the development of the core with the underdevelopment of the periphery, and both with the history of the world system (for further discussion see Taylor, 1985).

Critique of dependency and world systems theories

Dependency and world systems theories enjoyed wide support among critical social theorists and development planners in the 1960s and 1970s, and world systems theory remains a leading source of innovative ideas and historical research (e.g. Wallerstein, 1980, 1988; Kaplan, 1978; Goldfrank, 1979). However, dependency theory of the type proposed by Frank soon came under attack from the left. Here we summarize some criticisms of dependency as a specific explanation of underdevelopment, leaving more general criticisms of Marxist-type theories to Chapter 10.

Ernesto Laclau (1971) found that Frank had confused integration of the colonies into the capitalist world market with the creation of capitalist production relations in Latin America. In a Marxist understanding, he pointed out, feudalism and capitalism are separate modes of production defined in terms of production relations, and the forging of links with the world market is irrelevant in distinguishing between them. Frank's pre-occupation with exchange relations between centre and periphery flaws his attack on the theory of dualism and makes his assertion of Latin American capitalist underdevelopment misleading. For Laclau, Latin America remained feudal until the early twentieth century, and semi-feudal conditions are still widely prevalent today (see also Cheng, 1976; Brewer, 1980).

Characterizing Frank and others as taking the position that capitalist development is impossible in the periphery (Bienefeld, 1981) and that only underdevelopment is possible there, a number of writers (e.g. Weisskopf, 1976; Jackman, 1984) have shown that dependent countries can have economic growth rates higher than non-dependent countries, or more generally that capitalism can develop the productive forces in the periphery. Frank's mistake, in Palma's (1978) view, lies in the 'mechanico-formalistic' nature of his analysis which renders his theory static and unhistorical – Palma is referring to the 'mechanical' determination of internal by external structures. Instead Palma advocates more specific studies which include the possibility of capitalist development in Latin America (see also Palma, 1981). Similar arguments are assessed in Chapter 10.

The outstanding left critique of dependency and world systems theories came from the Marxist historian Robert Brenner (1977). An entire line of writers, he says, intended to negate the optimistic model of economic advance derived from Adam Smith – that widening trade and a deeper division of labour bring economic development – but ended up presenting a theory which, in its central aspects, is the mirror image of that model (see also Palma,

1978: 899–900). Thus Frank finds the dynamic of capitalist expansion to reside in the rise of a world commercial network, with growth or backwardness originating in the surplus-appropriation chain. Wallerstein carried this to its logical conclusion by defining capitalism as production for profit via exchange and focusing on the expansion of the world market. With this market came a world division of labour, the development of different methods of labour control in the various specialized zones, and the creation of strong and weak states in core and periphery. For Brenner, the main mistake of both analysts lies in displacing class relations from the main body of their development theories. Brenner argues that the incorporation of more productive resources into the world system does not determine the economic development process, nor does the transfer of surplus and build-up of wealth in the core, nor even specialization of labour control systems. Capitalism differs from all previous societies in its systematic tendency to economic development. But this is achieved through increasing labour productivity, which makes it possible for workers to reproduce themselves in less time than previously, and thus make a larger surplus (i.e. relative surplus labour in Marx's terms). Pre-capitalist societies were confined to extending absolute labour – extending the working day, gaining control over more workers, etc. But under capitalist relations, workers are free to be combined with machines at the highest possible level of technology, while competition forces capitalists to innovate. What therefore accounts for capitalist development is the class structure of the economy as a whole. This is exactly the position ignored by Frank and Wallerstein. The political conclusion is that while Frank's 'circulationist' argument could be construed as arguing merely for regional autonomy (i.e. development can be achieved through cutting the lines of surplus outflow) Brenner argues for changing the relations of production in favour of a new class system characterized by efficiency but also social equity.

Conclusion

Dependency theory played an important role in the critique of conventional theories – whether the theory of comparative advantage in mainstream economics, or modernization theory in mainstream developmental sociology. Dependency theory formulates a theory to account for the historical experience of peripheral societies proposing, in opposition to progressivist views, that contact with capitalism has led to underdevelopment rather than development. We conclude that such an over-generalization was necessary given the political and theoretical tenor of the times. A more typically academic statement, one which says very little with a lot of qualifications, would have been overwhelmed by propaganda that United States capital, aid and peace corps volunteers could work miracles of development for Third World people. Furthermore, there was a need at the time to expand Marxian theories from their established base in class analysis towards questions of inter-regional relations. This dependency theory achieved through the concept of the spatial transfer of surplus. To Baran's and Frank's eternal credit they recognized that surplus moves in space as well as between classes. Again, an over-emphasis on space, rather than class, was necessary to make the point – anything less would have been ignored. And, in partial response to critics, dependency and world systems theories can be synthesized with class-based theories. Dos Santos (1969: 80), for example, argues that several kinds of internal social structure are conditioned by international relations of dependence. Cardoso and Faletto (1979) theorize the complex relations between internal and external forces in peripheral societies in terms of an alliance between local dominant classes and international interests on the one hand and opposition from local dominated classes on the other. In certain circumstances, they add, segments of the local dominant class may seek alliances with the dominated classes to protect themselves from foreign interests (see also Evans, 1984). Likewise world systems theory has recognized that it must place working people at the centre of the analysis:

> Placing labor at the heart of the study of modern world history can unite the classical Marxist position of political praxis aimed at the working class, with the global dynamics of class struggle in a world social system. In that unity lies the best hope for peace and a more humane world order.
>
> (Bergquist, 1984: 17)

In brief, while Marxist criticisms of the dependency and world systems perspectives have validity, the differences between dependency and Marxism have been overstated. Dependency and world systems theories share the critical perspective and political position of Marxism and can be integrated into a left analysis. Dependency theory opened our eyes and made us see the world from the perspective of the oppressed masses living in its 'distant' corners. This is quite a contribution.

Chapter five

Historical materialism

Historical materialism was conceived by Marx and Engels during the social and technological upheavals of the mid-nineteenth century. They too were children of their time, sharing with environmental determinism the idea of rooting human history in natural evolution. But convinced by the evidence around them that a specifically human version of evolution was achieved by the growth of the forces of production and the development of consciousness, they gave their theorization an additional emphasis on the social production of existence. As Victorians, Marx and Engels believed in the transformative abilities of science and admired the material results of technological revolution. But they saw production from a critical vantage, as an emancipation but also alienation from nature, as a process of human self-creation but one directed by a few. The political result was that Marxist theory became not the scholastic pursuit of truth for its own sake, but the development of a theory to guide socio-political practice. Furthermore, as with structural functionalism, the theory they originated tries to uncover the hidden causes of social events. But, distinctively, emphasis is placed on the exploitative character of society and thus the need for a transformative politics. Marxism therefore shares common features with deterministic and functional modes of materialist thought emerging from the biological discoveries of the nineteenth century, but differs in ways theoretically significant and politically profound.

Idealism and materialism

We should first counterpose Marxist materialism with idealism, its opposite, and feudalism's finest intellectual achievement. Hegel's (1967 edn) idealism connects individual consciousness with a collective and transcendent World Spirit. Movements of Spirit precede human thought and material events, in some way causing them.

God 'wishes' an event to happen and moves in mysterious ways to effect it – for example, by influencing the human mind through spiritual means. Reality is the ground where Spirit achieves perfection. History is the evolution of an ever more perfect World Spirit.

In their youth Marx and Engels adhered to a radical version of German (Hegelian) idealism. However, they developed an alternative, indeed oppositional, conception of social existence, as their thinking matured, which they called 'historical materialism'. As they put it at the time:

> In direct contrast to German philosophy which descends from heaven to earth, here we ascend from earth to heaven. That is to say, we do not set out from what men say, imagine, conceive nor from men as narrated, thought of, imagined, conceived, in order to arrive at men in the flesh. We set out from real, active men, and on the basis of their real life-process we demonstrate the development of the ideological reflexes and echoes of this life-process. . . . Life is not determined by consciousness but consciousness by life.
>
> (Marx and Engels, 1981 edn: 47)

In materialism the mind is not a mysterious inner spirit with direct contact with the great Spiritual director in the sky, but the way the brain works – the brain being the natural product of evolution. Human consciousness comes not from God, but real experience in the material world. Thought starts by generalizing from an ongoing sequence of real events with the thinker becoming capable of interpreting experience and accumulating the resulting 'theories' as knowledge. In particular, ideas form and language is phrased to express them during social activity – making consciousness the supreme social product. And, for Marx and Engels, social activity always involves labour organized to transform nature. By playing thought back on production the human being changes the direction taken by evolution. This process takes the form of a dialectic between necessity and freedom.

Dialectics

Modern materialist understanding was made possible by economic development in early capitalist western Europe and in turn enhanced it. The upheaval wrought by the events of the proto-industrial and industrial revolutions, the discovery of the New World, and in general the shift from the constraints of feudalism into a freer social order, were causally related to a transformation in consciousness from spiritualism and religion towards materialism and science. As proponents of this revolution in thought, Marx and Engels saw themselves turning spiritual belief back on its feet, in that consciousness is the product of matter rather than its origin. Yet they retained, from Hegel's idealism, dialectical ideas like development through contradiction and transcendental change. In the dialectic, the natural and social worlds are seen not as sets of phenomena eternally the same, but as processes capable of rapid change. What brings change about, from a material point of view? Dialecticians begin with the '*inner*' relations which bind the elements of a thing together. Inner relations must be complementary and co-operative, so that an object has coherence. Inner relations may also be contradictory, giving an object the immanent potential for transformative change. New objects then arise from re-arrangements of the disintegrated components of the old. But there is also an external-relational dimension to dialectical thinking which is especially appealing to geographers and others fascinated by earth space. Objects also develop through '*inter*' relations with the external environment of other things. The particular character of an object is preserved by the frictions of distance; but also new components may be derived from external relations with other objects. Inner, or localized, movements give rise to new characteristics more readily in favourable outer, or broader, contexts. As an object grows its needs transcend the local and its ability to transmit change accumulates. Yet spatially transmitted changes from a new object cannot have transformative effects unless objects affected elsewhere are already internally unstable. The historical process is a synthesis between these inner and outer dynamics; the two aspects of change may alternate in significance; the types of their interaction are multiple.

Dialectics therefore traces an 'object', like a society, to its origins in nature and the decomposition of previous societies, see it developing in relation to other changing societies, and understand this development process in terms of quantitative growth and periodic qualitative transformations.

The materialist dialectic is a deterministic conception like environmentalism. But the space of determination is broadened to include the social environment created by human activity, and the structure of determination is expanded to imply multiple causations and interactions. Materialism shares with organic thinking the premise that there is a necessary order to social life, having a sense of historical direction similarly ordered by natural necessity. But it differs from naturalistic teleology in that history is made by increasingly conscious subjects. That is, humans become increasingly able to control the character and direction of their lives. So while it may be possible to find in Marxism a vulgar and mechanical determinism, such as the 'reading' of cultural characteristics directly from an economic causal script, this is a possibility realized only by those predisposed to an inaccurate simplified understanding.

Production as the transformation of nature

In materialism, therefore, the origins of human life are sought not in some act of creation by a 'Superior Being', but in the natural evolution of a distinctive kind of animal. For Marx and Engels, the writing of history always begins with these natural bases of life, and their modification through human action. As with other animals, the assimilation of natural materials is 'the everlasting nature-imposed condition of human existence . . . common to all forms of society in which human beings live' (Marx, 1976: 290; for elaboration see Timpanero, 1975). However, humans distinguish themselves from other animals when they *produce* their means of subsistence – i.e. when they consciously and exactly transform natural resources into materials which satisfy their needs:

> Labour is, first of all, a process between man and nature, a process which man, through his own actions, mediates, regulates, and controls the metabolism between himself and nature. He confronts the materials of nature as a force of nature. He sets in motion natural forces which belong to his own body, his arms, legs, head, and hands, in order to appropriate the materials of nature in a form adapted to his own needs. Through this movement he acts upon external nature and changes it, and in this way he simultaneously changes his own nature. He develops the potentialities slumbering within nature, and subjects the play of its forces to his own sovereign power.
>
> (Marx, 1976: 283)

For Marx there is no eternal or essential human character. Character is created under natural and social conditions never entirely of our choosing. 'Human nature' emerges and changes during the struggle with others to gain a livelihood from the rest of nature.

Originally, human labour was similar to the animal's hunting or gathering – it was simply necessary activity which made further life possible. For Marx the first transformative moment in natural history came when humans put consciousness and deliberation into effect, most significantly in the making of 'instruments of labour'. 'The use and construction of instruments of labour, although present in germ among certain species of animals, is characteristic of the specifically human labour process', especially instruments of a mechanical kind – the 'bones and muscles of production' (Marx, 1976: 228). Tools and instruments allow nature to be transformed in an intentional way. Shaping natural materials into tools and instruments which shorten necessary labour time ('necessary' in terms of providing the essentials of life) is the economic key to social evolution.

Development of the human ability to transform nature gives the possibility of higher material standards of living and thus the potential for a liberated existence. How do the productive forces advance? As the automatic consequence of the exercise of rationality? For Marx, the social relations people enter into for their existence determine the possibility and direction of productive development. Social relations are therefore Marxism's most essential analytical category.

Production as social relations

The analytically distinguishing feature of Marxism is its emphasis on the social relations between individuals in the production of their existence. We can conceive these relations broadly to include relations between the individual and the collective (society), between groups within a collective, and between societies over space. In examining social relations more precisely, it should be remembered that even relations fundamental to existence, functional relations that is, are characterized by a dialectical interplay between co-operation and competition, collaboration and struggle.

For Marx the most essential aspect of social relations is control over productive forces and resources: nature itself as a means of production; human effort; and the means created by labour for the further working of nature – the social means of production. In this understanding a second transformative moment in history comes when the means of production, even labour itself, comes to be controlled by a ruling elite. This creates a fundamental social cleavage between those who control the productive forces and those who perform the work. An aspect of this, crucial for economic development, is the extension of the working day beyond necessary labour time:

> Wherever a part of society possesses the monopoly of the means of production, the worker, free or unfree, must add to the labour necessary for his own maintenance an extra quantity of labour in order to produce the means of subsistence for the owner of the means of production.
>
> (Marx, 1976: 344)

Marx's term for the extraction of unrewarded surplus labour time is 'exploitation'. Because exploitation enhances co-operation in the collective labour effort, it is a fundamental process by which productivity is enhanced and nature counteracted. The contradictory aspect is that some people achieve greater control over nature and people than others. For Marx this has profound implications for consciousness, politics and socio-cultural life as a whole. Entire modes of production come into being as certain ways of enhancing productivity are directed by particular social relations. Marx's own summary of this complex structure runs as follows:

> In the social production of their existence, men inevitably enter into definite relations, which are independent of their will, namely relations of production appropriate to a given stage in the development of their material forces of production. The totality of these relations of production constitutes the economic structure of society, the real foundation, on which arises a legal and political superstructure and to which correspond definite forms of social consciousness. The mode of production of material life conditions the general process of social, political and intellectual life. It is not the consciousness of men that determines their existence, but their social existence that determines their consciousness.
>
> (Marx, 1970: 20−1)

First, let us consider what Marx does not say. He does not argue that a 'machine' called 'forces of production' stamps out 'parts' labelled 'economic structure, political superstructure, and social consciousness'. Dialectical terms like 'correspond' and 'condition' cannot imply such a mechanical determination. Marx does argue that the level attained in the development of the productive forces − society's ability to transform nature − limits and directs its cultural and political development, that is its entire mode of existence. Beyond this very general connection we have to look at the particular determinations binding production with the other aspects of social life.

Thus, religious consciousness is thought, by Marx, to be determined by the level and type of productive control a society achieves over nature:

> the ancient social organisms of production . . . are conditioned by a low stage of development of the productive powers of labour and correspondingly limited relations between men within the process of creating and reproducing their material life, hence also limited relations between man and nature. These real

limitations are reflected in the ancient worship of nature, and in other elements of tribal religions.

(Marx, 1976: 172)

With the development of the forces of production, people come to rely on each other (via exchange) more than directly on local nature. Yet they relate through objects exchanged via markets, rather than as co-operators bound by direct agreement in social planning. Alienated relations maintain the precariousness of existence; the social need for religion, however, takes a different form: 'For a society of commodity producers . . . Christianity with its religious cult of man in the abstract . . . is the most fitting form of religion' (Marx, 1976: 172). Only when natural determination is finally countered by communal relations at a high level of productive forces will the conditions for the existence of religious consciousness disappear:

> The religious reflections of the real world can, in any case, vanish only when the practical relations of everyday life between man and man, and man and nature, generally present themselves to him in a transparent and rational form. The veil is not removed from the countenance of the social life-process, i.e. the process of material production, until it becomes production by freely associated men, and stands under their conscious and planned control. This, however, requires that society possesses a material foundation, or a series of material conditions of existence, which in their turn are the natural and spontaneous product of a long and tormented historical development.

(Marx, 1976: 173)

Again, notice what Marx does not say. The contents of religious consciousness cannot be exactly predicted from a theoretical analysis of the natural/social base of society. But the general structure of consciousness (its religious character) and even the overall type of religion (worship of nature or abstract humanity), are determinable from a structural analysis of the material conditions of existence.

Let us take the analysis further. Societies are exploitative when uncompensated surplus labour, or its products, are taken from the direct producers. Surplus is not easily extracted. Particularly at a low level of development of the productive forces, when the margin of survival is narrow, exploitation may mean the difference between life and death at times of natural scarcity. So the exploitation process is seen by Marx as an arena of struggle, the dominant using a combination of economic, political and ideological force to ensure control over socially-produced surplus, and the dominated resisting through overt means like organization and rebellion, and hidden means like reluctant compliance. In such a context, consciousness must take ideological forms which rationalize and legitimize exploitation. Organized religion is one such form.

In addition, a society characterized by exploitation and conflict must develop institutions for ensuring elite domination and for collectively reproducing the conditions and infrastructures of production (Hirsch, 1978: 64–5). Many of these reproductive functions are accumulated in the state, governed by an appropriate kind of politics. Again, however, the exact character of the state can only be found through examining its particular conditions of existence:

> It is in each case the direct relationship of the owners of the conditions of production to the immediate producers – a relationship whose particular form naturally corresponds always to a certain level of development of the type and manner of labour, and hence to its social productive power – in which we find the innermost secret, the hidden basis of the entire social edifice, and hence also the political form of the relationship of sovereignty and dependence, in short, the specific form of state in each case. This does not prevent the same economic basis – the same in its major conditions – from displaying endless variations and gradations in its appearance, as the result of innumerable different empirical circumstances, natural conditions, racial relations, historical influences acting from outside, etc., and these can only be understood by analysing these empirically given conditions.
>
> (Marx, 1983: 927–8)

Hence for Marx there are structural connections between the economic base of a society and the state apparatus. These limit and direct the kind of state which comes into existence, but people living in specific times and places create its more exact form.

The Marxian concept of mode of production thus entails a system of social relations which organize the forces of production in the transformation of nature. The social objectives are: the production of material goods used to reproduce labour power; and a surplus of products, used partly for investment in new means of production, and partly to support and protect the life-style of the rich and famous. The social ability to transform nature limits and directs consciousness, while the state monopolizes violence, rationalizes inequality and guarantees the continued reproduction of the social order. For Marx this whole process is suffused with social, political and ideological struggles generated by contradiction at the very heart of society – in the relations which bind social actors together as producers.

Social transformations essentially involve a shift from one mode of production to another. Marx envisages these as violent episodes undertaken by desperate people when all the productive possibilities of the old social order have been exhausted:

> At a certain stage of development, the material productive forces of society come into conflict with the existing relations of production or – this merely expresses the same thing in legal terms – with the property relations within the framework of which they have operated hitherto. From forms of development of the productive forces these relations turn into their fetters. Then begins an era of social revolution. The changes in the economic foundation lead sooner or later to the transformation of the whole immense superstructure. . . . No social order is ever destroyed before all the productive forces for which it is sufficient have been developed, and new superior relations of production never replace older ones before the material conditions for their existence have matured within the framework of the old society.
> (Marx, 1970: 21)

Crises in material development sharpen and intensify ongoing class struggles, giving the possibility for broad social change, including political and ideological transformation. This happens only when the productive possibilities of the old society near exhaustion. And the new relations gained through struggle do not materialize out of thin air, or from utopian thought alone, but from embryonic relations already present in the dying body of the old society.

Marx therefore thought it possible to theorize 'laws of social transformation' – laws being understood as tendencies or probabilities – leaving the specifics of historical change to be worked out by empirical research. Marx himself had time only to begin an outline of the main modes of production which have characterized human history, and investigated only one (capitalism) in detail. However, from his notes, posthumously published as *Grundrisse* (Marx, 1973: 471–514), it seems he envisaged society passing through the following historical types:

1 The original *Tribal or Natural Society* characterized by communal appropriation of nature.
2 *Kinship Society* in which the patriarchal head of the clan organizes production and controls access to nature.
3 *'Asiatic Society'* in which the communal possession of land is

vested in a supreme ruler, making the direct producers actually propertyless. Part of the surplus is exacted as tribute, while other parts are used for communal reserves and expenses (like war and religion). This dominance of the despotic ruler depends on the provision of collective means of production and communication, and control of external means of defence.

4 *Ancient Society* in which clans are divided into higher and lower ancestral lineages, with previously communal lands similarly divided between private and state property. At first private lands are worked by free peasant families, contributing surplus labour to the state in the voluntary form of military service. But warfare brings slaves, and the enlargement of state lands increases the power of the dominant lineages (patricians). Hence, in the case of Rome, conquest and the development of slavery, concentration of land ownership, trade and the money system are contradictions signifying eventual systemic decline.

5 *Germanic communities* located in peripheral forested areas, where long distances separate clan groups occupying their own lands. Here the commune exists only as occasional tribal gatherings, not as a city or state. Public property takes the form of hunting, grazing and timber lands. The patriarchal head of the clan continues as main organizer of production.

6 *Feudalism*. Resulting from the fusion of the Germanic and Ancient modes in Europe, this mode retained features of each – such as common lands, yet with the nobles' monopoly over territory. Serfs perform surplus labour for the lords, independent mercantile towns extract surplus from the countryside, class and unequal exchange relations contribute to the breakdown of the feudal order.

7 *Capitalism* employs wage labour under conditions of private ownership of productive property. Ancient rights to land and productive resources virtually disappear from memory. Nature becomes a set of objects useful for the making of profit. The social forces of production develop to a degree previously unthinkable, science partly replaces religion, the state and law protect property rights. Contradictions in natural and social relations push towards a new society characterized by highly developed but communal forces of production – *socialism*.

Rather than exploring this last phrase (see Chapters 9 and 10), we should first present some of the subsequent developments in Marxist thinking. Obviously we cannot present a complete history of Marxist thought. But certain key debates have framed the recent discourse on Marxism, and we shall follow two. The first is the structural Marxism of Althusser; the second the feminist critique and restatement of historical materialism.

Structural Marxism

The above formulation contains a tension between structural imperatives (such as change in the forces of production) and people's struggle to change the conditions of their lives (such as class struggle) – that is between the unfolding of a system and the acts of people in creating history. This tension emerges as different schools of Marxist thought, and has been widened by those critical of the method or liberative intent of Marxism. Post-war France, for example, witnessed a debate between existential phenomenology, which argued for a subject-centred historical process, and structuralist thought (drawing on structural linguistics, anthropology and psychology) which argued for a 'decentring' of the subject (Benton, 1986). Structuralism's message is that human subjectivity and class consciousness are continually formed within rules set by the existing social order. Hence the analytical focus is moved to the social system in general.

Drawing on the passage from Marx quoted earlier, which argues that social relations and the way surplus is extracted are the hidden bases of the entire social system, Althusser and Balibar (1970) reconceptualized social totalities as 'structures in dominance'. They thought it possible to elucidate necessary structural relations between the various 'levels' or 'instances' of a society (economy, consciousness and politics) by asking more precisely how the form of surplus extraction determines the 'super-structure'. Under capitalism, surplus is expropriated at the same time, and in the same space, as useful products are being made. This hidden form of exploitation can occur without the direct use of 'extra-economic' coercion – for example, there is no need for the state to force workers directly to produce a surplus of values. Therefore the economic instance is said to 'dominate' the capitalist mode of production. By comparison, in the feudal mode of production, serfs reproduce themselves on plots of land and in time periods separate from the surplus labour services they perform for the landlord. They have to be forced to 'contribute' labour services through extra-economic coercion in the form of violence by the armed retainers of the lord, backed by the monarch. Under feudalism, therefore, the political instance is said to be dominant. Hence, Althusserian structuralism argues:

that economic relations, centrally those between owners and direct producers, are always determinant (in the last instance) with respect to the other levels or 'instances' in a society, and with respect to the configuration of society as a whole, but . . . this determination by the economic structure takes the rather indirect form of assigning to the other, non-economic levels, their place in a hierarchy of dominance with respect to one another, and the kind of articulation between them.

(Benton, 1986: 72)

Thus, there is a law of determination by social relations which operates differently for specific modes of production.

Furthermore, for Althusser, revolutionary change, from one mode of production to another, occurs through a 'condensation' or 'fusion' of several contradictions occurring in the different levels of a social structure. Change itself is a complex process in which dominance may be displaced from one instance to another – for example from the political to the economic during the transition from feudalism to capitalism (Taylor, 1979: chs 5 and 6). In other words, the various aspects of social existence are realigned following significant change in the social relations of production. Structuralism is proposed as a formal way of discussing these changes.

In this conception each mode of production has a characteristic structure, typical contradictions, and a dynamic, or course of development. A central tendency in a mode (like the economic tendency for the rate of profit to fall in capitalism) is counterbalanced by other forces (like the cheapening of the costs of machinery, or the use of new labour supplies) to produce the complex rhythms of change which typify an epoch. Any society has several interlocking rhythms: because a mode of production contains several divergent tendencies in dynamic tension with each other; and because several modes of production are present in an actually existing 'social formation'.

With this last analytical category we can begin to emerge from the heady realm of abstract theory to the world of concrete social practices. 'Social formation' is an intermediate level of structural analysis between the highly abstract conception of mode of production and the empirical details of particular events, places and times. The term social formation implies that we are looking at a certain society in terms of the articulation of its constituent modes of production. The word articulation has two meanings, both intended here. First, articulation means 'speaking coherently': modes of production are structures of necessary activities and relations informing practices at the level of the social formation. Here the purpose of mode of production analysis is to provide a guide to the (frequently ancient) structures hidden behind the myriad acts of everyday life. Second, articulation also means 'join together or connect'. Any social formation is made from a specific combination of several modes of production or even, more closely, from a combination of the phases of development of several modes of production, like a decomposing 'Asiatic' society and an advancing mercantile capitalism. Social formations take regional forms because the articulation of modes of production varies with locational position, depending for example on nearness to the point of origin of a new mode of production, or with the qualities of the particular natural environment being transformed by social labour – the results of geographic relations such as these can be called 'regional social formations'. Similarly, in historical terms, a social formation contains features traceable to the modes of the past, is dominated by a specific mode in the present, and has signs of the mode of production contending for future domination. Social formations are the ways in which general structures of existence appear in actual life situations.

Articulation of modes of production

Stimulated by the Althusserian debate, Marxists have re-theorized the connections, or articulations, between different modes of production, with the objective of elucidating the general tendencies in inter-societal relations. Articulation is thought of in terms of historical transitions (one mode giving rise to another) and in terms of geographical relations across space (one mode affecting another at a given historical moment). Articulation theory provides a way of understanding the history of development in terms of its different qualities and speeds as modes of production come to dominate social formations. Societies organized by dynamic modes of production, with powerful states and persuasive ideologies, are able to expand in space – indeed there are forces like resource scarcity and the need for markets which prioritize spatial expansion, or even make it necessary. The set of contacts between a dynamic, expanding mode and other modes, with different dynamics and patterns of expansion or contraction, is the main content of a structuralist geography of development.

Most work has focused on the relations between capitalism and pre-capitalist or non-capitalist modes of production. As pointed out by Wolpe (1980: 1–6), Marx's texts provide the bases of opposing views on the relationship between capitalism and other modes. The first view is that the appearance of capitalism signals the inevitable disintegration and incorporation of pre-capitalist modes: the implication is that little account needs to be taken of the inner dynamics of pre-capitalist societies. The second view involves a recognition of many different relations between capitalist and pre-capitalist modes of production, relations which are changed through struggle – capitalism does not establish immediate dominance, its destructive effects may be retarded by the internal solidity and organization of pre-capitalist modes. These different positions in Marx have been important for socialist political strategy in pre-revolutionary Russia and China and in Latin America.

In the more recent Marxist debate on articulation, the concepts of modes of production and social formation have similarly been interpreted in different ways – Wolpe (1980: 6–19) refers to a 'restricted version' of mode of production limited to the forces and relations of production (Hindess and Hirst, 1975: Banaji, 1977) and an 'extended version' which also includes mechanisms of reproduction and laws of motion (Balibar, 1970; Bettelheim, 1972). The latter proves more insightful for articulation theory. Thus Bettelheim (1972: 287–316) develops an argument of great significance for development theory. Social formations, he says, are complex entities composed from a number of modes of production – workers, for example, may be involved in capitalist and non-capitalist relations, as peasants and wage earners. Yet the world of social formations is dominated economically, politically and ideologically by the capitalist mode of production. Domination entails polarized development of the world's productive forces, fast development in the dominant countries and slow in the dominated, and thus the expanded reproduction of economic inequalities. This polarized development essentially results from the initial development of machine production in the industrialized countries, a development rooted in the production relations of these countries. The subsequent domination of the world by capitalist production relations entails an international division of labour favourable to further development of the dominant social formations and unfavourable for the dominated countries. World domination by the capitalist mode of production favours the maintenance (or in some cases the formation) in the dominated countries of production relations, politics and ideologies which 'block' the development of the productive forces. All of this supports the view that inequalities between rich and poor countries are prior to the exchanges between them (cf. Emmanuel, 1972), although such exchanges may subsequently worsen the original conditions of inequality.

Furthermore, Bettelheim continues, the capitalist mode of production has a two-fold tendency to reproduce productive forces and relations at the national and international scales, with the latter tending to break up the former as capitalist production becomes world-wide. At the 'national' (or social formational) level there are specific forms and degrees of domination by the capitalist mode over other modes, with a definite pace of growth and rhythm of crisis, level of wages, form of socialization of labour etc. At the international level there is again a specific pattern of domination and subordination of the different social formations with their uneven paces of development. Inside social formations in which the capitalist mode of production is *predominant*, other modes of production tend mainly to be dissolved and their human agents incorporated into capitalist production relations. But there is also a secondary tendency, conservation–dissolution, in which non-capitalist production is restructured while being subordinated, and is therefore 'conserved' – agriculture within capitalist social formations, for example. Inside social formations in which the capitalist mode is *not directly predominant*, various blocking and constraining mechanisms make the *main* tendency conservation–dissolution. This produces a heterogeniety of material and social conditions, often interpreted (poorly accordingly to Bettelheim) through the metaphor of 'dualism'. In such heterogeneous social formations large numbers of producers may only be linked to capitalist institutions, such as the market, to a minor extent so that, for example, prices for peasant products do not have the value of production (i.e. cost of reproducing the peasant family) as their lowest limit, but may be lower than this for indefinite periods. On the other hand, peasants are obliged, by debt among other things, to produce and sell even at these low prices. This has many implications for widening class inequalities and uneven spatial development. In general, Bettelheim finds the notion of the exploitation of one region or country by another better defined in terms of social formations, each with a specific make-up, fitting into a complex, hierarchical international structure. World domination by the capitalist mode of production is based on increasing exploitation of workers in the dominant 'imperialist' countries, and of working people in the dominated countries.

The theme of the transformation of pre-capitalist modes of production by the expanded reproduction of capital is also taken up by Barbara Bradby (1980). Following Rosa Luxemburg (1951), Bradby uses the term 'natural economy' to refer to pre-capitalist systems of social production oriented directly to needs (of the family for example) with industry and agriculture being closely connected. Non-commoditized economies like these are dissolved as labour processes are separated from the land as an immediate condition of production, and as production is oriented towards exchange rather than use value (see also Peet, 1989a). The process of dissolution is complete when land and labour power become commodities, and the objective of production becomes the creation of surplus value. However, not all natural economies dissolve with the same speed: Marx, for example says that the Asiatic mode of production is more resistant than others to penetration by capitalism. Therefore, an analysis of the destruction of natural economy must take into account first the dynamic of the extended reproduction of capital (or more generally the internal dynamic of capitalism), second the internal structural characteristics of pre-capitalist modes, and third the articulations between the two.

Bradby finds that Marxist theories of the first, the expanded reproduction of capital, have stressed: capitalism's ineffective demand for its own surplus, either at all stages (Luxemburg, 1951) or at certain (late) stages (Lenin, 1975); its need for cheap labour supplies, available because workers' families are maintained by income from pre-capitalist sectors (Meillassoux, 1972; Wolpe, 1972); and the different needs (raw materials, land, labour, markets) which capitalism has at different stages (Rey, 1973; Caldwell, 1977). In the case of the second, the internal dynamics of pre-capitalist modes have to be specified by looking at the principal relations of production and the reproduction of these relations. For example, in a study of a lineage-based system in Africa, Meillassoux (1972) shows how the social product is appropriated by the elders, who monopolize prestige goods, and acquire wives, dependants and (at one time) slaves as labour power, further increasing their wealth and reproducing an emerging hierarchical structure. When it comes to the third, the articulation between these two kinds of processes, Bradby can only pose some relevant questions, like whether capitalism necessarily attacks other modes, whether capitalism grows internally in pre-capitalist modes or is entirely an assimilation from the outside, what happens when exchange occurs between modes, and whether pre-capitalist remnants demonstrate incredible resistance or survive merely because areas, peoples or activities are of little use to capitalist industry.

In a further exposition of the ideas of Rosa Luxemburg (1951) Bradby (1980: 97–108) criticizes her 'strong thesis' that capitalism has a permanent need for an external market, but supports her 'weak thesis' that capitalism has occasional need for raw materials and labour from non-capitalist modes. Pre-capitalist modes put barriers in the way of quick and easy access to needed material and labour resources. Capitalism gains ascendancy to transform and destroy the old relations of production, and then assimilates them.

(The weak thesis thus ends up contradicting the strong, in that assimilation reduces the area of world space providing buyers of capitalist surplus products.) Capitalism's methods of destruction include direct military force, taxation by the (colonial) state and the introduction of cheap commodities. Open force is used first because of the urgency of capitalism's need for materials and labour. However, later processes of market competition, the competitive destruction of rural industries, and the eventual destruction of peasant agriculture by large-scale capitalist enterprise, are anything but peaceful as, for example, surplus labour is ejected from the countryside. Bradby herself finds no reason for the necessary use of open force at all stages in the expansion of capitalism: force is a temporary device to get results quickly and cheaply, such as getting access to raw materials by means other than fair exchange. Under other circumstances natural economy may be destroyed peacefully.

In a second critical exposition, Bradby (1980: 108–12) interprets the work of Pierre-Philippe Rey (1973) as showing that capitalism has not yet reached the stage where it can dispense with pre-capitalist modes for the reproduction of labour power or provision of raw materials. Hence too-rapid destruction of pre-capitalist systems would impede the functioning of capitalism. Development entails the widening of capitalist relations of production to increase the labour base from which surplus value can be extracted. But in underdeveloped countries today capitalism remains at the stage where it can widen the labour base only by reinforcing pre-capitalist relations of production. In such a context development is self-contradictory. Generalizing from the transition from feudalism to capitalism, Rey suggests three stages in the articulation between capitalist and non-capitalist systems: first, capitalism finds a labour force and agricultural provision especially in feudal modes, where the interests of the feudal and bourgeois ruling classes may coincide over long periods of time; second, capitalism becomes the dominant mode but still needs pre-capitalist modes to supply an increasing labour force – in such situations the pre-capitalist ruling class is seen as the enemy by peasants and small producers rather than the capitalist class, so that an anti-capitalist worker/peasant alliance is unlikely to form; third, capitalism provides itself with an expanding labour force without the intervention of pre-capitalist formations – this stage has not yet been reached. Bradby is critical of Rey's notions of capital as conscious and intentional, of the idea of the permanent necessity of capitalism's articulation with other modes, and of Rey's view that violence is a necessary part of transitions in pre-capitalist societies.

71

Bradby's (1980: 118–26) own contribution to articulation analysis comes in the form of a comparative study of highland and Amazonian Peru. In the Peruvian Andes, some of the indigenous *ayllus* (kinship, social and land units) were directly appropriated by the Spanish conquerors, while others reproduced labour power for the mines and agricultural estates. The Spanish broke the relations between the *ayllus* and the Inca state, but other reciprocal and communal work relations survived in transformed condition. This situation changed little in 400 years. Recently, however, competition from imports and large-scale agriculture on the Peruvian coast has increased, while the state has intervened through land reform – in some places rationalizing land holdings into large capitalist enterprises, elsewhere forming co-operatives. Bradby interprets these changes as a capitalist need for raw materials (large-scale meat and cereal production) and/or cheap labour from displaced peasants. She sees the pre-capitalist mode as susceptible to economic attack because of its specialization and division of labour, the peasants' 'highly individualistic spirit' and their limited redistribution of benefits. By comparison, a study of an Indian tribe in eastern Peru suggests increased capitalist interests in Amazonian land as supplier of raw materials but a more resistant internal social structure in that the pre-capitalist mode had little division of labour (each kinship unit was virtually self-sufficient) and the units were internally re-distributive. Her conclusion (Bradby, 1980: 126) is that 'capital is perfectly indifferent to what happens in natural economy', so that pre-capitalist societies may alternately be ignored, destroyed or even, in the case of some Brazilian Indians, physically exterminated. In brief she argues for empirical case studies to draw out the details of the many particular articulations.

The concept of articulation of modes of production theorizes the process of uneven development within and between social formations. Uneven development is structured by the reproductive requirements of the dominant mode and the level and types of resistance of the subordinate modes, with empirical analysis being necessary of the particular interactions and the formation of specific features, such as unemployment or indigenous capital formation. Articulation theory also analyses the alliances and oppositions of classes specific to social formations, the ideological combinations and inter-penetrations, and the various roles of the state. Ideas similar to this have occurred to theorists of otherwise widely dissimilar persuasion. Drawing on earlier conceptions from (East) Indian and Indonesian social science, J.H. Boeke (1953: 4) defines social dualism as 'the clashing of an imported social system with an indigenous social system of another style' and proceeds to explain that an economic theory of heterogeneous societies must explain the indigenous pre-capitalist ('primitive') society, the capitalist or other form of outside society, and the interactions between the two. Boeke however sees himself as generalizing from historical facts using a Weberian (ideal–typical) approach and, while rich in insights, his work lacks theoretical depth. Articulation of modes of production, therefore, is proposed as a theory of development superior to dualism, modernization and dependency theories (Taylor, 1979).

Structural Marxism of this kind has obvious implications for the geography of development. Modes of production, characterized most basically by their social relations, entail different capacities for the development of the productive forces – capitalism, for example, develops productivity under the coercion of competitive relations between capitalist owners and exploitative relations between capitalists and wage workers. But social formations are formed by the articulation of several modes, so the economic dynamic of society has several, often conflicting, developmental tendencies. Regional social formations have different developmental potentials, thereby taking a centre–periphery geographic shape. Surplus is extracted by ruling elites within a given social formation, and is transferred between formations according to principles of hierarchy and domination. Spatial systems of surplus extraction are protected and expanded by state action – imperialism and colonialism for example – and spatial inequalities are legitimized by ideologies (racism for example). Hence development can be usefully phrased in geo-structuralist terms.

Socialist feminism

Social feminists point to deficiencies in classical Marxism – that it misses activities and relations fundamental to existence – yet admire the general structure of the historical materialist understanding and share its equalizing, liberating intent. Socialist feminists are particularly critical of classical Marxism's emphasis on the economy and its relative silence on the question of women (Mitchell, 1966). The strongest statement on this topic is made by Hartmann (n.d.). She argues that the analytical categories of Marxism are 'sex-blind', in that the feminist question of the causes of gender inequality (male dominance over women) are lost during a structural Marxist analysis of class inequality (ruling class dominance over workers). A specifically feminist analysis is needed to reveal the systemic character of relations between men and women.

But most feminist analyses are insufficiently materialist and historical. Hence both

> Marxist analysis, particularly its historical and materialist method, and feminist analysis, especially the identification of patriarchy as a social and historical structure, must be drawn upon if we are to understand the development of western capitalist societies and the predicament of women within them.
>
> (Hartmann, n.d.: 3)

Mitchell (1966) differentiates between the several structures affecting women's condition – production, reproduction, socialization and sexuality. The first involves women's work in the non-domestic economic sphere, while the others concern women as wives or mothers. Each has different contradictions and dynamics. But all form a unity in women's experience, with the family triptych of sexual, reproductive and socializing functions dominant. Benston (1969) sees women performing domestic labour within the home and family as having a different relation to the means of production than men. The family is a productive unit for housework and child-rearing. Morten (1971) sees such activities as fulfilling the function of the maintenance and reproduction of labour power in (contradictory) relation to production. Della Costa (1973) emphasizes the quality of life and relations in domestic work as determining women's place in society regardless of place and class. Housewives are exploited workers, whose surplus is used most immediately by their husbands as an instrument of oppression – under capitalism, she says, women become the slave of a wage slave.

We can see two tendencies of materialist analysis emerging from critical statements like these. *First* there are those who wish to develop explicitly Marxian ideas in the direction of considering women (Vogel, 1983). For Hartmann's statement, that Marx and Engels were analytically sex-blind, is only three-quarters true: Engels had one eye half open. In a general statement similar to these quoted earlier Engels says:

> According to the materialistic conception, the determining factor in history is, in the final instance, the production and reproduction of immediate life. This, again, is of a twofold character: on the one side, the production of the means of existence, of food, clothing, and shelter and the tools necessary for that production; on the other side, the production of human beings themselves, the propagation of the species. The social organization under which the people of a particular historical epoch and a particular

country live is determined by both kinds of production: by the stage of the development of labor on the one hand and of the family on the other.

(Engels, 1972: 71–2)

Engels argued that the development of production was associated with the rise of private property, exchange, wealth differences and class antagonisms. Sexual relations similarly changed in that the position of women relative to men deteriorated with the advent of class society.

In a significant elaboration of the insights of Engels, Etienne and Leacock (1980) argue for the primary importance of social relations for understanding socio-economic and sexual inequalities and hierarchies. An inexact correlation between socio-economic and sexual inequalities suggests the origins are inextricably bound together. They develop a framework for considering relations between socio-economic and sexual hierarchies by defining four broad types of production relations in the course of human history:

1 Egalitarian relations among most gatherer-hunter and many horticultural peoples, as part of which women had autonomy, multiplicity of economic roles, and decision-making power.
2 Inequalities in ranking societies attributable to the growth of trade, specialization and the reorganization of production relations. In particular, a 'public' sector of the economy concerned with production for accumulation and trade was differentiated from a 'private' household or lineage sector concerned with production for subsistence and sharing. Men's responsibilities in hunting and warfare often led directly into trading and external political relations, and growth of the public sphere undermined women's position.
3 Stratified relations in pre-industrial society in which the patriarchal household becomes an economically independent unit, and women's work further privatized.
4 Exploitation in industrial capitalist society in which the subjugation of people generally is paralleled by the special subjugation of women (Etienne and Leacock, 1980: 8–16).

The main point of this analysis however is not the details of the kinds of gender inequality, but the attempt at linking modes of production with forms of gender relations. Not only does this begin to theorize the transition from egalitarian relations to domination, it dispels the myth that women have always ('naturally') been subordinated to men.

Second, the problem for some feminists with this kind of analysis lies in the continued, uncritical use of the same sex-blind Marxist terms – traditional Marxian analysis is simply pointed in the direction of women. New analytical categories are needed. Thus Hartmann (n.d.: 14) defines *patriarchy* as a 'set of social relations between men, which have a material base, and which, though hierarchical, establish or create interdependence and solidarity among men that enable them to dominate women'. The material base of patriarchy lies in men's control over women's labour power, a control maintained by excluding women from access to essential productive resources. Here the analytical potential lies in connecting the social institutions which coerce and legitimize unequal power relations with the personal processes of psychology and consciousness through which people, especially women, accept and rationalize their position in society.

Significant advances have therefore been made by feminists in broadening the Marxian conception of the material production of life. This broader conception includes gender as well as class relations, women's labour in the domestic and public spheres, child-rearing and socialization, and the family as the particular locus of reproduction. The argument presented earlier on material production is complemented rather than negated by such feminist conceptions. The main methodological problem remaining is to conceptualize the relations between these various aspects, or more basically to see them all as elements of a process of reproduction – some initial thoughts on this are presented in Chapter 10. For most of human history, productive and reproductive processes have occurred at the same time and in the same geographical location – as the barely distinguishable aspects of a whole way of life. More recently and increasingly, the various aspects have separated, as inequalities have widened. Indeed the contradictions between these various aspects of the life process have been a driving force in societal change. Class- and gender-dominated societies, characterized by exploitation, dominance and unequal life conditions, have developed most in material productive terms. This is the most powerful source of legitimation for the continuation of these otherwise unbearable inequalities. In terms of a materialist theory of development, therefore, attention to questions of gender brings greater completeness and deeper insights. Marxism should appreciate the feminist critique.

Conclusion

An adequate theory of economic development must satisfy several requirements. It must link the development process with the basic features of social existence. It must be grounded in a more general theory of societal dynamics. And it must hold the prospect of social change, including an explanation of how poor people themselves can improve their lot. This chapter has argued that Marxism, of a structural variety no less, comes closer to satisfying these requirements than other leading theories. Its materialist view focuses attention on the real processes in which people make their lives, and thus the institutions and relations which lie at the heart of any society. Dialectics is a general theory of change through contradiction which takes as one specific form the dynamics of societal transformation. A materialist dialectic roots class and gender struggles in societal contradiction, seeing these as transformative actions by the masses. And in socialism, Marx gives a vision of a social organization founded on material progress and democracy in all aspects of life.

The geographical version of Marxism – what we might call geo-structuralism – particularly emphasizes the transformation of nature during the productive process (see also Simmons, 1989). It therefore links modes of production to natural environments, retaining the crucial biological insights of environmental determinism and structural functionalism, but in a way which also emphasizes the relative autonomy of human thought and action. Such a naturally based theory of productive development has the capability of seeing inter-societal relations in a far broader, more insightful way than modernization theory or the dependency school. This potential is best realized in the concept of articulation of modes of production, in which spatial relations are reconceptualized as a total set of inter-societal connections, interpenetrations and influences.

Marxism is not a perfect theory. Major changes are still underway – for example the broadening of its earlier focus on the material production of existence into its *re*production through class and gender relations. Theoretical deficiencies remain, such as the placing of the individual into the context of the social. And the political forms of actually existing socialism, which so far have mainly occurred in societies long characterized by state domination, leave much to be desired as models of economic progress or social democracy. Western Marxism, however, has shown a capacity for debate and a commitment to a democratic form of socialism which allow for the necessary changes in philosophy, theory and political practice. Especially when compared with 'post-Marxist' ideas which overstress human freedom, contingency and randomness, structural Marxism remains the leading basis of a theory of development. The following chapters attempt to demonstrate this in the only credible way, by putting theoretical claims into practice.

Chapter six

The pre-capitalist world

The previous chapter gave an introduction to structural Marxism which placed new emphasis on two aspects of the production of existence: nature as the source of the production of life; and gender as a social-relational context in which life is made. These emphases widen the structural concept of mode of production to include more of the significant acts and aspects of human existence. However, the analytical concepts which result cannot be scientifically justified by logical coherence alone, but must show their effectiveness through interpretative use. This chapter uses the ideas of historical materialism to look at the pre-capitalist world.

Why is this important? Capitalism is a relatively recent phenomenon, but one with roots in hundreds of thousands of years of human history. The elements and relations of capitalism derive from predecessors in the pre-capitalist world. Capitalism first developed in a limited space and encountered pre-capitalist societies in its global expansion, both types of system being profoundly influenced by their encounters. There were many different dynamics of development prior to capitalist accumulation, but most people in the economically advanced countries know next to nothing about the history of the rest of the world. Hence for completeness of knowledge we must delve into global history before we can understand the capitalist system.

The approach lies first in outlining alternative 'schemas' of historical development – that is the ordering of modes of production in time and space. Three modes which have characterized long epochs of this development are then examined in more detail: primitive communism, lineage and tributary societies. Here we undertake a brief analysis of their structures to answer basic questions about the various conditions under which development has occurred in history. The objective as well is to trace essential elements of contemporary life to their historical and geographical origins – we have in mind issues like the origins of gender and class inequalities, private property and the state. These elements are recombined and transformed by capitalism which encounters them again, in earlier and somewhat different forms, through articulating with pre-capitalist modes during expansion into a global system. As a final prelude to this expansionary moment, the last part of the chapter reconstructs, in very broad outline, the regional geography of the world in 1400, emphasizing the civilizations which flowered in a variety of non-European environmental spaces. The ideology that capitalism is the last instance of a long history of superior European civilizations has to be countered by the knowledge that many civilizing leaps occurred beyond England's green and pleasant land.

Schemas of historical development

Do societies proceed along a unilinear path, so that spatial variations result only from different regional velocities of development? Or do societies change along a number of paths, so that regional variations result more fundamentally from entirely different processes occurring (with varying speeds) at different locations? The beginning of an answer is provided by concepts of historical 'schemas' of development.

As Melotti says:

> a schema or model of historical development is a simplified representation of the structures which characterize the various social-economic formations, and of their fundamental dynamics . . . an heuristic tool . . . [which] helps to lay bare the implicit 'logic' of historical development by stripping away the fortuitous accretions that blur its outline.
>
> (Melotti, 1977: 5)

In his early years, he continues, Marx presented a simplified schema of historical development derived from the experience of western Europe (Figure 6.1). This was not intended to represent a general path all people were destined to tread. Yet that is what the Europeans understood. And this interpretation was preserved in Stalinist and Maoist models, even being imposed on the schoolchildren of Cuba, Vietnam, Korea and Tanzania as a kind of Marxist cultural imperialism. Within this simplified conception there was a debate on recognizing, in the works of the later Marx, the separate existence of an 'Asiatic' mode of production. Based on this, Plekhanov and Trotsky saw two distinct but parallel lines of development in the West and East, while Wittfogel stressed the importance of environmental factors in forming these bilinear paths (Figure 6.2). Melotti, however, argues for a more complex

Figure 6.1 Unilinear schema of historical change

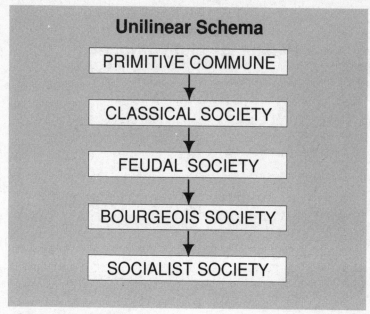

Source: Melotti, 1977: 8.

multilinear schema, in which original variations in primitive communism are retained through time in distinctive but interacting paths of societal development (Figure 6.3). For Melotti (1977: 7) Marx's history concerns people's real activities and, therefore, cannot be 'the unilinear development of a determined process; on the contrary, it is the multilinear and disjunctive expression of something which can take a wide variety of courses, and yet is not without "meaning" '. This, he thinks, bears closest resemblance to the ideas of the later Marx.

Hence the main difference between the multilinear and unilinear models resides in the concept of an Asiatic mode of production. Reconstructing Marx, Melotti argues that in 'Asiatic' societies (the Middle East, India, China but also meso-America and the Andean region) the state takes a despotic form, the individual has less autonomy, while contradictions develop less fully into social struggles. Asiatic societies cope with crises through a series of reincarnations which change outward appearances only. By comparison, European feudal societies had an autonomous sphere of

Figure 6.2   Bilinear schema of historical change

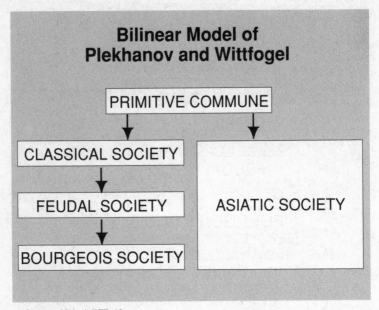

Source: Melotti, 1977: 12.

economic activity (referred to as 'civil society' by Marx) in which the urban bourgeoisie could pursue private profit – the city was the womb of capitalism within feudal society. Marx therefore thought that feudalism alone, and not the Asiatic mode of production, could give rise to capitalism. For Melotti such a conclusion could only be reached by a multilinear conception of history.

The question unresolved by Melotti is the theoretical status of the regional variants of development. At times one mode of production has a number of regional types (hence primitive communism is composed of a number of types of commune); at other times regional variants are labelled distinct modes of production (Asiatic mode in the East, feudalism in the West). The number of regional modes of production could be extended beyond those mentioned by Melotti, while the Maya and Inca do not fit easily or logically into the 'Asiatic' category. The conceptual terminology thus tends towards confusion. Yet the issue in contest is important. Is capitalism a mode of production uniquely produced by European history, or does it result from a global process which took only a

Figure 6.3 Multilinear schema of historical change

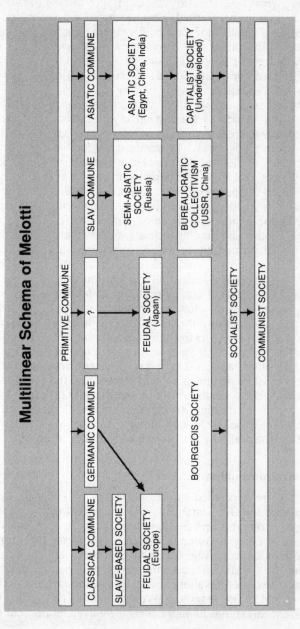

Multilinear Schema of Melotti

PRIMITIVE COMMUNE

CLASSICAL COMMUNE

GERMANIC COMMUNE

SLAV COMMUNE

ASIATIC COMMUNE

SLAVE-BASED SOCIETY

?

FEUDAL SOCIETY (Europe)

FEUDAL SOCIETY (Japan)

SEMI-ASIATIC SOCIETY (Russia)

ASIATIC SOCIETY (Egypt, China, India)

BOURGEOIS SOCIETY

BUREAUCRATIC COLLECTIVISM (USSR, China)

CAPITALIST SOCIETY (Underdeveloped)

SOCIALIST SOCIETY

COMMUNIST SOCIETY

Source: Melotti, 1977: 26.

certain form in Europe? The view adopted here is that capitalism emerged from the tributary mode of production, existing in a number of world regions, but appearing as a decentralized social formation (feudalism) in Europe for several hundred years prior to the rise of capitalism. By comparison more centralized tributary formations had greater stability and, for various reasons, tended more towards reincarnation than the generation of new social forms like capitalism.

This argument entails adopting a certain version of structuralist terminology. Mode of production is an abstract term theorizing general characteristics common to a large number of societies over long time periods. Social formations are combinations of modes existing in specific time periods and in particular regions. Societies are concrete, real structures bounded in some way (e.g. by national boundaries) in space and time. Localities are everyday life spaces occupied by smaller groups of people. This terminology, especially the retention of the term mode of production to mean something non-regionally and non-historically specific, and the use of the term social formation to mean something more abstract and general than society, is intended to preserve elements from the unilinear view in what is, essentially, a multilinear perspective. Thus, the similarities that occur by necessity in human history take the very general form of a limited number of modes of production – primitive communism, lineage systems, tributary societies, capitalism, socialism. However the human's autonomy of action, differing environments (physical and social) and temporal variations mean that the same mode takes many different regional forms, or appears as quite dissimilar social formations. And societies within the same social formation may be significantly different from one another, while retaining structural affinities. Capturing all this in one phrase, societies develop along a number of paths characterized fundamentally by one sequence of modes of production.

Primitive communism

All who are persuaded by the testimony of scientific evidence, rather than the Old Testament, now know that the human species emerged from the ape 5–10 million years ago. Archaeological findings at Olduvai Gorge in East Africa indicate that stone-tool-using, erect human beings definitely existed 1.8 million years before present (BP) and that gathering seeds and plants and hunting animals was the prevailing mode of livelihood until agriculture began some 15,000 years ago (Wenke, 1984). The startling conclusion from this is that human beings have lived 99 per cent of their

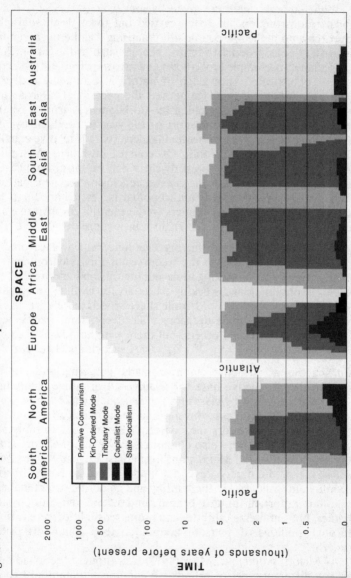

Figure 6.4 Modes of production in time and space

time as gatherers and hunters (Figure 6.4). If we want to know what kind of animal the human being is, and what is the historically typical form of society, we must reconstruct the structures characteristic of this long past.

While some insights are given by archaeology (Spriggs, 1984), most reconstruction has to be carried out through ethnographic research among the few people still practising a gathering and hunting lifestyle. In productive terms, peoples such as the bushmen of the Kalahari use simple tools (bows and arrows, digging sticks, etc.) but a sophisticated knowledge of nature in producing a diet of vegetable products, small game and the occasional large animal from an environment stretching 25–30 kilometres from a central water hole. Bushmen spend most of the year in bands of twenty-five people or less, with no formal leader. There is relative equality in terms of access to food. Of course, bushmen, Australian Aborigines, and tropical forest dwellers may be far different from our human ancestors. But the general conclusion reached, particularly by Marxist-feminist anthropologists, is compelling: the consensus is that gatherer-hunters were generally co-operative and egalitarian (Leacock, 1982: 159). In a little more detail:

> During most of human history everyone helped, according to their age and sex and to the resources of their environment, in acquiring food, in making tools and utensils, in building shelters, and in obtaining and working materials for clothing in climates where it was needed. . . . People shared food; there were no rich and poor. They made decisions collectively; some people were more influential than others, but there were no powerful chiefs.
>
> (Leacock and Lee, 1982: 1)

Putting this as an active claim, nomadic gathering and hunting formed the productive base for a universal primitive communist social order marked by class and gender equality (for a case study see Lee, 1982). Whereas conventional social science has come to accept that our ancestors were descended from apes, it refuses to consider that they were also communists. We can therefore share the conclusion of the Marxist anthropologist Eugene Ruyle (1988: 480–1) that humanity 'evolved under conditions of liberty, equality and solidarity in the hunting and gathering commune' and that 'it is important for us to bear in mind that not only our physical bodies, but our mental abilities and moral sensibilities were formed through millions of years of adaptation to a communist social order'.

As Melotti points out, Marx (1973: 672) thought there had been several different types of primitive communism (communist social formations in our terminology) with variations depending in part on geographic conditions. Recently more detailed, empirically-based work on primitive communist formations has been carried out in Marxist anthropology (e.g. Lee and Leacock, 1982) and by feminists concerned with discovering the origins of gender inequalities. Sanday (1981) believes, with Marx, that the natural environment and the mode of subsistence are the fundamental bases of a society's symbol system, sex role behaviour and authority relations. Hunting societies thus have certain general characteristics – they tend, she says, to produce distant fathers, masculine creator symbols and an outer, animal orientation towards the powers of the universe; gathering societies, by comparison, tend to produce involved male parents, feminine or couple creator symbols, and an inner, plant orientation; a dual orientation sometimes occurs in societies combining female plant gathering with the predatory hunting activities of men. In all societies women are associated with the power to give life, men with the power to take it. Depending on nature and historical conditions, one or both powers may be culturally valued. Furthermore, men and women tend to be more segregated and competitive in societies with masculine/outer configurations, and more integrated and co-operative in inner/plant-oriented societies. Male dominance, she concludes, is the likely outcome of the outer/segregated configuration when historical conditions (such as increased technological complexity, warfare, famine, migration and colonization) favour expansion of the male sphere and increased dependence of women on men (Coontz and Henderson, 1986: 27–9). The important point here is Sanday's discerning different 'culture configurations' (similar to social formations) in primitive society and her insight that such differences may be of great consequence in subsequent development.

Thus the earliest human societies were small, loosely organized groups whose survival depended on sharing and co-operation as well as flexible living and working arrangements. An informal division of labour by sex probably occurred in populations that developed specialized technology (like projectile weapons) for hunting big game. It was convenient for long-distance hunters to be males rather than females due to the risks for female childbearers or the difficulty for nursing mothers to suddenly leave their children. Yet there is nothing in such a division of labour that would of necessity create sexual inequality (see, for example, Lee, 1982). Further, while communal societies are associated with certain territories or resources, this simply gives them the right to be consulted by other users, rather than constituting monopoly over nature. Hence the relevant questions become: how did the original egalitarian communal societies move in the direction of sexual inequality, class and private property? How did some of the inegalitarian possibilities latent in primitive communism mature into dominant social forms, leaving communism as remnants in the distant desert and forest perimeters of the world?

Kin-ordered mode

These processes began between 15,000 and 8,000 years ago with the Neolithic revolution (Heiser, 1981). Most theories of the causes of this productive transformation point to environmental changes occurring at the time, the retreat of the Pleistocene glaciation and associated changes in plant and animal resource availability. Probably under conditions of resource stress, major additions were made to the forces of production through the domestication of plants and animals. Drawing a number of arguments together, Mies (1986: 54–6; also Childe, 1951) argues that as gatherers of plant foods women were the first to cultivate them. The regular cultivation of food plants signified an enormous increase in the productivity of female labour which, according to some, made surpluses regularly possible for the first time. Domestication occurred in three distinct areas within the broader zones of gathering and hunting – south-west Asia, south-east Asia, and meso-America and nearby Andean areas of South America (Figure 6.4). From these cultural hearths, agriculture diffused outwards into the rest of the world over the next few thousand years (Sauer, 1952).

Marxists look at this and see something else happening in addition. The change from gathering and hunting to crop production and herding was the productive basis of a momentous change in social relations. Coontz and Henderson (1986) argue that agriculture needs continual, organized work in the production and storage of food and this entailed giving more formal assignment of rights over resources to kin groups within the communist band. At first merely the logical extension of the communist social order, this process had results which eventually overturned that social order. Thus kin groups showed a growing concern over labour reproduction by controlling their fertile women. The sexual division of labour was formalized in kin institutions. The development of kin property gave greater emphasis to lineal descent and lineage heads became more powerful. The existence of distinct property-owning groups increased the possibility of differences at the local level in access to resources. Kin-corporate property rights increased the potential for inter-communal conflict and thus the importance of the male role as warrior. Kin societies developed more formalized exchange networks for people and goods. And one aspect of the exchange of people through marriage, significant for later class formation, was that the spouse that moved was separated from direct control over his or her natal group property, becoming a producer but non-owner in another household. An increasing redistribution, and the organizational tasks this created, had several results, not the least for (male) political roles. Hence agriculture and kin-ordering had tremendous consequences in transforming social relations. This laid the basis for social inequalities if it did not create them (Coontz and Henderson, 1986: 112–26).

Defining kinship as 'a way of committing social labour to the transformation of nature through appeals to filiation and marriage, and to consanguinity and affinity', Wolf (1982: 91–6) argues that in practice rights and claims to shares of social labour vary widely among kin-ordered societies. Where resources are widely available, for example in food-collecting bands, group membership expands and contracts among people in habitual inter-action with one another and the society retains characteristics of primitive communism. By contrast, where clusters of labour are expended cumulatively and transgenerationally to transform a particular segment of the environment, as in agriculture, the idiom of filiation and marriage serves to include or exclude people more rigidly in terms of rights to resources. In addition, the mythical charters which define lines of kinship-connection organize the exchange of persons between groups and allocate managerial functions unevenly in terms of elders and juniors or lines of higher or lower rank – that is, kinship is escalated into the political/legal realm, becoming a governing ideology in the allocation of political power. A major source of this power in the kin-ordered mode is control over the reproductive powers of women. Sources of contradiction are external oppositions between groups in competition for resources, and internal oppositions between men and women, elders and juniors, original settlers and newcomers, lineages rising to prominence and those falling from it. Leaders draw followings through alliances and redistributive dexterity, accumulating control over surpluses up to some limit set by the kin order. The tensions inherent in such inequalities are contained because they are particularized in everyday life (for example juniors confront elders as individuals rather than as classes), while myth and ritual dissolve them into generalities conveying messages about the nature of the universe. Conflict, however, may accumulate beyond the capacity of such coping mechanisms, producing breakup, fission and, more generally, social change. Finally, these tendencies towards inequalities are greatly enhanced when kin-ordered modes articulate with tributary or capitalist modes. Expanding spatial relations give opportunities for the seizure and transfer of surpluses beyond those previously available. This is why chiefs collaborated with European fur-hunters and slave-traders offering them access to arms, valuables and thereby a following outside the kinship system and unencumbered by it. In this last instance, the chiefly lineage is an incipient class of surplus-takers.

The most complete Marxian version of the transition from lineage to state/tributary society is provided by Friedman and Rowlands's (1977) model of the 'epigenetic evolution of civilisation'. They see societies as structures of reproduction, with the different 'levels' being relatively autonomous yet linked in two ways: from the ecosystem up is a hierarchy of constraints (negative determinations) which set limits of functional compatibility between levels, and hence limit their internal variations; and relations of production organize and dominate the entire process of social reproduction and determine its course of development. Evolutionary 'stages' are generated from previous ones in a process described as 'epigenesis'. Reproduction is also considered to be a spatial phenomenon in which a number of separate social units are linked through exchange and other external relations. External relations also determine the transformation of a society. Thus the specific evolution of a social formation depends on internal properties, local constraints and place in a larger system.

For the sake of simplicity, Friedman and Rowlands outline only one line of evolution from tribal to state society, merely indicating other divergent developmental pathways. In tribal systems, as we have seen, production is organized by local lineages, defined as households linked by ritual to a common ancestor. Nature is believed to be controlled by supernatural spirits. Ancestors intervene with the gods to bring wealth to a lineage, which converts the wealth into prestige or 'social value'. This creates a division between higher and lower lineages. Women are exchanged from higher to lower status groups in exchange for a bride-price. Surplus derived this way can be converted into more riches and an expanded labour force. Leading lineages feast the community and by the rules of reciprocity gain back more wealth. (The notion that gifts must be returned 'with interest', which once preserved egalitarian relations, now transforms them in that obligated kin groups begin to pledge labour when they cannot repay in kind.) For such a system to expand beyond a certain limit, dependent labour must be accumulated – from internal sources as debt slaves, and from external sources as captives. (Lerner (1986: 78) points out that the majority of the enslaved were women.) The positive feedback structure leads to increased ranking – a 'conical' clan headed by a chiefly lineage. This lineage comes to occupy the position of mediator in making offerings to the deity and is entitled to tribute and corvée labour, so the chief comes to control a sizeable portion of the total labour force of the community. The tribal system is also expansionist with alliance and exchange relations extending across a wider area to the further advantage of the emergent chiefs. The importing of slaves from surrounding groups creates a regional pattern in which centres of power expand at the expense of surrounding societies. The lineage system also culminates in the development of central places mainly consisting of ceremonial centres where ritual activities concerned with the fertility of nature and economic welfare are concentrated. However this movement towards state formation is not inevitable. Particularly in mountain regions, chiefdoms based on swidden agriculture tend to collapse due to decreasing productivity, and class stratification is therefore minimal (e.g. it is confined to the 'big man system').

Coontz and Henderson (1986: 129–48) add to this by suggesting that the matrilocality (men moving to their wives' families) or patrilocality (women moving to their husbands' families) plays a crucial role in the emerging stratification. They argue that patrilocality offers more opportunities for appropriating wives' labour and therefore for a local lineage to concentrate labour, wealth and power than matrilocality, thus enhancing inter-lineage inequalities. The subordination of female labour and reproductive power in patrilocal kin systems was a precondition for the emergence of other forms of stratification, such as the growth of the power of those men who could monopolize women. Social stratification also attached prestige to wealth- or power-generating mechanisms associated with the male side of the division of labour, devaluing womanhood as a social category.

Summarizing, all find that agriculture and kin-ordering were significant moments in social history – equivalent perhaps to leaving the Garden of Eden. A transformation in the organization of labour played on divisions already present under primitive communism. Heads of kin groups became chiefs endowed with mystical power. Womens' reproductive abilities were controlled by kin group and tribe. Positions held by men increased in relative power. Some peoples were alienated from their natural homes as slaves of powerful lineages. Centres separated in space from peripheries. And processes were set in motion which eventuated in the myriad social and spatial inequalities we know so well today.

Tributary mode

For Marx, changing relations to nature are an essential aspect of the transition from kin to class society. Speaking of the early kin-ordered 'clan communities' held together by blood, language and customs, Marx (1973: 472–4) says that they relate to the earth 'as the property of the community, of the community producing and reproducing itself in living labour' and that such a relation appears to the members of the community as 'natural or divine'. Without at first changing this fundamentally, a greater community can appear, above and beyond the local, as the higher proprietor of nature, leaving the smaller clan communities as hereditary possessors. This greater unity takes the form of a despot to whom part of the surplus labour is paid as tribute. Labour is also stored as communal reserves and expanded on war, religion, etc., and in that lies the source of other kinds of lordly dominion (priests, warriors). While the greater community may remain a 'more democratic' type of clan system, in which patriarchal heads of families relate to each other as equals (the 'Germanic system' which we can interpret as a type of lineage society), a more despotic form results from the marshalling of the communal labour force for the construction of aqueducts, means of communication and other public works (the Asiatic system). In such a system cities form at exceptionally favourable points for external trade or where the head of state and his retinue resides. Hence we find a transition from clan-organized society to one dominated by a line of rulers, nobles, priests and other members of a ruling class.

Subsequent Marxian accounts of the transition to tributary and state-dominated society have elaborated these skeletal remarks. Returning to Friedman and Rowlands (1977), who draw only on archaeological evidence gathered mainly in the Near East, but consider also findings in south and east Asia and the Americas, the original *'Asiatic' state* is seen as emerging in fertile valleys and riverine plains where the evolutionary tendencies of the conical tribal system can work themselves out to the fullest. In a fully formed conical clan structure, rank becomes absolutely determined and wives now move from lower to higher ranks as tribute. Surplus is not longer redistributed, but a major portion is absorbed in the transformation of the old tribal aristocracy into the state, the basis of elite power still being monopolization of access to the supernatural. In this period there is a growth of large ceremonial centres surrounded by smaller centres and villages, perhaps a two-tiered central place system. Central tribal domains dominate smaller surrounding domains. The internal structure is one in which a main line chiefs or kings leads a quasi-sacred aristocracy; the exploited class consists of commoner lineages and slaves produced by debt and capture. (Coontz and Henderson (1986: 151–5) add that while the state did not initiate the oppression of women or their ideological devaluation, its development worsens their position by centralizing and formalizing authority, undermining women's ritual power, restricting women to the domestic sphere which becomes divorced from the public sphere, and increasing the power of the husband in a more nucleated household.) Growth in the agricultural surplus permits an increased division of labour. Artisans are brought to the centre where new and more productive techniques are elaborated. Interregional exchange develops markedly. Regional specialization is not yet developed to any great extent, but already there is a pattern of combined development and underdevelopment.

Prestige goods systems also begin to appear in the tribal period, but develop more fully as extensions of the 'Asiatic' states. There is an increase in production of goods in the centre which are passed down to lower ranks where they enter into local exchange networks as necessary for ritual transactions. In this period there is a cleaner settlement hierarchy over a larger area, with a quantum leap in the level of trade, especially in prestige goods. Monopoly over the source of prestige items becomes a new form of social control. The theocratic state is split into a religious component and one increasingly occupied with external politico-economic relations. There is a marked dualistic development in the conception of the supernatural: for example, sky and earth are separated, male and female principles diverge in ideology. The massive increase in production for exchange implies a high demand for labour obtained by a slave trade between peripheral areas and the centre. Geopolitical expansion occurs.

Territorial and city states are formed as the expansion of the prestige-goods system encourages the development of new centres capable of their own production thus undermining centralized control. The political hierarchy breaks into a number of centres competing over labour and land. Conflict leads to large nucleated and fortified cities. The importation of food becomes an absolute necessity – this means larger trade systems and regional specialization (agricultural surpluses for exchange). Administrative institutions at the centre focus on trade and craft production. There are also tendencies towards centralization as the scale and complexity of decision making increase. Urbanization intensifies where possible, for example in areas of irrigation agriculture. Some prestige items take on the function of commercial money. With growing economic specialization a class of wealthy individuals appear, mainly from the old aristocracy, but also from middlemen and lower-ranking officials. Within the oligarchy there are those who control the means of production of the artisan industries or who are directly involved in trade and those who own land. Accumulated commercial wealth is invested in land and dependent labour. The class structure is transformed. Commoners are increasingly made into landless labourers and tend to be merged with the former slave category into a single class of expropriated producers. There is a separation of the relations of production from the state structure, of economics from politics, and a shift of the state into a more superstructural position. Religious dualism is elaborated into a more complex structure. The separation of religion from the relations of production may lead to a depersonalization of the former principles embodied in the deities, so that natural forces become separated from the figures that once represented them – the destruction of the segmentary structure of the supernatural. The former hierarchy of spirits becomes a pantheon of gods and goddesses which may become increasingly anthropomorphic. Religious institutions are now ideological rather than directly a form of economic control. The royalty owes its power to its ability to control labour, land and currency. Where the royalty loses economic control it may become a purely political force. There will be tendency for oscillation between periods of political fission and recentralization in the city-state, between democratic and autocratic periods or, in more dispersed territorial states, between feudal and despotic phases.

Friedman and Rowlands thus see themselves outlining a general model of development processes which combine with regional conditions to predict a range of societal variants (i.e. social formations); these include variants of the general process (like those discussed above), other truncated evolutionary lines, and some devolutionary lines. The general model predicts a multilinear evolutionary trajectory in which variant pathways are generated by the constraints of local conditions. Stages are sections of a continuous developmental and transformational process. Evolution is not stable in space, but shifts in its focus, often from centre to periphery, the different systems having different modes of spatial integration. Also the development of states implies, from early on, the necessity of exchange over wide areas to maintain social systems. Friedman and Rowlands present only one general trajectory in the above sequence whereas others may exist in the periphery and, when centres of development shift to these, synthetic developmental pathways emerge. As an important example of peripheral development they cite V. Gordan Childe's (1954) process of the emergence of secular urban centres on the margins of Near Eastern civilization, such as around the Mediterranean. This process may have affected northern European tribal systems incorporated as suppliers of raw materials. The early commercialization of this area before the emergence of centralized state control may be significant for later decentralized feudal/mercantile formations that led to European capitalism. The mercantile system which developed in Mesopotamia may also have affected the later growth of commercial city-states and trading empires in the Middle East and around the Indian Ocean (Friedman and Rowlands, 1977: 267–72).

The final result of this development in the pre-capitalist world was what Amin (1976; 1989) calls the '*tributary mode of production*', a society divided into two main classes: the peasantry organized in village communities; and the ruling class (including civil and military bureaucracies and a theocracy) which monopolizes political organization and exacts tribute from the rural communities. Amin analyses this structure using Althusserian structural notions.

As in all pre-capitalist modes, the extraction of surplus is transparently obvious in the tributary system. Most of production is consumed directly by the producers themselves, while the surplus levied by the ruling class takes the form of rents and fees often in kind or in labour. The reproduction of pre-capitalist social systems rests on the producers believing it necessary for the survival of the social and natural order that tribute be levied – that is, successful tributary reproduction rests upon the stability of power and an ideology which endows it with legitimacy. Pre-capitalist societies are therefore controlled by politics and ideology and to understand them historical materialism must strengthen its theory of culture. His own cultural hypothesis is that

all tributary cultures are based upon the preeminence of the metaphysical aspiration, by which I mean the search for absolute truth. This religious or quasi-religious character of ther dominant ideology of tributary society responds to an essential requirement of the social reproduction of these societies.

(Amin, 1989: 7)

Furthermore the central or peripheral forms of tributary society are characterized by the finished or unfinished degree of state formation and ideological expression. It is this unfinished character which makes the less advanced peripheral tributary societies (such as feudalism) more flexible and therefore capable of generating new forms of society. Thus while pre-capitalist civilizations form a single family characterized by the same general arrangement of economy and superstructure, Amin elaborates three variants and serveral associated formations linked with tributary modes. (1) If the natural and social conditions are favourable and the productive forces developed, the tribute is large, and considerable amounts are redistributed to craftsmen and merchants – this type embraces the great, long-lasting civilizations of Egypt and China. (2) Poor tributary formations embraced the civilizations of European antiquity and the Middle Ages. (3) Formations controlling long-distance trade circuits, or 'tribute-paying and trading formations' appeared usually for short periods in ancient Greece, the classical Arab world and the African savannah. Linked with tributary formations we find: slave-owning modes of production – these acquired considerable scope only in connection with the development of commodity exchange; and simple commodity formations – these being even more exceptional. Amin argues that eventually the development of the main line of rich tributary formations becomes blocked by slow technological progress, and a secondary, marginal (and geographically peripheral) line of development in feudal formations containing strong commodity elements becomes more dynamic and conflict-ridden, eventually disintegrating into capitalism (Amin, 1976: 13–25).

An alternative version which, however, converges with Amin's, is outlined by Karl Wittfogel (1957; 1985). Wittfogel reinterprets Marx to stress the natural origins of the 'powers of production'. In early societies, the naturally conditioned powers of production were crucial for the direction taken by development. The dry but fertile environments of the East could only be intensively used by hydraulic powers of production, that is manipulating water through irrigation and other hydraulic methods. But operations involving large amounts of water required widespread human co-operation, planned integration, organization, discipline and leadership – in a phrase centralized control over extensive labour supplies. Hydraulic agriculture characterized by huge water works (dams, canals, etc.) developed the peculiarities of hydraulic society in general – for example the huge spatial scale of the management of operations. Other types of large-scale organization and construction, like aqueducts and reservoirs, navigation canals, defensive structures, roads, palaces, tombs, temples and capital cities achieved a distinctive monumental scale because of centralized control over labour. Wittfogel divides hydraulic civilizations into societal types. *Core societies* may be compact (hydraulic agriculture predominates, as in Egypt) or loose (hydraulic agriculture exists only to a degree sufficient to secure political and organizational hegemony). *Marginal societies* may have some hydraulic features (the Mayan civilization) or may be influenced by hydraulic culture or organization but have little or no hydraulic base (Byzantium, Muscovite Russia). Lastly there are *submarginal societies* with un-coordinated, isolated hydraulic features like Minoan Crete, Etruscan society, Kievan Russia and Japan. In all the oriental systems, the bureaucratic state came to occupy an unrivalled position, coercing labour through the corvée and collecting taxes. The hydraulic state prevented the crystallization of non-governmental forces into institutions capable of counterbalancing its power – for example by restricting private property and monopolizing religion. Hydraulic society was thus able to prevent the maturation of internal contradictions, so that change came mainly from outside in the form of invasions. These, however, were soon accommodated and hydraulic systems became outstanding cases of long-term societal stagnation. By comparison, rainfall-fed agriculture in the West did not involve extensive co-operation and society took the more decentralized form of feudalism.

Wittfogel regarded this formulation as countering the fiction of unilinear and irresistable development. Like Melotti, he regarded his ideas as critical of the state socialism of the Soviet Union and China, which he saw as continuations of the despotic centralized regimes of the past.

In support of Wittfogel, it is indeed the case that state-dominated societies arose 5,000–6,000 years ago in south-west Asia, Egypt, the Indus Valley, China, Peru and meso-America – places with similar but not identical physical environments (Figure 6.4). All used irrigation to some degree and all displayed monumentalism. But early irrigation seems to have been relatively simple (i.e. not requiring much state control) and there is evidence that hierarchies, states, cities and monumental architecture began several centuries before large-scale irrigation. In south-west Asia, urbanism seems to have come first and irrigation second as a way of intensifying agri-culture around the cities (Wenke, 1984). This empirical argument does not, however, prevent irrigation playing a significant role in strengthening the powers of centralized states arising for the reasons given earlier by Friedman and Rowlands. Thus

great coordinated efforts at water control did take place in the years leading up to the founding of the first great Chinese Empire. But this was about a millenium after the Shang, who themselves depended on rainfall rather than irrigation for agriculture. The water control theory thus cannot explain the centralized absolutism of the Shang state, although it may explain the continuance and strengthening of this pattern in later times.

(Fairbank *et al.*, 1973: 30–1)

Wittfogel has been criticized for continuing the environmental determinism of the early twentieth century. But his quasi-Marxist version of determinism, focusing on the naturally-derived powers of production, avoids the racial implications of environmental determinism. Profound insights into differential societal development can be derived from Wittfogel's ideas (Peet, 1985b).

Centralized tributary systems marked the pinnacle of pre-capitalist civilization and economic development reached its highest level in the state-dominated societies of China, India and the Middle East. This involved a model in which taxes and obligatory labour were reinvested in irrigation and other public works to increase agricultural productivity. Surpluses were concentrated in ceremonial centres, where sponsored artisanship reached high levels of craftmanship and technology, while ideas reached the advanced state of mystical science – indeed capitalism at first drew on this record of accomplishment for its productive techniques. And it was with these ancient complexes, with histories stretching back several thousand years, that feudal Europe contended as capitalism emerged. To set the global stage for this contestation we conclude by briefly outlining the geography of the pre-capitalist world in 1400, just as the first signs of modern capitalism appeared in Europe.

Geography of the pre-capitalist world

We might first add a disclaimer. Accounts such as Friedman and Rowlands see societies passing along an evolutionary process from primitive communism to advanced forms of tributary society. Not all societies, they think, pass through all stages in the sequence, some societies devolve, and the end points vary in historically significant detail. Even so, the term 'evolution' has problems, especially for Marxism. Derived from biology, the concept of evolution describes a natural process eventuating in the human species, and therefore finds a progressive theme in the human imagination. But social evolution is progressive only in certain respects, the development of material production, liberation from natural dependence, and the partial growth of scientific consciousness to name but a few. As evolution 'progressed' the relations between people changed in what can be termed a degenerative way, that is away from the egalitarianism of primitive communism and towards class and gender inequalities. Indeed, as we have seen, exploitation of slaves, women and peasants deprived of land were the essential sources of material progress in the post-(primitive) communist world. It is exactly this tension between economic progress and social retrogression that necessitated the centralization of power in the state.

What did global society look like at the dawn of capitalism? Drawing the geographical, anthropological, archaeological and historical evidence together in a mode of production analysis, Wolf (1982: ch. 2) paints the following picture of the geography of the world in 1400 (on the organization of space *within* pre-capitalist societies see Dodgshon, 1987). Running across the Old World, from southern China to Spain, is a great chain of mountains crossed by a dry belt stretching from the Sahara to Mongolia. South of the pastoral desert and steppe lie cultivable subtropical and tropical forest and savannah. The distribution of the pastoral dry belt is continuous, that of the cultivable land archipelagic. Wolf (1982: 26) finds that 'the dichotomy between steppe and sown shaped much of the course of human action in the Old World, sometimes dividing pastoralist and villager, at other times promoting them into interaction'. Widely spaced cultivated regions formed an arc extending from Morocco to China. These regions were interconnected by trade, but only occasionally and partially by political conquest (for example, by the armies of Islam in the seventh and eighth centuries AD). And events at one end of the arc (e.g. the defeat of pastoral invaders before the Great Wall of China) promoted events at the other end (e.g. migratory invasions of Europe).

However to suppose that the mass of the world's population was in intimate contact was as erroneous then as it remains today. The local way of appropriating nature and the institutions and relations organizing this appropriation, in short the mode of production, structured life experience. Generally, the agricultural islands strewn across the pastoral sea were centres also of the tributary mode of production (Table 6.1 and Figure 6.4). The weighting of the arc towards the East was a consequence of the growth and persistence of the core, hydraulic or 'Asiatic' form of the tributary system, with its ability ot organize broad stretches of territory, expropriating surplus in support of the massive centralized structures of several glorious civilizations. In 1400, China, northern India and the Ottoman Empire of the eastern Mediterranean, together with smaller inland states in south-eastern Asia representing, to differing degrees, the centralized form of the tributary system, were the dominant centres of global civilization. Surplus drained in

Table 6.1 Agricultural societies (civilizations) AD 1400

Society	Region	Ruling class	Other elites	Main ideology (religion)	Mode of surplus transfer	Spatial organization	Trade	Dynamics
China	China	Emperor, nobles	Bureaucracy, gentry	Confucian ideals, Buddhism in south	Peasant taxes or corvée, serfdom	Hydraulic cores, outer regions	Spices, tea exported, turned in on itself after 1367	Cyclical invasions – dynastic change, expansion from cores
South-east Asia	South-east Asian mainland, Sumatra, Java	Divine God-king inland, prince and merchants on coast	Merchants, armed retainers	Hindu-Buddhism then increasingly Islam	Corvée labour, taxes, trade	Inland empires with cores, trading ports	Export spices, bridge between India and China	Trade expansion, state formation then decentralization
India	Northern and coastal India	Moghul emperor, rajas	Upper castes, brahmins, warriors, merchants	Hindu-Buddhism, Islam	Dominant caste segments paid rent to Raja. Tribute to emperor	Central state, smaller kingdoms, villages	Export of spices, textiles, gold imported	Cyclical, invasion and dynastic change, base unchanging
Ottoman empire	Anatolia, Balkans, eastern Mediterranean	Sultan, imperial household	Provincial governors, merchants, religious teachers	State-controlled Islam	Peasant tribute to military bondsmen of sultan, tribute	Core/ periphery, provinces	Bridge between India and Europe	Expansion and consolidation followed by increased regional autonomy
Muslim North Africa	Northern coast of Africa	Elite of landowners, merchants, state officials, religious leaders	Sultans in strategic centres	Islam	Taxes, rents	Regional composites tied by trade and religion	Trans-Sahara and across North Africa	Cyclical contests between elite alliances, nomad/ sedentary conflicts

West Africa	West Africa	Lineage elders/divine kings	Military and trading elites	Ancestor worship, Islam	Redistribution by elders, with tribute to king	Central lineages/local lineages	Gold, etc. exported across Sahara	State consolidation through conquest and trade, then collapse
East Africa (Zimbabwe)	Zimbabwe, Zambia, Mozambique	King and royal lineage	Chiefs of patri-lineages	Ancestor worship	Tribute of trade goods paid by clan chiefs to ruler	Clan territories focused on Great Zimbabwe	Gold, copper, etc. exported via Arab merchants	State formation then collapse into chiefdoms
Europe	Western, central and southern Europe	Landlord, king	Merchants	Catholicism	Corvée, rents	Feudal estates, autonomous mercantile cities	Regional and long distance to Orient	Political consolidation, expansion, peasant resistance
Central Andes	Peru, Bolivia, northern Chile	God-king aristocracy (Incas)	Heads of land-owning lineages	Natural gods, God-king	Corvée labour (MITA)	Zones, small states around cities	Interzonal reciprocity and with Maya	Cyclical-state formation, expansion, collapse
Meso-America	Mexico. Guatemala, offshoots to south-western USA and Mississippi	Emperor, military, elite, priests	Mercenaries, merchants	Natural gods	Tribute of slaves, labour and products, taxes	City states, dependent villages	Intercity and with Inca	Cyclical-collapse of Mayan empire, decline, new state formation (Aztecs)

Source: Based mainly on Wolf, 1982

an easterly direction: as late as the seventeenth century Sir Thomas Roe was saying 'Europe bleedeth to enrich Asia' (Bhattucharya, 1954: 222). Indeed it can be claimed that the results of economic and technical development in the Eastern civilizations, flowing through Arab contacts, made possible the development of Europe. As Fairbank *et al*. say:

> Consider how the main flow of influences over the long course of history has been from China to Europe, not the other way: first, the silk trade across central Asia to Rome, then the great series of inventions emanating from China – paper and printing that spread literacy, porcelain (chinaware) so easy to keep hygenically clean, the crossbow used by the Han armies, cast-iron, canal lock gates, the wheelbarrow, the stem-post rudder to steer ships at sea, the compass to navigate them, gunpowder, and all the rest. This material technology was paralleled by the Chinese primacy in the methods of bureaucratic government including civil service examinations, to say nothing of such arts as painting.
>
> (Fairbank *et al*., 1973: 243)

On the margins of this discontinuous array of high civilizations lay several centres where civilization was emergent rather than permanently established. In the West African savannah, the lineage system had shown signs of state formation since before AD 800, especially where lineage heads controlled vital resources valued in the trans-Saharan trade. A similar, if less continuous, process of state formation occurred around the gold and copper mines of East Africa. The North African coast was occupied by a series of city states based on interregional trade between West Africa, Europe and the Near East. And while Europe had been a dependent fringe of Asia in AD 800, 600 years later its many small principalities had fused into larger and more effective polities, capable of competing with their southern and eastern neighbours and launching major overseas adventures.

The New World had two centres of intensive agriculture, dense population, cities and impressive architecture. One lay in the central Andes in what, during the fifteenth century, would become the Inca empire. The other lay in meso-America, in contemporary Mexico and Guatemala, where power was shifting from the Mayan lowlands to the central Mexican plateau and eventually to the Aztecs. Two streams of meso-American influence affected cultural development in the desert south-west and Mississippi Valley of North America. Here, as elsewhere in the world, contact and

influence from tributary centres had led only to certain imperman-
ent signs of state formation (temporary urbanization, monument
building, etc.).

Otherwise, the vast stretches of global space were occupied by
kin-ordered and primitive communist societies. The tribal systems
of the steppes and desert margins of the Old World were at a lower
level of the productive forces than their sedentary neighbours.
However, following the Arab historian Ibn Khaldun, most com-
mentators find pastoralists to exercise superior military power
which enabled them to gain periodic control over even the most
splendid civilizations in North Africa, the Middle East, India and
China. This militarism then underwent disintegration as a result of
sedentarization. Moghadem (1988) hypothesizes that the self-
reproducing character of, for example, the Iranian social formation was caused by cyclical nomadic invasion and rule.

In terms of geographic shapes we can say that the tributary cores
of the world were surrounded by peripheries of kin-ordered
pastoral and agricultural social formations with which they had
complementary and contradictory relations. In turn, kin societies
had similar, if less permanent, relations with primitive communist
formations in forest, hill and desert margins. The world thus had a
layered, hierarchical geography, the cores were interconnected, and
the centre of power shifted eastward in space.

Conclusion

Where do new modes of production come from and how is their
socio-economic dynamic set in motion? This chapter began to
answer these related questions by examining theories dealing with
three pre-capitalist modes: primitive communism, kin-ordered
societies and tributary formations. These three 'stages' in societal
development roughly correspond to levels of development of the
productive forces: primitive communism corresponds with gathering, hunting and other non-agricultural techniques; kin-ordered
societies seem to have appeared with the domestication of plants
and animals and the increased commitment of family labour to a
particular piece of land or flock of animals; tributary formations
resulted from the growth of productivity and the concentration of
surplus in the hands of the state, and in turn vastly increased this
accumulation by organizing social labour on a massive scale. But
the notion in Marx of the growth of the productive forces bringing
the social relations of production into crisis and promoting structural change is intended only as a general framework for organizing
the more complex social, cultural and political forces which actually

carry out transformation. We therefore focused on the development of contradictory elements in the social order – class, unequal gender relations, the state and the elaboration of ideology as significant moments of pre-capitalist history. Mode of production theory, we think, is the only existing method which can link the various forces, struggles and dynamics of economic and sociocultural change. Pre-capitalist societies are best seen in terms of social formations articulating several modes of production. Societal transformation is the rearticulation of the components of previous formations with new elements emerging from their contradictions.

Thus kin-ordering and gender specialization were present in embryonic form in primitive communist societies: the transition to agricultural society transformed differences and specializations into inequalities. Similarly, state-like institutions existed in lineage societies (the conical structure of the clan) but were brought into prominence by the continuing growth of the surplus product. There is a persuasive argument that tributary societies developed in their various centralized and decentralized forms in different ecological settings. All tributary formations contained embryonic forms of capitalism, for example in their merchant classes trading for profit. But only in decentralized, weak-state formations could such elements achieve cultural and political independence from, or rival, the state and the landed nobility. The classes of tributary formations contended over productive resources and control of the surplus product, but the centralized might of military and religious-ideological power, periodically renewed through invasion by nomads, gave a cyclical shape to the dynamics of the 'Asiatic' civilizations of the East (and the Americas), while lesser centralized power gave the potential for transformation in the feudal peripheries.

Thus people as individuals and groups cause change, but they do so within structured conditions set by past events. An adequate theory of societal development must attend to human actions and their contexts, but it must pay special attention to the structural conditions which limit, direct and divert transformative activity.

Chapter seven

The origins of capitalism

The dynamics of tributary formations are usually described in terms of cyclical repetitions of centralization and decentralization, invasion and incorporation, urbanization and partial collapse back to the village. In a challenge to this interpretation of the 'never-changing East', Jim Blaut (1977; 1989) argues the contrary position, that pre-capitalist society was dynamic in a developmental sense and, more controversially, that several centres of incipient capitalism sprang up in the Old World during the two or three centuries prior to 1492. Blaut maintains that 'feudalism', which he calls the dominant mode of production in all the pre-capitalist world, was crumbling everywhere, giving way to centres of protocapitalism – particularly around the highly interconnected port cities of Canton, Malacca, Calicut, Sofala, Cairo, Timbuktu, Venice and Antwerp. In all three Old World continents, hinterland regions were being penetrated by capitalist production in the fifteenth century – examples include Flanders, southern England, northern Italy, the Nile Valley, Malabar, Coromandel, Bengal, northern Java and south-east coastal China. Hence Blaut concludes capitalism was equally close to its moment of triumph in Asia and Africa as in Europe, so that no single centre was the birthplace of capitalism. Europe's sole advantage was its location relative to the New World. By plundering the Americas, Europe accumulated capital, made a more rapid transition to capitalism, and gained control of Asian and African trade bringing their rise to a halt. What had been a uniform process of development became uni-centred.

Blaut's strongest case lies in his documenting the increase in world trade which preceded the rise of capitalism. The question is: does such an increase in trade and merchant activity necessarily lead to capitalism? Trade has occurred for the last 5,000 years and while its increase may have a disintegrating effect on pre-capitalist societies this did not, and need not, lead to capitalism. Marx's argument on the question is worth repeating:

> Trade always has, to a greater or lesser degree, a solvent effect on the pre-existing organizations of production, which in all their various forms are principally oriented to use-value. But how far it leads to the dissolution of the old mode of production depends first and foremost on the solidity and inner articulation of this mode of production itself. And what comes out of this process of dissolution, i.e. what new mode of production arises in place of the old, does not depend on trade, but rather in the character of the old mode of production itself.
>
> (Marx, 1981: 449)

Hence, the solvent effect of trade depends on prior conditions, or the internal structure of the society. The last chapter argued that the dominant mode prior to capitalism was tributary society, rather than feudalism, but that this mode appeared as several different social formations – feudalism being a decentralized version of the tributary mode. We can reach the further conclusion that an increase in societal interaction through trade would have a quite different effect on these various social formations. Trade-dominated social formations already existed in south-east Asia and North Africa without breaking the fundamental structure of the tributary system. Hence we have to take the contrary position to Blaut, and argue that the transition from pre-capitalism to capitalism was indeed influenced by the increase in world trade of the fifteenth and sixteenth centuries, but that European feudalism was also disintegrating as the result of internal class struggles. In the dialectic between internal (class) and external (trade, conquest) changes we can discover the exact origins of the capitalist system.

Marx on the origins of capitalism

For Marx, the early agricultural societies were aimed primarily at making use values for the reproduction of the family and the community. Nature and resources are regarded as an extension of the human individual – 'the inorganic nature of his subjectivity' (Marx, 1973: 485). But this relation to land and soil as the property of the individual is mediated by the commune in some historically developed form. The survival of the commune depends upon the reproduction of its people within the existing conditions and relations. Production, however, destroys these conditions, the commune falls, and with it the old system of relations to nature. Marx thought that Asiatic society hangs on the most tenaciously because 'the individual does not become independent vis à vis the commune' and because 'there is a self-sustaining circle of production, unity of agiculture and manufactures' (Marx, 1973: 486). By comparison, in the West, social relations to nature are changed by productive development in classical times (the growth of slavery, concentration of land possession, exchange and money, external conquests), and a process of societal change unleashed which resulted eventually in capitalism. Capitalism, therefore, was not some prior intention towards which all history tends. It came about through the dissolution of previous societies and the recombination of their elements in new forms.

On the one side we find the alienation of labour from any residual kind of proprietorship of nature (whether in communal or individual peasant form) and the freeing of workers to be employed for money wages. It is exactly this alienation from nature which Marx regarded as more advanced in Europe and less advanced in the 'Asiatic' societies. In medieval England, communal property was a Teutonic institution (from the Germanic clan system) surviving within the feudal social formation. Using violent means, the nobles began to usurp common lands at the end of the fifteenth century. Marx chronicles a series of such acts, increasingly supported by the state, in the sixteenth century (the Reformation and sale of church lands), the seventeenth century (the yeomanry or class of independent peasants disappeared while state lands were sold) and the eighteenth and nineteenth centuries (common lands were expropriated by acts of 'enclosure'). 'By the nineteenth century, the very memory of the connection between the agricultural labourer and communal property had . . . vanished' (Marx, 1976: 889). The last great process of expropriation took place in the Celtic fringes, still organized under the clan system, with the so-called 'clearing of the estates' of highland Scotland. Here the noble heads of the clans claimed the right to convert clan territory into private estates and, when this was resisted, drove their kinfolk out, burned their villages, and converted the land into sheep farms and deer reserves. Marx calls such moments of the usurption of feudal and clan property 'just so many methods of primitive accumulation. They conquered the fields for capitalist agriculture, incorporated the soil into capital, and created for the urban industries the necessary supplies of free and rightless proletarians' (Marx, 1976: 895). Along with such 'freeing' of labour from its natural 'inorganic body' went the destruction of the ownership of the instruments of labour (as in craft and artisan work) and the breakup of relations in which workers themselves belonged among the objective conditions of production, as slaves and serfs. These then were the internal changes needed for the worker to become free, objectless, pure labour capacity confronting the objective conditions of production as 'non-property', alien property, value-for-itself, or capital.

On the other side, what was required so that workers found themselves confronted by capital? Wealth in the forms of stocks of money has long existed in pre-capitalist societies. The period of the dissolution of feudalism was also characterized by the rapid accumulation of monetary wealth through trade and plunder. Indeed the dissolution of feudalism and early capital accumulation were related in that (as we have seen) trade tends to dissolve property relations based on use-value, while money acts as a 'highly energetic solvent' (Marx, 1973: 507). Calling the original stock-piling of capital 'primitive accumulation', Marx distinguishes between two geographical sources in capitalism's formative years. Money had long been piling up internally through usury, especially practised against landed property, and more importantly through local and regional commerce as merchant's capital. And capital was accumulated with particular rapidity from external sources, the plundering of the world, or those parts vulnerable to European depredation, and the reorientation of global trade so it focused on western Europe. Here Marx's bitter words bear repeating:

> The discovery of gold and silver in America, the extirpation, enslavement and entombment in mines of the indigenous population of that continent, the beginnings of the conquest and plunder of India, and the conversion of Africa into a preserve for the commercial hunting of black skins, are all things which characterize the dawn of the era of capitalist production. These idyllic proceedings are the chief moments of primitive accumulation.
>
> (Marx, 1976: 915)

Monetary wealth derived from these sources ended up in the hands of adventurers, merchants and banks. And from the ranks of tenant farmers and manufacturers came organizers capable of using capital productively. In this way, the two main elements of capitalist production, free labour available for wage employment, and capital in the hands of profit seekers, emerged from the breakup of feudalism during the 'age of discovery'.

Of course this is merely a shorthand way of categorizing the complex moments of capitalism's emergence. But Marx's idea that capitalism is the synthetic result of two tendencies, internal societal dissolution and external plunder and trade, is a useful guide to the rich complexity of historical events. We might note that this is but one example of the dialectical notion that transformational change comes from the contradictions internal to a thing – here the struggle between feudal classes – and the external relations between one thing and another – here the spatial relations between Europe and the rest of the world. In the following sections we fill this argument out by looking at the debate on the transition from feudalism to capitalism.

Debate on the transition from feudalism to capitalism

Marx's brief remarks on the origins of capitalism in the dissolution of feudalism were the subject of a significant debate between Paul Sweezy and Maurice Dobb in the 1950s. In essence the debate involved differing conceptions of feudalism and differing versions of the tensions pulling it apart. Drawing on Pirenne (1936), Sweezy (1978) argues that feudalism was a system of production for known community needs (use-values), immersed in tradition, and needing an external source of transformative change. As with Pirenne, the conductors of change were the merchants living in cities, places where economic life was oriented towards exchange-value and profit making. Waves of change spread from these commercial cities creating regions of capitalism in an otherwise feudal space, with merchants serving as the organizers of the new form of capitalist production. Dobb (1963; 1978), by comparison, sees feudalism as a mode of production in which the direct producers were forced to fulfil labour obligations to their lords, with class struggle occurring over the rights and conditions of surplus expropriation. Ruling class demands for additional revenue (to strengthen military power, support growing extravagance, etc.) could only be met by extracting a larger surplus from the peasantry. This, Dobb says, provoked mass emigration, labour shortages and the crisis of European feudalism in the fourteenth and fifteenth centuries. The noble reaction in western Europe was to commute labour services, leading to a peasant-artisan system out of which capitalism arose, but in eastern Europe it was to tighten feudal bonds, ensuring its undeveloped status until the nineteenth century. Merchant capital began to penetrate petty commodity production in sixteenth-century England via two routes: by merchants themselves organizing the small producers; and by small producers reorganizing on a capitalist basis. The latter, Dobb thinks, proved the more revolutionary way. The capitalist bourgeoisie came from the ranks of the artisans rather than the rich merchants.

The Brenner thesis

Building on Dobb's position, Robert Brenner (1977; 1985) argues that feudalism was limited in its developmental potential because of heavy surplus extraction and the way surplus was used – 50 per cent of the unfree peasant's total product was squandered by the lords in military expenditure and conspicuous consumption – and because land and labour resources were immobilized by the unfree social relations necessary for this form of surplus extraction. The lords' most obvious method of increasing income from land was not capital investment and new techniques, but squeezing the peasants. Available agriculture improvements were ignored. Caught in an exploitative relationship, the peasantry was also unable to return the nutrients taken from the soil, for example by investing in animals for ploughing and manure. Demographic/environmental crisis, as well as class struggle, was thus endemic to feudalism.

The class struggle set off by crisis in the fourteenth and fifteenth centuries achieved different regional results. Outcomes were not arbitrary, but were bound up with historically specific patterns of class development and contention – things like class solidarity and consciousness, popular organizations and political resources. In western Germany the peasantry had constructed a network of village institutions for economic regulation and self-government, in part because they inhabited a landscape characterized by the 'chaotic' development of small and scattered parcels of land. These institutions provided a powerful defence against the lords. By comparison, eastern Germany had been laid out in large, consolidated strips, and peasant co-operation and institutions of self-government were little developed. Peasant resistance to the lords through warfare in both western and eastern Germany was largely a failure. What was successful in western Germany was a process of stubborn resistance by which the peasants were able to forestall noble reactions to peasant actions, the eventual result being the dissolution of feudal restrictions. By comparison serfdom was intensified in eastern Germany.

However, the collapse of serfdom more generally in the West did not automatically lead to capitalism or even economic development. In England, the peasants strove for freehold control over their customary lands. But the landlords prevented a massive loss of land: customary peasant land left vacant during the demographic collapse of the late fourteenth and fifteenth centuries was added to the lords' demesnes; and the lords retained the right to charge 'fines' when peasant land was sold or inherited. Fines were unsuccessfully resisted by peasant rebellions in the sixteenth century. As a result the lords retained control over most of the cultivable land of England by the end of the seventeenth century, consolidated large farms, and leased them to capitalist tenant farmers who employed the former serfs as wage labour. The tenant farmers, in effect, entered into an alliance with the lords which ensured them a share of increased revenues from investment, and left them free to bring about technological improvements. This meant stable food prices, allowed a high proportion (40 per cent) of the English population to move out of agriculture (mostly into manufacturing), and provided a growing home market for industrial products. For Brenner (1985: 54) it was 'an agricultural revolution, based on the emegence of capitalist class relations in the countryside, which made it possible for England to become the first nation to experience industrialization'.

By comparison in France peasant struggle gained not only freedom from serfdom, but also rights to land. An important aspect of this was that in France the centralized state seems to have developed in a class-like way, as an independent extractor of surplus through its power to tax land. Hence the French state could develop as a competitor with the lords, whereas in England monarchical centralization developed in relation with, and dependent on, the landlord class. The French absolutist state therefore had an interest in limiting the landlord's exactions, intervening against them to ensure peasant property. (A similar development occurred in the 'mini-absolutisms' of the west German princes.) By the early modern period a different class structure had been created in the French countryside, characterized by small peasant proprietorship – peasants owned 45–50 per cent of the cultivable land at the end of the seventeenth century, while the lords' demesnes were also split into small rented plots. The peasants were under no compulsion to operate profitably, demographic growth led to the subdivision of their landholdings, while taxation ruined them. Hence rising population, growing markets and higher prices led to a Malthusian crisis rather than agricultural improvement:

> Thus ironically, the most complete freedom and property rights for the rural population meant poverty and a self-perpetuating cycle of backwardness. In England, it was precisely the absence of such rights that facilitated the onset of real economic development.

> (Brenner, 1985: 62)

It bears repeating that for Brenner capitalism differs from all previous modes of production in its systematic tendency to economic development through the expansion of relative rather than absolute surplus labour: under capitalism, surplus is achieved through increases in labour productivity rather than extending the working day, or controlling more workers. For this, innovations must be made in the forces of production, and these require the plough-back of surplus by a profit-seeking, competitive, owning class. In addition, only where labour has been separated from the means of production are capital and labour 'free' to be combined at the highest level of technology (or in the most efficient place). What therefore distinguishes capitalist economic development is the class (property/surplus extraction) system of social relations. The capitalist dynamic of development came as the unintended consequence of class conflict in the European countryside (Brenner, 1977).

Conclusion

Transitions between pre-capitalist modes of production can only be theorized in general terms: particular actors, actions and motivations are lost in the remoteness of the long sweep of history. But the transition from the tributary to the capitalist mode is more immediately present. We can flesh out what previously was only a skeletal (structural) outline. Indeed our knowledge of the main historical events intensifies to the extent that differing interpretations, each well backed by evidence, appear even among Marxist theorists. Feudalism gave way to capitalism under two broad patterns of change. First, external relations were transformed by 'discovery', conquest and interregional struggle so that surplus accumulated in Europe on an unprecedented scale – the capital equivalent of a transformation in the forces of production. The development of trade, the reorientation of production towards exchange, and the rise of mercantile cities were externally-derived forces acting to dissolve the existing social relations. Second, these internal relations were already in crisis as the result of the intensification of contradictions internal to the feudal order. Feudalism was the most unstable social formation in the tributary mode of production because class struggles over land and surplus and mercantile struggles to accumulate profit were only intermittently and partly contained by local states themselves in contention. Here the Dobb–Brenner argument is compelling: the class struggle had differing regional outcomes which structured the subsequent geographical pattern of development in Europe. The outcome in the English countryside, a three-tiered system of noble owners of land, tenant farmers and peasants ultimately made landless and forced to work for wages, proved compatible with economic development: a system of surplus extraction and investment emerged 'in which the methods the extractors were obliged to use to increase their surplus corresponded to an unprecedented, though enormously imperfect, degree to the needs of the development of the productive forces' (Brenner, 1977: 68). These social relations meant that surplus was reinvested in production rather than squandered on cathedrals. We therefore reach the conclusion that the outlines of the new capitalist social organization came from a process of disintegration, reassembling, and the formation of new elements which was largely 'internal' or localized, albeit in the context of rapidly changing global conditions. Capitalism is feudalism's errant offspring.

Chapter eight

The development of global capitalism

In its inherent dynamism capitalism is qualitatively different from all preceding modes of production. But this dynamism rests on exploitative social relations and in this capitalism continues, indeed intensifies and completes, the tendencies observable over the previous several millenia for human co-operation to be achieved via the force of ruling class domination. The previous chapter argued that capitalist relations of production are the basic social structures promoting the economic development of modern Europe – capitalist social relations guide a form of competitive efficiency in which private (non-state) owners of the means of production strive endlessly for profit, and workers deprived of their own means of livelihood are forced to work hard for a living wage. It took three centuries or more for these relations to assume a form which we would recognize today. This was not a simple process of evolution, in which a social form which everyone recognized as most efficient naturally emerged as dominant. Rather it was a process of class struggle, between the old and new ruling class, between those losing their ancient rights to land and those usurping these rights, and between the state and the people.

In this chapter we turn to the other aspect of the capitalist revolution, the external arena in which the new society, forming in a peripheral area of Eurasia, struggled for global dominance. To understand this long history we must translate the emerging internal social relations of capitalism into parallel external spatial relations.

From early in its development, capitalism proved an adept method of organizing external relations to bring maximum benefit to the home country and minimal advantage to the foreign. This chapter looks at two general forms of external domination: mercantilism and imperialism. Lasting from the fifteenth to the nineteenth centuries, mercantilist forms of expropriating surplus involved the plundering of ancient stockpiles of wealth, unequal trade relations, and the production of bullion and exotic commodities using coerced labour. These methods did not necessitate (yet sometimes involved) political control over foreign territory. In the second half of the nineteenth and first part of the twentieth centuries, imperialism entailed more direct methods of control over external productive processes, markets and resources. Its main features, therefore, were the massive use of state-organized force and the expansion of territorial control to widen the range of economic use and deepen its intensity. Both forms of articulation between capitalist and non-capitalist modes involved the widespread use of violent force (cf. Bradby in Chapter 5, pp. 69–72), and both were characterized by the polarization of development and underdevelopment (cf. Frank in Chapter 4, pp. 46–7).

In expanding to become global powers, the European capitalist societies encountered social formations based in several pre-capitalist modes of production – lineage societies in Africa, kin-ordered and primitive communist societies in North America, various kinds of tributary formation in meso-America, the Andes, the Middle East, India and China, primitive communism in Australia, and so on. The structural character of each social formation presented quite different opportunities to the Europeans, in some places enabling almost unlimited use, in others ensuring virtually complete exclusion for centuries. Also each social formation had its own dynamic, so that a different phase of expansion or contraction, consolidation or dispersal, interacted with the various phases of development of west European capitalism (mercantilism, free trade, imperialism). The degree to which advantage could be taken, the types of benefit Europe could gain and the effect this had on pre-capitalist societies are the various moments of the global process of articulation.

Mercantilism

We shall call the transitional social formation between feudalism and capitalism 'mercantilism', a phrase usually reserved for the economic doctrine dominant at the time. Mercantilism, however, was more than an economic ideology. It was a total system of institutions, thought patterns and politico-economic practices suited to an emergent region – something akin to the character, behaviour and beliefs necessary for an aspiring member of the *nouveau riche*.

The general goal of mercantilist policy was increased national power symbolized in the political might of the state. National political power was thought to rest on economic means, and production was understood as the application of labour to natural resources. The aim of state policy was to increase control over larger amounts of both kinds of productive resource, with harsh methods used to extract work often from paupers, criminals and slaves. Some kinds of labour were deemed productive, especially in agriculture and the new manufactures (for example cloth production in rural cottages and workshops), while other labour, like professional services, was though to be unproductive. Colonies were desired to enrich the mother country by providing raw materials and consuming manufactures. The state granted trading monopolies over entire spatial arenas to joint stock companies, with the king and members of the court benefiting through stockholdings – examples were the British Muscovy Company, the Virginia Company and the East India Company. A country was considered prosperous when it had a favourable balance of trade, specifically an increased inflow of bullion. Mercantilism was announced by plunder at the moment of conquest, showed its presence by the forceful reorientation of trade so that profit accumulated in Europe, and proclaimed victory by establishing coercive forms of production.

Mercantilism broke with medieval precedent in that it was an amoral system in terms of the ends pursued and the methods used to achieve these ends. The political welfare of the state replaced the spiritual welfare of the individual. People were taken as they were, pursuing their own interest, but were guided in a direction which would enhance the well-being of the state. And morality took second place to practicality so that, for example, the (highly profitable) slave trade was a valuable national resource or, as another example, the population of the colonies was increased regardless of whether by women, horses or sheep. Mercantilism was against church interference in the pursuit of economic ends, and was often religiously tolerant of sects considered good traders (for example Dutch toleration of Sephardic Jews driven from Spain and Portugal). Finally, mercantilism was, as far as possible, rationalist rather than mystical, believing in the application of science to practical problems in the social and economic spheres (Newman, 1952: ch. 2; Hecksher, 1935).

As interpreted by Perry Anderson (1979; see also Beaud, 1983), mercantilism developed contemporaneously with the absolutist monarchies forming in fifteenth- and sixteenth-century Europe and reaching their pinnacles of power in the seventeenth and eighteenth centuries. 'Absolutism was . . . a redeployed and recharged apparatus of feudal domination, designed to clamp the peasant masses back into their traditional social position – despite and against the gains they had won' (Anderson, 1979: 18). The absolutist state was also an agent of modernization, introducing standing armies, permanent bureaucracies, national taxation, codified legal systems, and forging a national market. More significantly, from our perspective, the absolutist state exercised national force in the external arena, waging war on behalf of its own interests, and those of the nation's merchants and manufacterers.

'Discovery' of the Americas

The prelude of Columbus's voyage was the Ottoman conquest of the eastern Mediterranean seaboard signified by the fall of Constantinople in 1453. Moslem middlemen used their monopoly over the trade between Europe and the East to mark up tenfold the prices of spices, silk and other luxury goods. Portugal took the lead in finding an alternate sea route to the East, rounding the Cape of Good Hope in 1486, and reaching India in 1498. In 1492 Spain became a nation state, conquering the last Moslem city and expelling all Jews from the country – causing a financial crisis. What the new state (and Europe) lacked was gold, the universal means of payment.

By Columbus's day, the Greek knowledge that the earth is round had been re-learnt by all educated Europeans. The problem was the great distance across open seas to be sailed by boats which usually hugged the shore. Columbus's error lay in believing that the islands off Asia were but a short distance across the Atlantic – indeed for this reason his project of a western voyage was rejected by the king of Portugal. Favoured by Queen Isabella, he eventually reached an agreement with the Spanish monarchy that gave him 10 per cent of whatever trade resulted with the East and a loan to finance his voyage. By sailing from the Spanish Canary Islands, Columbus adopted a southern course, catching the north-east 'trade winds' which made his voyage successful, whereas earlier more northerly attempts had been blown back to Portugal by the westerlies. Greeted in the Bahamas as a god from the sky, Columbus dwelt only on the innocence of the 'Indians' (!), the fact that they had only cane spears, and that 'should your Majesties command it, all the inhabitants could be taken away to Castile, or made slaves on the island. With fifty men we could subjugate them all and make them do whatever we want' (Koning, 1976: 53–4). Columbus sailed on to Cuba and Hispaniola, believing he had reached China, before returning to Spain with six Arawak Indian survivors of the voyage. These were followed on Columbus's second voyage by 500 Arawak slaves, of which 300 survivors were sold in Seville, whereupon most died. Frustrated in his attempt to find gold, Columbus instituted a system whereby every inhabitant of the (mythical) 'gold fields' of Hispaniola had to furnish a gold tribute on pain of having his or her hands cut off. During two years of the Columbus brothers' administration, half the population was killed, or committed suicide. Twenty-five years later the entire population of the island had vanished. However, the Indian women passed syphilis to the Europeans, a disease incurable until recently (Koning, 1976).

Mercantilism had shown the world its intent and methods.

Mercantilism in the Western Hemisphere

Since the continent was already inhabited, the 'discovery' of the Americas by Columbus may more accurately be characterized as the forging of trans-Atlantic links. This brought three regions into contact: mercantilist western Europe, the lineage/state societies of West Africa already known to the Portuguese, and the tributary, kin-ordered and primitive communist societies of America. Each regional formation was characterized by a certain articulation of modes of production and had a given developmental potential. In the Americas the main types of social formation confronting mercantilist Europe were: (1) tributary societies, densely populated and already able to deliver sufficient surpluses to maintain a non-productive elite, as in highland Central and South America; (2a) primitive communist areas where hunting and gathering peoples, if caught alive, were useless as a disciplined agricultural or mining labour force (northern Mexico, Amazonia, Uruguay, Argentina), and (2b) areas with little labour, but in a good position for export crop production, like the sea coasts of northern Peru, the Caribbean islands, and north-eastern Brazil; (3) societies characterized by dispersed kin-organized agriculture as part of a subsistence economy – much of the Caribbean, parts of Brazil, Bolivia, central Chile, and Paraguay. Where the land could be used for mining or crop production, the Indians were impressed by various means into work gangs or domestic slavery. Elsewhere an external source of labour was necessary (Pearse, 1975).

As foot soldiers of mercantilism, the Spanish conquistadors were interested in pillaging stored wealth ('they crave gold like hungry swine') and, failing that, gaining control over a labour force to work local resources into new wealth (Galeano, 1973: 29). After the initial contact in the Caribbean, the immediate focus of Spanish interest lay almost exclusively on regions of type 1. Here the Spanish took over the apex positions in centralized tributary social formations, instituted the *encomienda* to exact tribute and labour service, and used this to mine gold and silver and grow food on haciendas organized on expropriated Indian land. The effect on the Indian population was disastrous: Mexico's population declined from perhaps 25 million in 1519 to 6.3 million in 1548; that of Peru from perhaps 7 million to 1.8 million by 1580 (Stavrianos, 1981: 96). The mining of bullion was an enclave industry contributing little to the economic development of what quickly became *Latin* America. When mining declined in the seventeenth century, a process of economic involution turned these regions into feudal backwaters.

Mercantilist attention then shifted to regions of types 2b and 3, where dependent colonial economies, based on slave labour, were established to export raw materials and agricultural products to Europe and, of course, generate profit. Sugar production was started in coastal Brazil by Dutch mercantile interests and on the Caribbean islands, where British capital predominated. In these areas the people had either been exterminated during the first plundering wave of European contact or were hunters and gatherers of only marginal use as coerced labour. Instead the Europeans turned to the next nearest source of agricultural labour – the lineage societies of West Africa – to work the plantations.

As a case study of the plantation space economy we can take Frank's (1969b) model of the underdevelopment process in Brazil. Portugal had previously controlled a large production of sugar in the Madiera Islands, and when prices rose precipitously in the sixteenth century, expanded cane production to north-eastern Brazil (which Portugal was granted as part of the Pope's division of the world in 1494). Initially Portugal allowed Dutch capital to use indigenous slave labour (which did not work well), but later black slaves from the African coastal trade were employed. Large profits were initially made; but even in the 'golden years' wealth was concentrated in the hands of a few owners and merchants, who transferred the profits to the European metropolis and made little investment locally, while equipment and consumer goods were bought in. The sugar economy generated a satellite economy of its own in the inland livestock regions, and this in turn forced the Indians to withdraw further into the interior or be used as cheap labour. Frank claims that the structure of underdevelopment was thus impregnated into the social and economic structure of Latin America through its incorporation into the world capitalist system.

At the end of the seventeenth century, the Dutch established further plantations in the West Indies, cutting the price of sugar in half. Brazil's ties with the metropolis weakened, a process of involution began, and a precarious subsistence economy was established. Also between 1600 and 1750 Portugal itself underdeveloped, becoming a satellite to Britain. Hence, after gold and diamonds were discovered in the central region of Brazil in the eighteenth century, the gold flowed through Portugal to be accumulated and invested in Britain. Furthermore, when manufacturing (iron, textiles) began to develop in Brazil, the Queen of Portugal in 1786 ordered the factories and workshops closed because they competed for labour with Brazil's 'real and solid wealth' which lay in 'the fruits and products of the earth'. In the early nineteenth century Brazil was forced by Britain to open its ports to free trade. Competition destroyed whatever Brazilian manufactures had grown up. The economic depression of the late nineteenth century and penetration by British imperialism put Brazil entirely out of a development race it should have won had natural resources decided the matter (Frank, 1969b: 145–67; on the position of women in Brazilian society see Saffioti, 1978).

In *Capitalism and Slavery*, Eric Williams (1944) explores the interconnections between Britain, West Africa and the Americas. The early British colonial possessions, he argues, were of two types: small farmer colonies in most of North America; and producers of tropical and subtropical staples like the Caribbean islands. The main problem in staple production was a lack of labour. The Spanish tried to use Indian labour under various systems, but failed to find an efficient method. The British used indentured servants, convicts and prisoners from English invasions of Ireland and Scotland. But a change in mercantilist policy at the end of the seventeenth century away from the accumulation of precious metals and towards the development of manufactures, for which a large cheap labour force was desirable, led to a change in the state's attitudes towards emigration. In addition, indentured servants were expensive and temporary. Hence, for Williams, black slavery had an economic rather than merely a racial basis – it was used because it was cheaper.

The slave trade was made a monopoly of the Company of Royal Adventurers Trading to Africa, incorporated in 1663 for a thousand years, and founded by the most worthy members of mercantilist society, leading 'humanitarians' holding high office in England. The triangular trade connected England, France or colonial North America, which supplied ships and manufactures, with West Africa supplying 'human merchandise', with the plantations of the Americas, which supplied colonial raw materials (sugar, tobacco, indigo, molasses, cotton), in turn used in European or North American manufactures. The small plantation island of Barbados was considered more valuable to Britain at the end of the seventeenth century than New England, New York and Pennsylvania combined. William's thesis is that the profits made in this system of production and trade were a mainstream of capital flowing to Britain. Capital accumulated in Liverpool and Manchester was reinvested in canals and cotton factories, while profits from the West Indian trade financed James Watt's invention of the steam engine. The industrial revolution, he maintains, was financed by slavery (Williams, 1944; Frank, 1979). As Galeano puts it:

> Traffic in slaves raised the shipping center of Bristol to the rank of Britain's second city and made Liverpool the world's greatest port. Ships sailed with cargoes of duly blessed weapons, cloth, gin and rum, baubles and colored glass, the means of payment for Africa's human merchandise and for the sugar, cotton, coffee, and cacao of American colonial plantations. At the end of the eighteenth century, Africa and the Caribbean were providing work for 180,000 textile workers in Manchester; Sheffield produced the knives, Birmingham produced 150,000 muskets a year. African chiefs received the products of British industry and delivered the human cargoe to slave captains. . . . Many of the slaves came from forest areas and had never seen the sea; they mistook its roaring for that of some underwater beast waiting to devour them, or (according to a slave trader of the period) believed not entirely without reason, that 'they are carried like sheep to the slaughter and the Europeans are fond of their flesh'. The cat-o'-nine-tails could do little to contain the Africans' desperate suicides.
>
> (Galeano, 1973: 93–4)

What, by comparison, was the effect of the slave trade on West African society? In *How Europe Underdeveloped Africa*, Walter Rodney (1974) argues that economic expansion was occurring in West Africa between the tenth and fifteenth centuries. African manufactures, like 'Moroccan' leather (actually made by Hausa and Mandinga specialists in northern Nigeria and Mali), bark and cotton cloth, and copper articles were produced by guild-like institutions, within a system characterized by increasing specialization and division of labour. Money was replacing barter. Socio-political change accompanied an expansion of the productive forces. Rodney maintains that African society retained its communal features even as the lineages achieved different levels of economic and political power.

West Africa's misfortune lay in its being the non-European source of labour disciplined to agriculture and industrial pursuits nearest to the Americas. Ten million slaves, Rodney estimates, were landed alive in the Americas, the Atlantic islands and Europe and, given high mortality rates, several times this number were taken or killed. This massive loss to the African labour force was made more critical by the prime age and health of the workers involved. Thus while other continents experienced rapid population increase after 1500 (and population growth is at least a strong pressure for economic development), Africa's population remained roughly the same for four centuries. The West African societies intensively used as sources of slaves, previously leading forces in regional development, were the most negatively affected by the kidnapping and warlike activities of the slave trade. African societies were fragmented at a time when national economies were emerging elsewhere. Interregional links within the continent were broken, Europeans and other outsiders became middlemen (often replacing indigenous middlewomen) and African societies were made dependent on the triangular trade. The trade goods exchanged for slaves were of the consumer variety rather than productive implements which could be used in African development. Vital inventions were made in western Europe, with capital accumulated from the slave and sugar trades being reinvested in technological improvement. Competition from modernized European industries destroyed African cloth production, iron smelting and other manufactures. Europe developed into industrial capitalism; Africa was underdeveloped.

These were some of the mechanisms by which societies in West Africa, the Caribbean, and South America were differentially underdeveloped following contact with Europe. The more difficult and controversial question is how the Europeans were able to fulfil their mercantilist intentions. In the African case, Rodney (1974: 78–82) argues that Europe was technologically more advanced in terms of improvements in a few key areas (ships, cannon, some metal goods) and had the further advantage of supplying new, unusual and desirable manufactures to Africa. Perhaps more significant were the communal social relations of Africa, associated with political fragmentation (only a few states had territorial solidarity), which the Europeans could exploit. In effect, certain aspects of African society became weaknesses when exposed to pressures from other societies at slightly higher levels of technical development or with different socio-political organizations. However Europe's advantage was not sufficient for conquest or permanent political control of large stretches of African space.

In the case of the American civilizations, the argument has been made that excessive centralization proved their downfall – once the Aztec and Incan emperors Montezuma and Atahualpa fell into Spanish hands, their empires became 'bodies without heads'. But then, what first enabled Cortes, with 400 men and 100 horses, or Pissaro, with even fewer supporters, to overcome empires which could field armies numbered in the tens of thousands? Stavrianos (1981: 80–1) finds the explanation ultimately to lie in 'the devastating effect of millennia of isolation'. By this he means: first, that the American civilizations were technologically thousands of years behind – for example they did not smelt metal ores, and had only stone, wood or bone tools and weapons and cotton armour; second, that the Americans were 'psychologically vulnerable' – Montezuma greeted Cortes as a long-departed white serpent-god which prophecy had foretold would return from the East, and having never seen horses thought he was opposed literally by horse-men; and third, that the American peoples had no immunity against European and African diseases – so that the indigenous population of Spanish America fell from 50 million on contact to 4 million in the seventeenth century.

In brief, Europe could achieve domination over the social formations of the Atlantic rim because of prior differences of socio-political and technological development. The position of Europe on the Eurasian continent also played a role in the sense of providing ideas, goods and diseases which were instumental in the conquest of the Americas. It is exactly for explaining this latter aspect that spatial relations, societal exposure or isolation, have to be an integral part of theory at the level of the social formation. Theory aside, the result was that the initial differences in level of development and mode of social organization quickly widened to Europe's extreme advantage. Domination of the Atlantic was of fundamental significance in the sixteenth and seveteenth centuries as Europe struggled to accumulate wealth and power. Capitalism's first great leap forward was financed by American plunder, African slavery and the Atlantic trading system.

Mercantilism in the Eastern Hemisphere

The situation was different in the East. As Wolf (1982: ch. 8) argues, when the Europeans expanded trade to Asia in the sixteenth century they found lands and peoples organized by centralized tributary states. These confined mercantile companies to 'factories' (trading posts) around the perimeters of south and east Asia for as long as three centuries. There they had to compete with the Muslim mercantile system which had spread from the Middle East to the East African coast in the ninth century, and to India and south-east Asia in the thirteenth and fourteenth centuries. Using gun-bearing sailing ships, especially galleons carrying cannon, the Portuguese were able to capture Muslim ports and large parts of the spice trade (pepper, ginger, cloves, nutmeg, mace) but not monopolize it. The Portuguese were succeeded by the Dutch East India Company in the seventeenth century, a company able to control production and dominate the trading kingdoms of the smaller kingdoms of the south-east Asian coasts. Conceding Indonesia to the Dutch, the English East India Company concentrated on the Indian subcontinent, which indeed became the jewel in the British commercial crown. How this happened is described in detail by Ramkrishna Mukherjee (1974; see also Davey, 1975).

Mercantilism in India

In north India (ruled by the Mogul emperor) and the south Indian Vijayanagar empire, the village community was the predominant socio-economic institution. Based in agriculture, but with a sizeable complement of artisans, villages were relatively self-sufficient peasant communities. The usufruct of land was held by peasant families, with 'ownership' vested in the village community administered by a headman and council of leading householders and elders. The primary internal social mechanism was the *jati*, or division into immutable social units (castes) whereby everyone had a definite socio-economic position and specific work to do. (Mukherjee interprets the origin of castes in terms of the successive incorporation of earlier tribal peoples into the more advanced village-agricultural system.) Village communities were further stabilized by the spiritual sanctions contained in the doctrine of *karma* and the theory of reincarnation – that is, position in society results from the previous life, while behaviour in this life affects the next. An older class system (*varna*) grouped castes in hereditary levels composed of spiritual and political leaders, artisans and agriculturalists, and servile people. Local chiefs (*zamindars*) had a claim to the surplus product and, after the conquest of north India by nomadic Muslim invaders, Mogul officers and nobles were assigned *jagirs* (claims on surplus). The apex of power was constituted by the Mogul emperor and his household. Both in south India, and the growing north Indian Mogul empire, one-third of the product was expropriated as taxes, this exploitation being sanctified by religion and enforced by the state.

As in Europe, the tributary system (which Mukherjee calls 'feudal') began to change starting in the fourteenth century. The underlying force for change was commercialization and the growth of manufactures, but the complex manifestations of change ranged from increased state intervention into village life (the farming-out of tax collection to the *zamindari* rather than relying on the village council), secularization of political and economic life, and an attack on the ideological basis of the caste system (the Bhakti movement led by merchants and artisans). The significant difference between the European and Indian 'feudal' trading revolutions, however, was that neither Indian states nor merchants developed their naval power to the level reached by the Europeans; more generally, mercantilism did not develop to the same degree. This deprived the Indian merchant class of the spectacular profits made from long distance trade (weakening them as an independent social force) and made the Indian state dependent on successive European mercantile interests – for example, the state was forced to grant 'concessions' and trading monopolies to foreigners. The English East India Company was exactly such a concessionaire, gaining a charter of trading rights from the Mogul emperor in 1618, establishing factories around the coast during the seventeenth century (especially Bombay, Madras and Calcutta), but unable as yet to do what the Spanish and Portuguese had done in the Americas – conquer territory.

But while flowering with mercantile wealth in the first half of the eighteenth century, the Mogul empire was decaying from within. The share of the product taken as rent by the state, which had been about one-third, rose to one-half. Attempts to convert Hindu north India into an orthodox Sunni Islamic state resulted in mass uprisings led by the traditional Indian nobility. At the same time, the now decadent Mogul nobility squabbled over supreme power, previously vassal states became independent, and semi-independent principalities were declared all over the empire – for example the *subah* of Bengal. And during 1759–61 north-western India was invaded by an Afghan army. In brief what is more accurately defined as a precariously centralized tributary system in India disintegrated into a series of feudal social formations.

These cyclical events, endemic to the more unstable versions of tributary systems, could now be taken advantage of by the East India Company, which had long regarded the conquest of the subcontinent as a logical culmination of mercantile policy. Joining in dynastic squabbles and inter-principality wars, the company extended its control of the fortified port of Calcutta into Bengal province in 1757–65, annexed Mysore (in southern India) by 1799 and in the first half of the nineteenth century became master of most Indian territory, leaving dependent 'native rulers' to control the rest.

What does a mercantile company do when it rules? Mukherjee (1974: ch. 5) makes the following assessment. Until the company usurped power, international commercial transactions had faced the grave difficulty of unequal exchange relations in favour of India – hence the East India Company had to buy spices, cotton and silk goods with American silver. With the mercantilists as rulers, what had always been a fine line between trade and plunder became so fine it disappeared. Beginning with Bengal, the company enforced trading relations so unfavourable as to make the reproduction of producers' families impossible. Indian textile artisans were forced (by flogging) into becoming bond slaves of the company; Indian merchants were prohibited from buying commodities directly from producers so that the company monopolized internal as well as external trade; Indian peasants were forced to deliver export crops at nominal prices, or for nothing. This destroyed the progressive forces which were, at the time of conquest, leading Indian economic development and challenging certain ancient institutions. Simultaneously, to stabilize a ravished society, 'reform' measures were introduced which codified Indian law and supported customs according to orthodox Brahminism (for the Hindus) and Islam (for the Muslim population), further suppressing the more liberated views of the Bhakti movement. To give a few examples, widow burning, which had been abolished in the Mogul empire, was now carried out under British supervision; child marriage was reinvigorated; the caste system, which had come under attack in the fifteenth to eighteenth centuries, was reestablished. In the direction of 'modernization', the ancient communal right to land became the (European-style) right to private property. A high-caste group of landowners grew at the expense of a peasantry weakened by mercantile exploitation. And whereas the state had previously maintained the central irrigation system, under the company (with its mercantilist attitude of 'let us get what we can today, let tomorrow take care of itself') these constructions became historical ruins. The land taxes, now gathered so efficiently by the company that they doubled in amount, were exported as 'personal fortunes' by British adventurers and as 'earnings' by the company. Mukherjee (1974: 398–9) finds that the increased power to extract taxes, tribute and 'presents' from the immense wealth of the Indian subcontinent 'contributed significantly [through an expansion of credit] to the industrial revolution in Britain'. Mukherjee (1974: 343–74) and others (Davey, 1975: 43) put the extraction of surplus from Bengal in the period 1757–80 at £1.7 million a year, with the total rising to £3–4 millions annually from all India by the early nineteenth century, this at a time when capital employed in buildings and machinery in the British textile industry was £1 million in 1783 and £9.25 millions in 1802; indeed revenues from India in the late eighteenth and early nineteenth centuries were one-quarter to one-third of the amount of gross domestic capital formation in Britain at the time (Mitchell, 1988: 857). Obviously there was no necessary connection between Indian profit and industrial investment, in that profit could also be spent on luxury consumption, but Mukherjee's assessment of India's contribution to financing the industrial revolution is realistic in terms of the amount of capital involved. Meanwhile the company's rule in India produced such devastating effects (like widespread famine) that the 'Sepoy Revolt' of 1857, led by Indian soldiers, forced the British state to take over the administration of what became part of the colonial empire in 1858.

Mercantilism in China

The last great act of mercantilist destruction took place in the world's most glorious pre-capitalist civilization. The Chinese empire was unified under a centralized tributary system between 246 and 221 BC in the Ch'in dynasty. The social system, composed of classes rather than castes, consisted of the imperial clan, scholar-administrators, rich landowners, merchants, artisans, a mass of peasants and a small number of slaves. Tribute was extracted as taxes and, more importantly, as corvée labour (one month a year) on roads, canals, palaces, imperial tombs and in military duty. Apart from these obligations the people were left to administer their own village affairs. The early empires, like most other despotisms based on agricultural taxes, had a strong prejudice against merchants – hence the bureaucracy was drawn from the richer landowners. And the entire system was bound together ideologically under the Confucian belief that people must play their assigned roles in a fixed authoritarian structure but that the first duty of the ruler was to set a proper example of sound ethical conduct. Fairbank *et al.* (1973) describe the structure of classical China in terms of a relatively small centralized governmental body floating on a sea of semi-isolated peasant communities and finds some validity in the Chinese concept of dynastic cycles (heroic founding, great power, long decline, total collapse) lasting two to three centuries.

Behind this historical pattern, however, lay technological, economic, social and cultural changes fundamental to Chinese and global development. Between the eighth and thirteenth centuries China experienced a leap in agricultural productivity (through double cropping, refinement of the water control system, new crops like tea and cotton), rapid advance in textile, lacquer and porcelain production, and innovations like gunpowder, printing and paper currency. Trade burst out of its earlier government-imposed straitjacket to be organized by guilds in commercial cities.

However, the resilience of the centralized tributary structure is shown by the failure of this economic transformation to overturn the Chinese system, which was reincarnated in a somewhat different form: the class system became more egalitarian and less aristocratic, property could be accumulated by small private owners, while traditional ideology was rejuvenated as a neo-Confucian orthodoxy. The revival of classical values, including the ancient disdain of commerce, signalled a return to the agrarian-centredness of the past. From the mid-fourteenth to the beginning of the twentieth century, China returned to traditional ways. This six-century-long period of slow change left Chinese civilization undeveloped relative to a Europe undergoing dynamic transformation. China was a huge (300 million) rural social formation whose capital was mainly the land itself, improved by centuries of arduous labour, and the irrigation facilities, and maintained by the continued application of raw labour power. In comparison with Europe there was little means or incentive for technological improvement and, in any case, no class interested in economic innovation – capital accumulation was precarious except under official protection. As Fairbank *et al.* (1973: 440) summarize, 'the Chinese economy around 1800 was notably at a different stage of development from that of Europe. It was also differently constructed and was thought of in entirely different terms'.

In the nineteenth century two interacting processes came together to bring about the collapse of the last great tributary system. Internal signs of decline were evident from around 1800, the basic pressure coming from growing difficulties of peasant livelihood, yet bureaucratic and military ineffectiveness. Class struggle took the tributary forms of secret societies, religious uprisings and regional revolts among peripheral and incorporated peoples. Restoration of central power was achieved in part by appeal to traditional Confucian values, in part with the force of Western arms. External pressure was exerted by European and United States mercantile interests, which had long coveted the products of Chinese agriculture and craft industry (tea became the national drink in Briatin in the eighteenth century). For the Europeans the problem had long been a lack of Chinese interest in foreign goods – thus King George III's ambassador of 1793, on asking for the opening of trade with Britain, drew the imperial reply: 'our celestial empire possesses all things in prolific abundance' (Fairbank *et al.* 1973: 257). Chinese products had to be bought with Spanish pieces of eight – a mercantilist's nightmare! The problem was solved by the British conquest of India and the establishment in the nineteenth century of a triangular trade between England (cotton and manufactures), India (raw cotton and opium) and China (tea and silk). Here we will follow just one thread of a miserable tale – the opium trade (Greenberg, 1951).

Opium was indigenous to China but not widely smoked until the nineteenth century. The British East India Company organized opium production on a large scale in Bengal, perfecting a brand specifically for China, packaging it, and then disowning it. Prohibited in China, the drug was smuggled in by private British, Indian and Chinese merchants, with the help of bribes to Chinese officials. Such was the corruption that Mandarin navy boats, supposedly preventing smuggling, were used to import opium. By the 1830s the ancient inflow of silver was reversed and the drug's effects so disastrous that an imperial edict was issued against it, followed by fines, house-to-house searches, and the massive imprisonment of addicts. European merchants urged intervention and between 1840 and 1842 the First Opium War was fought between the Chinese army, brandishing swords and spears, the provincial navies, using junks filled with archers and antiquated cannon, and the East India Company's iron-hulled steamer *Nemesis*, with two 32-pounders on pivots fore and aft. The result of this unequal contest was that China was forced to open five ports to the British, and other ports to France and the United States, with further concessions being made in the 1850s following a Second Opium War. The treaty ports organized the tea and silk export trade, but the Chinese market for British textiles remained limited (the self-sufficient village production system had not broken) so imports of opium were used as exchange and with that, by the end of the nineteenth century, one in ten of the Chinese population was an addict, and the world's oldest civilization lost in debt and corruption.

The treaty ports established along the coast provided points of contact between the enormous production and commercial system of the Chinese interior and the international trading system. The valuable silk and tea industries were incredibly labour intensive. Silk culture, for example, involved feeding the silk worms fine-cut mulberry leaves five or six times a day, or twelve tons of leaves for a crop of 700,000 worms, which yielded 116–175 pounds of raw silk. Growing and processing the finest green tea involved several rounds of picking and 'tatching', collecting, storing and packing. After this the chests of fine tea were carried on bamboo frames on 'coolies'' shoulders, never being allowed to touch the gound lest they be damaged – all this for a crop sold to middlemen for the equivalent of $5.33 for a chest of 133 pounds of common tea and double that for fine tea in the mid-nineteenth century. Tea would then be subjected to high imperial duties at the coast (Fairbank, 1964: 291).

After winning concessions in 1858–60, the treaty powers sought to keep the emperor in full domestic sovereignty. The Chinese Maritime Customs Service, administered by British officers until 1899, and thereafter by United States personnel, proved

> useful both to Western traders and to Chinese administrators, enabling the Chinese government to meet some of its immediate problems, and western merchants to exploit their Chinese market more effectively. . . . The aim of the western trading powers in China was to trade but not to govern.
>
> (Fairbank, 1964: 463)

In the late nineteenth century, after tea plants had been carried to the East India Company's plantations in the foothills of the Himalayas by the appropriately named botanist Robert Fortune, China's tea exports were eclipsed by even cheaper production elsewhere. China became one of the poorest components of the Third World periphery.

Mercantilism was therefore a highly efficient system for changing the orientatiion of world trading relations from its previous Eastern focus to one centred on Western Europe: thus the historic outflow of capital from Europe to the more advanced centralized tributary civilizations of the East was slowed, stemmed and finally reversed in the late eighteenth and early nineteenth centuries. Plunder and slave production in the Americas channelled capital into the early phases of Europe's modern process of economic development. We find convincing Mandel's calculation that the value of Latin American bullion, the booty extracted from Indonesia by the Dutch East India Company from 1650 to 1780, the profits from the French slave trade and from slave labour in the British Caribbean, and the profits from India in the late eighteenth century, which together made up over £1 billion, were far 'more than the capital of all the industrial enterprises operating by steam which existed in Europe around 1800' (Mandel, 1969; Hayter, 1981: 45–6). And it is difficult not to concur with the main thesis of underdevelopment theory, that the early development of Europe had so devastating an effect on the rest of the world as to provide the basic explanation for their continued poverty today.

Industrial revolution, free trade and imperialism

At crucial points in the discussion of mercantilism reference has been made to European manufactures, which in some cases (armaments especially) proved decisive in relations with non-European societies. In the Middle Ages, European industrial goods had been made in mercantile cities by craft members of guilds. Towards the end of the medieval period manufacturing moved to villages and country towns as merchant capitalists used the 'putting out system' (supplying raw materials to independent craftspeople and marketing the finished products) to avoid the restrictions and high costs of the guilds – the attraction of the countryside being cheap labour employed part-time in agriculture (Dunford and Perrons, 1983). Making textiles, leather and metal goods, proto-industrialization was a pronounced internal phase of the development of capitalism in England, Holland, Belgium and Germany. It led eventually to a class system polarized between merchants, master craft workers and independent producers on the one side, and a mass of poor workers, increasingly separated from land, on the other – the beginnings of an industrial capitalist class system.

The industrial revolution, which began in England around 1760, was thus a qualitative leap preceded by 200 years of quantitative change. This had already produced a country unusual for its time in that England was no longer a peasant economy engaged in subsistence agriculture, but a market economy with highly developed commercial and manufacturing sectors and an accumulated money surplus in the hands of capitalists rather than traditionalists. So how was the industrial revolution started? Here the enormous advantages gained in the external arena have to be taken into account. One argument maintains that market growth in the eighteenth century made traditional methods of production inadequate, thus requiring technological and organizational transformation. The market grew rapidly because population numbers rose in western Europe, doubling between 1750 and 1800. Rural areas of cottage industries and new factory and mining towns were 'demographic hothouses' producing children in good times and bad (Seccombe, 1983). But the market for industrial goods also grew because exports, while fluctuating wildly (50 per cent a year), increased rapidly, indeed more rapidly than domestic sales between 1750 and 1770. Thus by 1805 British cotton manufacturers exported two thirds of their output. The export market was not tied to population numbers, but grew by destroying competing producers often through the use of war and colonization. This required that the state be willing to wage war on behalf of its manufacturers, something the British government proved more than willing to do. There were other ties to the external arena, and especially to the underdeveloping world. The cotton industry, driving force of the first industrial revolution (1760–1840), drew its raw material from peasant and plantation production in the Caribbean, the southern states of the United States, Africa and India. And as several Third World theorists maintain, it was financed in good part from mercantile profits made through destructive exploitation of the global system. In this explanation, therefore, the industrial revolution was the modern outgrowth of the mercantilist system, located in the most 'successful' mercantilist country, Britain (Hobsbawm, 1968).

The main advantage of the new industrial system was competitive efficiency. This rested on rapid technological change, in cotton spinning in the eighteenth century, and throughout the textile industry in the early nineteenth century, with dramatic results in terms of labour productivity: spinning 100 pounds of cotton took eighteenth-century Indian hand workers 50,000 hours; even with the early crude spinning-jenny and water-frame this was reduced to 2,000 hours in England in 1780; further innovations (the steam-driven 'mule') reduced the labour input to 135 hours in 1825 (Dunford and Perrons, 1983: 200). With advantages like these we find (mercantilist) protection of manufacturing declining in the early nineteenth century, to be replaced by free trade as official state policy in Britain in the 1840s.

What effect did the industrial revolution have on the world's previous manufacturing centres, like India? By manipulating import duties the British government discouraged Indian manufactured exports and encouraged imports from Britain into India, reversing the main direction of the flow of textiles between 1813 and 1830. As railroads brought all the subcontinent within reach of Manchester, first the manufacturing cities were destroyed by competition (Dacca, 'the Manchester of India' fell from a population of 150,000 to 30–40,000) and then the village craft industries disappeared. Even the Governor-General of the East India Company was moved to remark that 'The bones of the weavers are bleaching the plains of India' (quoted in Hayter, 1981: 68). The ancient 'self-sufficient' village community system, based in a symbiotic relation between agriculture and manufacture, was captured as a source of agricultural export crops. Instead of exporting cotton textiles, India became a source of raw cotton exports to China and Europe (Mukherjee, 1974).

Imperialism

The destruction of civilizations, the movement of millions of slaves, the raiding of ancient treasures, the capturing of world trade were the external conditions under which capitalism could come into existence. These interacted with and shaped the development of the social relations and forces which constituted the internal structure of capitalist life. Capital derived from mercantilist use of the world's peoples, strengthened the power of capitalists and developed the forces of production. Once the capitalist mode had achieved domestic hegemony in Britain, once the forces of production had achieved obvious dominance, the early device for state control over primitive accumulation – mercantilist protection – could be dropped and 'free' trade between unequal partners relied on for continued global economic dominance.

However by the second half of the nineteenth century there were several large industrial countries competing for global domination and, at times of depression (such as the 1870s and 1880s), struggling for economic survival. The development of continental European, North American and Japanese industries also involved the intervention of the state, initially for protection, later for creating the conditions for expansion. This was the context in which a 'second imperialism', perhaps more violent, certainly more voracious, than the first mercantilist version, emerged from Europe, the United States and Japan.

In the late nineteenth century the word imperialism, which had formerly been used to mean dictatorial government, was extended to include political sovereignty of a nation over alien peoples and territories. The usual date for the onset of modern imperialism is 1870. But we should note certain events hidden by this generalization – throughout the nineteenth century European Russia expanded into Asia, the United States and Canada pushed their frontiers into North America, and Britain, as we have seen, was actively expanding its politico-economic influence in India even as free trade was debated in the Houses of Parliament. Even so, the rapidity of the onset of global expansionism around 1870 does mark a qualitative advance. After 1870, a new era of empire building began in earnest in which the European powers partitioned virtually all the Eastern Hemisphere amongst themselves – between 1870 and 1900 the European states added 10 million square miles of territory and 150 million people to their area of control, one-fifth of the earth's land surface and one-tenth of its people. The principle arena of conquest was Africa, although the Middle East, south-east Asia and the Pacific also received attention. European expansion was characterized by the most extreme belligerence, with ruthless 'sporting wars' (in Bismarck's words) fought on the slightest pretext against pre-capitalist peoples. The result was that Britain extended its empire over one-fifth of the globe controlling one quarter of its people, gaining an empire on which 'the sun never sets'. France took possession of much of North and West Africa and Indo-China, Germany parts of Africa and the Pacific, Italy and Belgium were active in Africa, the United States in the Pacific and Caribbean, and Japan in east Asia and the Pacific (Cohen, 1973).

Why did the Euro-American social formations show such a suddenly renewed and ferocious appetite for foreign domination? Schumpeter (1952) seeks the explanation in socio-psychological compulsion – that is, instinctive inclinations towards war and conquest coming to the surface as people and nations struggled to avoid extinction. Others see imperialism as an act of state power, the political expression of modern government. Radicals influenced by socialist ideas note a correspondence between the maturation of industrial capitalism, with its tremendous material demands, and the redevelopment of imperialism. John Hobson (1902; Zeitlin, 1972), a British journalist radicalized by his experience in the Boer War, formulated an argument linking the internal class relations of industrial capitalism with an external need for territorial control. For Hobson, the crucial issue was an otherwise indisposable surplus of capital. Because of the limited purchasing power of workers, capitalist societies have a tendency to economic stagnation unless a place can be found to invest unneeded capital. Imperialism was therefore a contest between the industrial capitalist powers to monopolize external markets for capital exports. Externalization was not inevitable; capitalism could be reformed by increasing labour's consumption and stimulating the capitalist system through internal sources. This conclusion was disputed by socialists influenced by Marxist theory, who saw some kind of external imperialist action as an inevitable aspect of the capitalist system. Beyond this Marxist theories differ on the internal drive behind external conquest.

The Austrian socialist Rudolph Hilferding took Marx's idea of monopoly capitalism (competition concentrates capital in fewer hands) one stage further to include capital accumulation by banks (finance capitalism). Finance capitalism, he said, is diametrically opposed to *laissez-faire* capitalism in that in seeking domination it needs a state strong enough to pursue an expansionist policy and acquire colonies. This is given justification by racial ideology, but is essentially a matter of economic necessity since 'any faltering of the onward drive reduces the profits of finance capital, weakens its powers of competition and finally turns the smaller economic area into a tributary of the larger' (quoted in Mommsen, 1980: 37). Imperialist expansion of all kinds (export of capital, gaining of external markets, opening of new territories) accelerates the accumulation of capital, and in an expansionist phase capitalism is less vulnerable to crisis. The idea of the export of capital was retained by Vladimir Lenin (1975) in an explanation of the global origins of the First World War. Lenin found the developing capitalist powers struggling to repartition the global system of investment domains, with the late-comer Germany attempting to acquire colonies. In a somewhat different version, Rosa Luxemburg (1951) saw the contradictions of capitalism focused on the inadequate purchasing power of workers, with consumer markets being sought elsewhere, in non-capitalist societies. As these would not submit voluntarily (to having their manufactures destroyed, for example), there was a need for state violence and political control to force trade on disadvantageous terms. Other theories stress labour needs, or energy and raw material supplies Caldwell, 1977). Despite their differences of emphasis all radical theories of imperialism have essentially the same logic – external imperialism served to relieve contradictions internal to the capitalist system.

This radical position has been questioned especially on the issue of connections between the maturation of capitalism and the onset of imperialism. Empirically, the connection is disputed by pointing to the fact that several imperial powers (Italy, Portugal, Russia) were not mature capitalist countries in the late nineteenth to early twentieth centuries, while several mature capitalist countries (Sweden, Switzerland) were not imperialistic (Cohen, 1973). Yet it remains the case that all major industrial capitalist countries were also imperial powers. Likewise the 'purely economic' motivation of imperialism is questioned – the European powers took non-profitable colonies (with few export or investment opportunities) in the belief perhaps that the white man's burden was to bring civilization to the world. Yet again an excess of zeal in pursuit of an ideology can hardly be used to question the theory of economic interests originating that ideology. In other words, these are quibbles rather than theory-shaking criticisms. We can therefore proceed to examine the results of imperialism, taking as a case study the African arena of struggle. (See also Magdoff, 1982; Rhodes, 1970; Galtung, 1971; Szymanski, 1981; Brewer, 1980.)

Imperialism in Africa

The Marxist notion of socio-economic necessity has to be retained if we are to explain the despicable acts performed by imperial Europe in terms other than an irrepressible biological urge. Here we shall use a case study of the articulation between European capitalism and the lineage/state systems of Africa. The available literature affords the possibility of extending mode of production analysis in two significant directions (which in Chapter 10 we shall call mode of reproduction analysis) so we shall emphasize changing gender and natural relations with the onset of imperialism.

In a brilliant summary, abstracting from the complexities of many diverse situations, Jeanne Henn (1984) presents a feminist—materialist survey of the African pre-colonial production system. African farmers used the hoe rather than the plough (except in Ethiopia) and relied on female rather than male labour. The basic production unit was the extended family household, with families embedded in wider networks of economic and political obligations based on kinship ties. The patriarchal head of the household controlled resources and labour, land was cleared by dependent men, and food production, storage, preparation, craftwork, child care and domestic and personal services were performed by women. In stateless societies, socio-political linkages were formed on the basis of kinship, but positions of leadership rarely resided in a single person or group. As women were not usually heads of household, they took no part in the council of elders, although they often formed parallel, if less powerful, organizations. State societies ranged from hierarchical (conical) lineage systems to complex empires grouping several different societies under a single political centre, and integrating subjugated peoples via tributary systems (ivory, slaves and women were given to the king or ruling group), feudalistic labour services and systems of direct slavery. Most societies were patrilineal, making women's economic position precarious, for a woman worked on her husband's land and did not have land rights in her natal village.

In a study of environmental relations in one such state society, the Sokoto caliphate of northern Nigeria, Michael Watts (1983a; 1983b; see also Jaffe, 1985) shows how peasant reproduction was secured in a hazardous climatic environment through the network of relations and reciprocities embedded in the kin/state mode of production. Drawing on Scott's (1976) work on the 'moral economy' of the peasantry, Watts identifies several dimensions of response to climatic hazards (the volatility of rainfall on the margins of the Sahara) in the peasants' subsistence ethic, in their risk-averting behaviour, in communal reciprocity and redistribution of the social

Table 8.1 Subsistence security and adaptive structure in pre-colonial Hausaland

Safety-first or risk aversion	Norm of reciprocity	Moral economy
Agronomic risk aversion, intercropping, crop mixtures, crop rotation, moisture preservation, crop experimentation, short-maturing millets, etc., exploitation of local environments (famine foods), secondary resources (dry season crafts), domestic self help and supports	Inter-family insurance, risk sharing, extended kin groups (*gandu*), reciprocity, gift exchange, mutual support, elite redistribution to the poor, storage, ritual sanction, anti-famine institutions, patron-clientage, communal work groups	Regional and ecological interdependence between desert edge and savannahs, trade in foodstuffs from surfeit to deficit regions. Role of the state: (i) central granaries based on grain tithe (ii) State relief and tax modification
Agronomic/domestic level	Community level	Regional/state level

Source: Watts, 1983b: 29

product by the state (Table 8.1). This, he says, is not to suggest a 'Rousseauian pre-capitalist bliss, a glorified peasant life somehow optimally adapted and ultra-stable'. Rather:

> various individual and collective practices, some of which are still extant, permitted a margin of security and dealt with normal agriculture risks. This pantheon of adaptive strategies was, moreover, firmly grounded in the social and economic architecture of the Sokoto Caliphate. Peasant security, and by extension the hazardousness of place, was intricately bound up with the nexus of horizontal and vertical ties which were coterminous with the social relations characteristic of a tributary system of production.
>
> (Watts, 1983b: 30)

Hence while famine was not unknown, a series of measures were taken to minimize the impact of climatic variations. Indeed it is exactly Watts' point that the northern Nigerian social formation was formed through the adaptation of the kin and tributary modes of production to a volatile environment.

Modern capitalist expansion in Africa proceeded in two phases: the ending of the slave trade and the opening of legitimate ('free') trade; and the political partitioning of the continent under imperialism. The movement to abolish slavery was phrased in religious and moral terms. But it was also led by anti-mercantilist forces, people who believed that free trade and wage labour were preferable forms of economic organization, especially as revolts in the Caribbean made free workers cheaper than slaves. A reduction in the ideological and economic power of the slavery interests enabled the abolitionists to be successful. The 'legitimate trade' (as the abolitionists called it) mainly involved West African exports of palm oil (raw material for soap, lubricants, candles), palm kernels (margarine) and ground-nuts (cooking oil, soap), with textiles, alcohol and hardware being imported from Europe. The commodities were raised under the African family labour system and as the nineteenth century progressed the terms of trade rose in Africa's favour. By the mid-nineteenth century substantial portions of African production and trade were dependent on the European connection (Stavrianos, 1981: ch. 14).

In the second half of the nineteenth century, and especially after 1870, there was a dramatic change in this informal system of contacts as the (political) scramble for Africa began. Why was political control over African territory necessary? Capitalism by this time was a system of mass industrial production which could no longer rely on the vagaries of mercantilist trade, but had to secure a raw material base, protect lines of communication, and where possible find guaranteed markets. Several major industrial powers stalked the global scene – informal 'gentlemen's agreements' over spheres of influence no longer sufficed in a cut-throat world made worse by economic depression. The problems thrown up by these industrial pressures were beyond the means of even the largest private company to resolve. The European merchant houses, which previously had been content with the coastal trade to Africa, pressed their governments to use force to maximize business opportunities and keep out rivals. However as Rodney (1974) reminds, we should not forget racism as a motivation for colonization. Whereas Britain granted dominion status to its white colonies, it withdrew self-government from the West Indies when white planters were replaced by blacks in the legislative assemblies. Englishmen likewise opposed self-government in Africa on grounds of black incompetence. When Durham University affiliated with an African college in 1874, *The Times* suggested the university next affiliate with the London Zoo! 'It was economics that determined that Europe should invest in Africa and control the continent's raw materials and labor. It was racism which confirmed the decision that the form of control should be direct colonial rule' (Rodney, 1974: 141).

The principles of imperialist expansion in Africa were set by the Berlin Conference of 1885–6: (1) notice of intent given to other European powers; (2) claims legitimized by effective occupation; (3) intra-European disputes settled by arbitration. Of the battles between African warriors, who made mass frontal attacks in a vain show of bravery before retreating to mud-walled cities, and European and Indian armies, with repeating rifles, machine guns, iron steamers and artillery at their disposal, we need say little. By 1914 the continent was partitioned into colonies distributed among the European powers, although African resistance continued into the 1920s. The first political act of a European colonial power was the drawing of boundaries, the prime consideration being the balance of European power rather than natural or ethnographic realities (with severe geopolitical consequences for contemporary Africa). The main concern of the colonial administration was to make the conquered pay for their oppression, given the tiny budget allocated by European governments. This led to various systems of indirect rule mainly through 'traditional chiefs' advised by colonial officers – what used to be a communal form of authority, a system of negotiated agreements, became a series of petty dictatorships, aimed at producing taxes, labour, products and resources for the Europeans, again with disastrous consequences for the present-day socio-political structure. And finally, Christian missionaries consciously tried to change African culture, using religion, medicine and education, into a Europeanized version amenable to the colonial system. Resistance came from peasant resentment of the growing power of the chiefs (especially the alienation of communal lands for cash crop production) led by 'trousered blacks', educated by the missionaries, yet driven by their experience and knowledge into translating tribal resistance into claims for national independence.

In political territories stabilized by such methods we find the African traders being replaced by European companies, the development of commodity exports (mainly agricultural and mineral products) and the mobilization of local labour directly through the corvée (i.e. demands made on the chiefs to deliver a certain number of workers) or indirectly through the coercion of hut and poll taxes, all this labour being grossly underpaid. Following the discussion by Amin (1972; 1981) we can define three social formations derived from the differential integration of African societies and resources into world capitalism:

1 *West African peasant production*. The British and French colonial governments encouraged peasants to grow export crops needed in Europe (ground nuts, cotton, palm oil, cocoa, rubber). European companies were given trading monopolies able to dictate prices which were low for African exports high for imports (tools, clothing). The trading monopoly was the direct instrument for the extraction of surplus, with firms paying dividends (to European shareholders) of 25 per cent in poor years, 90 per cent in good years (Amin, 1973).

2 *Concessionary system* in the Congo Basin. Where equatorial rainforest precluded dense populations and mass peasant production systems, King Leopold of Belgium granted land concessions to private European companies to exploit territory and people. On these concessions a horror story rivalling slavery unfolded, especially during 1895–1905 when the strong demand for rubber led to excessive demands for deliveries of the prized commodity. Africans who did not meet their quotas were mutilated by chopping off a hand or foot and baskets of preserved limbs were presented by labour organizers to the Belgian authorities as evidence of their zeal. Under such conditions the population of the 'Belgian' Congo was, literally, cut in half.

3 *European settler areas, plantation and mining companies*. In the highlands of eastern and southern Africa, 'grants' of land were made (by colonial governments!) to European settler farmers or

plantations. Such land grants were useless without labour. A variety of measures induced the 'lazy Africans' to work on farms and in the mines: head taxes on males, who therefore had to work in the money economy to earn a cash income; and the reserving of arable land for white settlement only, again forcing the African people to work for Europeans. The universal characteristic of African jobs in colonial farms, plantations and mines was extremely low wages, inadequate for family subsistence. Wages had to be supplemented with food and services from the non-capitalist sector – or to put the matter more accurately, the unpaid labour of rural women subsidized the gin and tonics of the British settlers. The result was a deterioration in rural family welfare – indeed the impoverished female-headed households of southern Africa are the contemporary result of more than a century of capitalist growth based on migrant labour (Stavrianos, 1981; Rodney, 1974; Henn, 1984).

Re-examining gender and environmental relations in one region, peasant production of export crops in West Africa, we return to the work of Henn (1984) and Watts (1983a; 1983b) to witness the effects of colonialism. Henn's main argument concerning the traditional African production system was that women wielding hoes did most of the hard work. In the period of 'legitimate trade', and even more under colonial administration, African food production was reoriented to export crop production. The transformation of the African household from a largely self-sufficient production/consumption unit into a peasant farming or pastoral unit established international capitalist dominance over rural Africa which continues to this day. While this changed the form taken by the labour effort, there is debate on whether it changed the gender relations of production.

Some scholars (Boserup, 1970; Van Allen, 1974) suggest that women's economic independence and traditional authority were undermined by incorporation into commodity production; others question whether women ever had significant independence in the pre-colonial era, and say that colonial intervention may have weakened patriachal control over women. All, however, agree that women's workload increased because of the extraction of surpluses from the African population (via taxes, forced production of export crops, food levies on villages, removal of young men to work in European plantations and mines or as forced labour on state railways). Research on the Beti peoples of southern Cameroon during the depression year of 1934, when cash crop prices were low and taxes high, shows women working 70 hours a week (compared with

46 hours in the pre-colonial period), while dependent males worked 55 hours and male heads of households 25 hours a week (Henn, 1978). During the commodification of the African economy, male heads of households retained control over family property, established ownership over cash crops, and with the compliance of the colonial authorities maintained patriarchal control over family labour (Henn, 1984). Profits accumulated in Europe were made from the bent backs of African female labour.

Watts (1983a; 1983b) points to a different aspect of the articulation between capitalist and pre-capitalist modes. In northern Nigeria (Hausaland) capitalism took the form of merchant capital protected and aided by the colonial state. The colonial administration sought to divert the surplus, previously exacted by the indigenous ruling elite, to their own coffers. But the colonial state's rigid demands for taxes paid in cash prior to harvest time, took no account of the realities of Hausa rural life. In addition the extended structure of the family changed, social and familial solidarity lost its original significance, the moral economy was ruptured. Larger areas of land were diverted to cash crop production at the expense of foodstuffs. A previously self-sufficient region became dependent on imported consumer goods and even basic food supplies. To the extent that the pre-capitalist character of Hausaland was eroded by colonial integration, Watts concludes:

> the adaptive capability of Hausa communities and the margin of subsistence security accordingly changed. In the process, peasant producers – particularly the rural poor – became less capable of responding to, and coping with, drought and food shortage. Traditional mechanisms and adjustments disappeared, the extension of cash cropping undermined self-sufficiency in food stuffs, a dependency on volatile world commodity prices (for cotton and groundnuts) amplified an already high tax burden and households became increasingly vulnerable to environmental peturbations such as droughts or harvest shortfalls.
>
> (Watts, 1983b: 30)

As a result, four major famines occurred during the colonial period, in 1914, 1927, 1942 and 1951. Watts (1983b) and Franke and Chasin (1980) attribute the catastrophic famine events of 1968–74, and the several near-famines since, to the changes wrought in the Sudano-Sahelian societies by colonialism and neo-colonialism. Environmental crises in the Third World must be understood in terms of the incorporation of pre-capitalist societies into the capitalist world system (see also Gakou, 1987; Austen, 1987).

Colonialism lasted until the late 1940s and 1950s with some countries achieving political independence only in the late 1970s. However this decline in Euro-American political control occurred only when the economies of Third World societies had already been captured, in structure and orientation, by the capitalist world market – 'independence' has therefore been more accurately termed 'neo-colonialism'. With imperialism world history took a new turn and global geography found a new focus. Increasingly the dynamic of European capitalism became the central source of societal change in what became a global system so that, by the late twentieth century, there is essentially one global dynamic, admittedly with several regional versions and counter-currents. This entails the increasing homogenization of time with the incorporation of global space. It also entails the imposition of permanently limited developmental opportunities on a world of people.

Conclusion

Relations between capitalist and non-capitalist social formations have taken a number of forms, depending on the stage in the development of capitalism, the structure of external relations and the politico-military capacity to fulfil them, and on the other side the position, solidity and dynamic phase of a series of non-capitalist formations. Mercantilism was accompanied by plunder during the first years of direct domination (the Spanish in America, British in India), with a more permanent extraction of surplus via unequal trade relations enforced by state power. Where goods were produced under mercantilist relations, slavery and other forms of coercion were used; in such systems surplus was extracted directly, in the production process, and therefore politico-military coercion had to be applied. This required political control over territory and thus mercantilist colonies. Colonization could occur extensively only in the Americas where indigenous resistance was lower than in the Old World. Elsewhere, in the East, mercantilism could achieve minimal political control over Asiatic societies until the British conquest of a disintegrating India in the late eighteenth and early nineteenth centuries.

'Free trade' between European and North American manufacturing, mechanized and improved with the aid of capital drained from the global system, devastated the craft industries of the Third World, while colonial governments encouraged plantations and enforced peasant production of export crops and raw materials. This transformed economic diversity into monocultures subject to

143

deterioration in terms of trade, wild fluctuations in prices, and continued extraction of surplus by European trading companies. Imperialism therefore completed the process of underdevelopment started by mercantilism.

The decisive difference between mercantilism and imperialism as capitalist forms of external relations was the development of the forces of production in western Europe during the industrial revolution. On the one hand, this *necessitated* the permanent use of Third World resources, the widespread integration of peasant producers in the world market (and the transfer of some rural labour from commodity production to mines and plantations), and capitalist access to Third World markets which was more reliable if these were monopolized – all of these favoured political domination through colonial control. On the other hand, the industrial revolution transformed both the means of warfare and those of communication and *enabled* the colonization of the Third World. Under imperialism, the dominant external relation of late nineteenth-century capitalism, Europe extended political as well as economic control over most of the earth's surface. This increased the speed at which Third World societies were changing and involved a decrease in the control they exercised over the direction of change. The Europeans usurped control over the destinies of the people of the earth.

Chapter nine

Global transformation through industrialization?

Capitalism was made possible by the raiding of stored wealth, the reorientation of trade routes, the imposition of unequal exchange, the forceful movement of millions of people in world space, and the conversion of the people and territories of whole continents into colonies where all aspects of existence were subject to the purposes of the Europeans. The term 'Third World' thus came to signify a spatial sequence of societies characterized by monoculture where previously diversity had prevailed, economies declining through disinvestment because indigenous surplus was captured by the European centre, and low productivity where craft skills had previously been common. The poverty of the Third World is not natural, inevitable or even historically typical. Instead the dependency school's thesis of the development of underdevelopment proves a highly generalized yet accurate appraisal of the effects of the expansion of Euro-American capitalism on the rest of the world's societies.

Conditions did not change fundamentally when most of the colonies achieved political independence after the Second World War. Control of the state did not necessarily mean control over the development process. The term '*neo-colonialism*' has thus come to signify a national economy controlled by external interests, either in the direct form of foreign ownership of productive resources, or the more subtle form of the setting of basic conditions of production by external institutions. Economy dominates polity, says Marx: the governments of the former colonies must now adhere to economic conditions set in the centres of world power, often the same capital cities which once issued political directives under direct colonialism.

Perhaps the most pernicious aspect of the Third World's underdevelopment was the de-industrialization concomitant with industrial revolution at the centre of global capitalism. Why is industry so important? 'Industry' refers to the final processing of natural materials into material objects which directly satisfy needs

145

(consumption goods) and provide means of further production (investment goods). Industrial manufacturing takes place under conditions controlled more completely by human action than agriculture or mining, where nature intervenes in an unpredictable way. Therefore, industry can be expanded in a planned manner, so that growth rates in industrial capacity of 10 per cent a year or more are possible. Ideas can be materialized as new technologies in a more organized, coherent manner, so that productivity from a given capacity can grow at rates of 5 per cent to 10 per cent a year. An economy can therefore be transformed, in terms of structure and productivity, by industrial development over a period of twenty to thirty years. Additionally, industry has the potential to spread material benefits evenly among the mass of human participants. Large numbers of workers live in urban-industrial areas, sharing essentially similar productive and reproductive conditions. Industrial labour is more collectively organized and more active in the pursuit of its share of the product than any other mass of workers in history. As a result, industry is inextricably linked with high levels of economic development: 'No major country has yet become rich without having become industrialized. . . . Greater wealth and better living standards under any political system are closely connected with industrialization' (Sutcliffe, 1971: 69–70).

The good news is that things are beginning to change in terms of the industrialization (or rather re-industrialization) of the Third World. The share of global manufacturing held by Third World countries, which had been about 8 per cent for some time, suddenly rose to 11 per cent by 1980 (UNIDO, 1979: 33, 224). It became almost realistic to call for a new international economic order, in which the Third World's share of industrial output might rise to 25 per cent by 2000 – at least this was the figure set by a United Nations organization meeting in Lima, Peru in 1975 (UNIDO, 1975). The bad news is that significant industrial growth is limited to a small group of Third World countries – ten newly industrializing countries (NICs) account for three-quarters of the growth (UNIDO, 1979: 42). Questions have also been raised about the quality of the industrialization process – whether cheap-labour, fly-by-night manufacturing can be considered 'industrialization'? Optimistic answers have been quick to follow.

In a typical statement of the model favoured by most international development agencies in the 1970s and 1980s, Bella Belassa (1981) argues for a stage of development theory emphasizing the importance of choice of economic policy in setting a course and pushing a country through the various phases of industrialization. Industrial development begins in Third World countries as a response to the needs of the primary sector (i.e. processing raw materials, providing simple inputs, etc.). Then a first or 'easy' stage of import substitution entails the local manufacture of previously imported non-durable goods. These industries are conducted at a small scale and require unskilled labour, but provide rapid growth as tariffs on imports enable local production to gain increasing shares of the market. With the completion of import substitution further growth is confined to (small) increases in local consumption. Maintaining high rates of growth entails either second-stage import substitution or exporting. Second stage import substitution – the replacement of imports of intermediate goods (petrochemicals, steel), producer durables (machinery) and consumer durables (automobiles etc.) by domestic production – was undertaken in the post-Second World War period by the Latin American countries, some south Asian countries, and the eastern European countries. Problems such as the small size of the market (when industries are characterized by considerable economies of scale) led to the need for considerable state protection; in fact in several underdeveloped countries the cost of protection amounted to 6 or 7 per cent of the GNP. Belassa finds that economic growth was distorted in environments protected from outside competition, agriculture suffered and countries following this strategy lagged behind. This led to policy reforms like reductions in import protection and subsidization of exports. Export-oriented policies were adopted by Japan in the middle 1950s, Korea, Singapore and Taiwan in the early 1960s, and the Latin American countries in the middle to late 1960s. Korea, Singapore and Taiwan, which implemented 'free trade regimes' (exporters could choose to use local or imported inputs in their manufacturing), increased industrial exports rapidly in the early 1960s, and in the late 1960s and early 1970s various incentives for exporting led to further growth in manufacturing employment and to higher incomes. Countries in Latin America (e.g., Brazil) that reformed their system of incentives also experienced (somewhat lower) rates of increase in exports and employment. Countries which retained inward-looking strategies (India, Chile, Uruguay) remained at the bottom of the industrial growth league. For Belassa (1981: 16–17) the evidence is conclusive: 'Countries applying outward-oriented development strategies had a superior performance in terms of exports, economic growth and employment whereas countries which continued inward orientation encountered increasing economic difficulties.' Choice of economic policy was the differentiating factor, and export-led industrialization is the promise of the future for the underdeveloped world. Belassa (1981: 22–3) argues that east Asian countries with high educational levels could replace Japan in exporting skill-intensive products; the Latin American countries could expand their capital-intensive production, whereas countries at lower stages of industrial development could export products requiring unskilled labour. This would widen the circle of industrial development to eventually include all. Belassa's argument, a version of modernization theory, essentially concludes that the Third World can follow the path of the First through a process of industrialization into economic development.

Similar conclusions were reached by some left analysts. Bill Warren (1980) argues for the progressive nature of capitalist development from a Marxist perspective. Capitalism's unique achievements have been to release individual creativity and organize co-operation in production; there is also an important connection between capitalism and parliamentary (bourgeois) democracy. Capitalism can therefore be an instrument of social advance in pre-capitalist societies. However, following Lenin, a version of Marxism was popularized – underdevelopment theory is the most recent case – which argues that imperialism (and subsequently neo-colonialism) are socially retrogressive, preventing or distorting economic development and creating relations of dependence between rich and poor countries. Contrary to these views, Warren finds empirical evidence that many underdeveloped countries have favourable prospects for successful capitalist development. Indeed capitalist social relations and productive forces have grown rapidly in the Third World since the end of the Second World War, especially in industry, but also (more slowly) in capitalist agriculture. Far from retarding or distorting development, colonialism acted as a 'powerful engine of progressive social change, advancing capitalist development far more rapidly than was conceivable in any other way both by its destructive effects on pre-capitalist social systems and by its implantation of elements of capitalism' (Warren, 1980: 9). Thus the overall effect of the policies of the imperial countries favours the industrialization of the Third World. Within a context of growing interdependence, the ties of dependence are now being loosened by the rise of indigenous capitalist systems: we are in an era of declining imperialism and advancing capitalism.

Industrialization and development

This hardly exhausts the arguments raised by Third World industrialization. More detailed analyses focus on the more exact nature of the recent industrialization process and its connections with economic development. A provocative debate between Martin Landsberg and Charles Barone, using the case of the Republic of South Korea, captures some of the main arguments.

Landsberg (1979) argues against the progressiveness of the recent export-oriented industrialization. He maintains that, in the post-Second World War period, Third World development was constrained by dependence on imported manufactured goods, paid for by primary exports subject to violent swings in demand and lowering prices. Fearing internal pressures for change, the national bourgeoisies of a number of Third World countries sought to initiate self-expanding capitalist development via import-substitution industrialization (ISI). But the logic of imperialism kept this from succeeding: industrial development became dependent industrialization under the leadership of outside capital, while Third World economies were plagued with balance of payments deficits and foreign debt. By the 1960s the bourgeoisie was forced to admit that ISI was a failure and that a new strategy was necessary. Foreign exchange pressures dictated that Third World development be tied to the external market, yet industrialization remained the goal, hence export-oriented manufacturing was chosen as the linchpin strategy in a few countries which became known as the NICs. Central to the growth of Third World industry was the mechanism of international subcontracting – that is transnational corporations contracting Third World firms to make products or provide services especially in NICs with few local resources and little competition for labour (Hong Kong, Singapore, Korea and Taiwan). Depending on foreign trade, these countries offered inducements for transnational capital – things like tax holidays, free trade zones and repressive labour conditions. Landsberg maintains that this established only a new form of international capitalist domination. He gives the following reasons:

1 Export industrialization blocks the development of an internally-articulated, self-expanding economy and creates dependent industrialization.
2 Subcontracting operations specialize in the use of low-skilled assembly workers to complete specific parts of the manufacturing process, making it unlikely that linkages will appear locally, technology be transferred, or that the skill level of the work force will be upgraded.
3 This kind of production invests minimally in the local economy and can be easily moved elsewhere if wage rates increase or other local conditions change.
4 Transnational corporations retain control over research, design

and technology, making Third World corporations dependent, rather than leading in the direction of indigenous capitalism.

5 Competition within the Third World between the NICs and countries of the outer periphery (Indonesia, the Philippines, Thailand, Haiti, El Salvador, etc.) deteriorates the NIC's position and increases the profits and power of the transnational corporations.

6 Cyclical downturns and stagnation in the centre countries particularly hurt export-dependent Third World economies. Protectionism in the centre adds to this.

7 Feminist writers add the point that most of the new industrial employees are women, who suffer terrible working conditions, low pay and sexual harassment on the job, and rejection by their traditional societies off the job or after temporary employment (Fuentes and Ehrenreich, 1987; Nash and Fernandez-Kelly, 1983).

Landsberg concludes that export-oriented manufacturing leads to growth in industrial production and the size of the industrial workforce, but does not lead to an indigenous self-expanding capitalist economy. Moreover, in the context of a stagnating global capitalist system this will eventually bring increased poverty and suffering for workers and peasants in the Third World. However, it will also bring increased anti-capitalist struggle.

Barone (1983) offers a Marxist defence of the progressive nature of the recent industrialization using the case of South Korea to refute Landsberg's arguments. His position is that countries such as Korea are extremely repressive exactly because successful capitalist development is taking place. They also represent anomalies which challenge radical dependency theory. Landsberg's arguments are countered as follows:

1 Korea is no more dependent on exports than many developed West European countries, hence export 'dependency' does not necessarily imply underdevelopment. Landsberg's 'indigenous self-expanding capitalism' is only an abstract ideal.

2 Despite poor working conditions and severe repression, real incomes have more than tripled in Korea since the early 1960s, the well-being of the population has improved, and levels of inequality are similar to those in the United States. Indeed much (three-quarters) of the demand for manufactures now comes from the growing domestic market.

3 Industrialization is neither shallow (in terms of the proportion of the economy it constitutes or the type of product made) nor has it been at the expense of agriculture.

4 While Korea relied heavily on foreign capital and technology in the 1960s, it has been able to reduce this dependence in the 1970s and 1980s, so that wholly Korean-owned enterprises account for 75 per cent of mining and manufacturing output and 90 per cent of employment. Also under 'state capitalism' the South Korean government has played a leading role in planning development, limiting the size of foreign investment and directing it to sectors which Korea otherwise would lack.

5 South Korea has been at the forefront of the growth of Third World corporations and now compares with Italy in terms of the number of multinational corporations, and these are in industries like shipbuilding, metal products and electronics rather than textiles and clothing.

6 Korea has been able to control and direct the transfer of technology through its Ministry of Science and Technology and has, more recently, focused on the development of an indigenous technological capacity.

7 While specific information is lacking, subcontracting probably does not represent foreign control over Korean businesses and, in any case, the country is developing the ability to market its own products through state agencies and the growth of large Japanese-style trading firms.

In general, Barone concludes that Korea is not a case of dependent industrialization and that dependency theory fails to explain the history and nature of its development. Following Brenner (1977) he suggests that change in Third World societies can only be understood via an analysis of internal class structure and struggles.

Applying this notion to South Korea, Barone (1983: 52−63) argues that a centralized version of the tributary mode of production concentrated power in the hands of the monarchy and aristocracy until the late nineteenth century. Compelled by the imperialist powers to open its doors to foreign trade, Korea was engulfed in class struggles, with Japan intervening to rule the country between 1910 and 1946. Forced development under Japanese control left only a modest industrial and commercial bourgeoisie so that, following independence, further development was limited, especially under the Syngman Rhee regime (1948−60). Following a military coup, the Park regime instituted centrally-directed capitalism as a way of progressively developing the forces of production under the slogan 'economic growth first, democracy second'. Barone (1983: 61) attributes the installation of this system to 'the absence of an effective bourgeoisie' and the 'past history of reliance on centralized authority'. Its main features are state control of banking and thus control over interest rates, credit and the allocation of financial capital; centralized capitalist planning, with mechanisms for ensuring compliance; and public enterprises in infrastructure and advanced industrial sectors. Korea Inc. is characterized by state dominance over business and labour, but growing dissent from students and workers. This state (bureaucratic) capitalist structure with origins deep in Korean history and culture, facilitated, guided and controlled the rapid development of capitalism. Barone (1983: 64) sees such an internal process as interacting with the 'forces and needs of international capital accumulation' and being shaped in part by foreign intervention. But dependency theory would force us to ignore indigenous class forces and internal dynamics which his brief recapitulation of Korean history has shown to be crucial (see also Browett, 1986).

In replying to Barone, Landsberg finds his work mislabelled as dependency theory (Hart-Landsberg, 1984). Instead he attempted a Marxist analysis of the forces shaping the world capitalist system and the countries in it. It is exactly such a global perspective, he continues, which Barone lacks – one would never know that South Korea's economic expansion was largely export-led or that US and Japanese capital played key roles in shaping it. This leads Barone to seriously underestimate the role of transnational capital in shaping South Korea's economic development, and to overemphasize its ability to control its own destiny. Landsberg then proceeds to counter Barone's main points concerning South Korea, marshalling facts, arguments and quotations to show that the economy remains externally reliant and dependent on foreign capital and technology. South Korea's present achievement is best characterized as 'dependent industrialization', while signs point to even greater dependency in the future.

In subsequent work, Hart-Landsberg (1987) argues that the South Korean economy is unstable and extremely exploitative, with the benefits from growth unevenly distributed, the main portion going to military and governmental leaders, a few South Korean conglomerates, and US and Japanese capital. South Korean workers, he says, pay a heavy price for their country's 'miracle'. The oppositional movements of the post-1987 period threaten the social basis of the economy (by forming unions, raising wages, etc.), but are part of a struggle to 'reduce the country's extreme dependence on exports and foreign capital, achieve better internal balance regionally and industrially, ensure production for mass domestic needs, and raise the standard of living of farmers and workers under conditions they themselves can control' (Hart-Lansberg, 1987: 40).

Debates like this, in which polar positions are taken and different aspects of a process explored, are useful in the development of specific arguments. The problem is that both positions may be right, or have elements of truth, so that the argument goes on for-ever, with the reader agreeing first with one, then with the other. To find resolution we are forced to a different level, a more general analysis capable of synthesizing partly contradictory movements. It is time to return to a structural analysis of global productive systems.

The regulation school

One such approach is formulated by a diverse group of French scholars known as the 'regulation school'. Althusserian structural-ism came under sustained criticism in the 1970s (e.g. Thompson, 1978; Giddens, 1981). French Marxists in the regulation school (we focus on Michel Aglietta and Alain Lipietz) likewise found Althusser's static reproduction paradigm inadequate for concep-tualizing the dynamic transformation of capitalism (Lipietz, 1985: xvi). Members of the school began to develop structural concepts in new directions using novel terms. Their concept of the economy begins with the labour process and builds outwards into the general structure of production. Thus the concept *'regime of accumulation'* refers to

> the stabilization over a long period of the allocation of the net [social] product between consumption and accumulation; it implies some correspondence between the transformation of both the conditions of production and the conditions of the reproduction of wage earners. It also implies some form of linkage between capitalism and other modes of production.
>
> (Lipeitz, 1986: 19)

Regimes do not materialize automatically, but need means of coercion and institutions of persuasion to assure the cohesion of peoples' strategies and expectations. The body of norms, habits, laws and regulating networks which ensure that individual behaviour is consistent with a regime of accumulation is called the *mode of regulation*. Regimes and modes succeed because they ensure some regularity and permanence in social reproduction. However, modes of regulation should not simply be assumed to have the 'function' of making regimes of accumulation work. 'Rather, a regime of accumulation and forms of regulation get stabilized together because they ensure the crisis-free reproduction of social relations over a certain period of time' (Lipietz, 1986: 20). External relations are said to play a regulating role for capitalism of the global centre: imperialism, for example, temporarily resolves contradictions of central capitalism. But in Lipietz's (1986: 20–1) view imperialism was not created specifically (intentionally) to resolve contradiction, and other solutions could have been found – 'we should not confuse results with causes' and must remember 'the open-endedness of history, the class struggle, and capitalist competition' as well as 'the autonomy of national social formations and the sovereignty of states'.

In my view (Peet, 1989b) this does not emerge as a coherent view of structural causality. For example, there is a denial of structural functionality on the one hand and a reliance on ideas remarkedly similar to it on the other: Lipietz's denial that regulation has the function of making accumulation work is a very short step away from his affirmation that the two 'get stabilized together because they ensure the crisis-free reproduction of social relations'. Lipietz calls imperialism and the new international division of labour 'chance discoveries'; yet they are characterized by intenton, unequal (monopoly) power, limited fields of possible choices, constraints of compatibility, etc. Lipietz gets himself into such quandaries because he over-reacts to the critique of Althusserian structuralism, is too anxious to reassert the open-endedness of historical processes and thus is forced to deny the structural logic on which the coherence of his argument depends.

Even so, this proved to be an attractive set of notions, especially for geographers. The French regulation school divides the history of capitalism into regimes based essentially on the prevailing labour process: *manufacture*, dominant in the capitalist countries between 1780 and 1870 but continuing in some industries until today; *machinofacture*, dominant between 1870 and 1940; *scientific management (Taylorism)* and *Fordism*, beginning at the turn of the century and dominant from 1940 to the late 1970s; and *neo-* or *post-Fordism* beginning with the economic crises of the 1970s and rapidly expanding in the late twentieth century (Dunford and Perrons, 1983: ch. 9). Fordism was pioneered by Henry Ford in the immediate pre-First World War years, and generalized in the United States from the 1920s. Ford linked two innovations: the semi-automatic assembly-line, adopted between 1910 and 1914; and the $5.00, 8-hour day, inaugurated on 5 January 1914. Ford argued that he had made a huge investment in machinery which had to be used 24 hours a day in three shifts of 8 hours – eight because that was the longest a worker could keep going day in and day out.

The problem also lay in stabilizing an immigrant work-force and counteracting radical unionism. In fact, with Ford's reforms, thousands of job seekers descended on Highland Park, Detroit, labour turnover dropped by 90 per cent and absenteeism halved. Ford could report that the $5.00 per 8-hour day was 'one of the finest cost-cutting moves ever made'. Gramsci (1971) points out that Ford's goal was to create a new kind of worker, thoroughly Americanized and committed to conventional morality and the family, who would never need to join a union. Should indirect regulation not be sufficient, Ford's 'Sociological Department' with its 100 investigators, made sure that Ford's workers were spending their time well.

In Aglietta's (1979) version of regulation theory, consumption is thought of both as an organized set of activities subject to the general logic of the reconstitution of energies expended in social activities (especially production) and as a regulatory process which preserves the abilities and attitudes implied by the hegemonic social relations. The norm of consumption under (mass-producing) Fordism involves individual ownership by the working class of commodities like automobiles and standardized housing which permit 'the most effective recuperation from physical and nervous fatigue in a compact space of time within the day, and at a single place, the home' (Aglietta, 1979: 159). Fordist consumption entails the creation of a functional aesthetic, the calculation of consumption habits, and their social control. The resulting 'consumer society' of the post-Second World War period seemed to resolve the contradictions of capitalism and abolish its crises. But in the late 1960s, Fordism entered a period of crisis, for instance as the limitations of the intensification of labour were reached in the physical and mental capabilities of the workers and as class struggles intensified at the point of production. Neo- or post-Fordism, based on automatic production control, responds to the crisis by introducing a new flexibility of production design and location. For Aglietta (1979: 385–6) it also means 'massive socialization of the conditions of life' and 'a strong totalitarian tendency under the ideological cover of liberalism'.

The appeal to geography of these notions lies in their incorporation of the dimension of space. Each regime is associated with a distribution in space of its economic and social components, together with the politico-cultural regulation mechanisms tied to them. Lipietz (1987) sees capitalism deriving an absolute productivity advantage over other modes of production through more complex forms of co-operation in manufacturing. At first this form of growth did not produce a parallel expansion in social demand, which was created externally – the mainspring of imperialism was the search for new sources of demand outside capitalism. Once commodity production and the wage system had sufficiently developed, the outside world also became an outlet for direct capital investment. As an intensive regime of accumulation centred on mass consumption, Fordism became generalized in the capitalist social formations of the centre after the Second World War. This produced economic growth rates of 4 per cent a year, except in the United States (where Fordism was no longer as dynamic) and Britain (which departed from the model of Fordist production because of the strength of its craft unions and the lethargy of its financial bourgeoisie). International trade was of secondary significance to the post-war Fordist model – the driving forces being the transformation of production processes and the expansion of the internal market through increased mass purchasing power. However peripheral social formations still supplied labour and raw materials, with United States military domination assuring continued control over these resources. In the 1930s in Latin America and the 1950s in South-east Asia some countries developed an import-substitution industrialization policy. Although initially successful, the strategy ran into difficulties in the 1960s because it failed to enter the 'virtuous circle' of central Fordism (in terms of limited technology, restricted worker and peasant markets, and restricted foreign earnings from raw material exports). These regimes were therefore caricatures of Fordism or were '*sub-Fordist*'.

Central Fordism showed signs of crisis in the 1967 recession. The essential reason was a slowing down in the rate of productivity growth because the limits of Taylorist and Fordist work organization principles had been reached. This change in internal dynamics led to new socio-spatial strategies. An attempt was made to raise productivity by expanding the scale of production. This meant increasing international trade between the centre countries and gaining marketing footholds in the immediate peripheries of southern and eastern Europe, the American south, and areas around Japan. Fordism is characterized by a division of labour between conception, skilled manufacturing and unskilled assembly work, and multinational corporations can spread these across different labour pools. Early experiments with relocating unskilled tasks in search for lower wages occurred in the 1960s, again in the immediate periphery, including Latin America and South-east Asia. This required certain conditions to obtain in the peripheral countries – like political regimes autonomous from landed interests and import substitution industrialists, and also regimes not based in the popular masses.

NICs opting for a new regime of accumulation via 'export substitution' employed a number of logics, of which two are significant.

1 *Primitive or 'bloody' Taylorism*. This refers to the transfer of limited branches of production with high rates of exploitation (in terms of wages, length of the working day, and labour intensity) from the centre to peripheral countries like South Korea before 1973, and to Taiwan, Singapore and Hong Kong, with a second wave now including Malaysia, the Philippines and China. Women's role in domestic production prepared them for participation at low wages. And the state managed labour in terms of holding down or reducing living standards, restricting unionization, etc. While this raises profit levels in the centre, it raises other problems for Fordism like reducing demand as well-paid workers are replaced by those making minimal wages. In the periphery, the model is redolent of the last century, and it is not long before the working class reacts in the nineteenth-century manner.

2 *Peripheral Fordism*. Countries with autonomous local capital, markets formed by sizeable middle classes, and elements of a skilled working class (South Korea since 1973, Mexico, Brazil) were able to develop a new logic in the 1970s, referred to as peripheral Fordism. It is Fordist in that mechanization and a growing consumer market are involved, but peripheral in that skilled manufacturing, engineering and other production processes are mainly outside such countries – hence industrialization is accompanied by the importation of capital goods and skilled assembly products which are paid for by exports of unskilled assembly goods to the centre. This model achieved spectacular success in the 1970s, 'completely discrediting' the development of underdevelopment thesis, for it showed the periphery could industrialize.

However, the early 1980s saw the rise of workers' struggles (in South Korea and Brazil), financial bankruptcy in Mexico and other signs of crisis. The centre economies were likewise marked by contradiction between the productivity crisis of Fordism and the stimulation of demand through Keynesian policies – one result being inflation. But the monetarist policies of the conservative governments elected in the late 1970s and early 1980s ended the period of inflation and growth. A crisis in the peripheral Fordist countries became inevitable as markets in the centre dried up, yet debt payments remained. The expected financial crash did not happen, however, because Third World debts have been continuously renegotiated. Third World debts will never be repaid in full. The question is to what extent they will be cancelled and to what extent postponed (Lipietz, 1987: 165).

Recent work developing regulation school ideas has tried to capture the nature of the emerging post-Fordist regime using the term *'flexible production system'* (Piore and Sabel, 1984). Scott (1988) argues that the typically rigid mass production processes of Fordism are giving way to changeable, computer-enhanced processes, situated within systems of malleable external linkages and labour market relations. Storper and Scott (1989: 27) find the turn towards flexibility marked by a decisive reagglomeration of production within a wider international division of labour. The older foci of Fordist mass production, unionized with rigid labour relations and with governmental restrictions on producers, were avoided as flexible production began its ascent in North America and western Europe – for example high technology industries located in the suburbs of large metropolitan areas and in previously unindustrialized communities. In the Third World the spatial margin of production is expanding while industry also converges on major growth centres (Scott and Storper, 1986: 306). However, this work leaves open the question of whether industry will reagglomerate in robotic form in the centre countries, or whether mass production industries will continue to migrate to the Third World, leaving the centre with control activities, research and development, and service industries concentrated around global cities.

Transformation through industrialization?

Since 1965 several Third World countries have seen manufacturing output rise at annual rates of 10–20 per cent over periods of as long as twenty years (Table 9.1). The quality of manufacturing industry, as indicated by the presence of sophisticated manufactures like machinery, transport equipment and chemicals, has also improved, in some cases sharply. Countries with rapid growth in manufacturing (8 per cent a year or more) have seen worker earnings rise and, more generally, GNP per capita increase at rates of 4–8 per cent a year. The potential for industrialization to transform Third World economies definitely exists and has already had dramatic results, albeit in relatively few countries and, with the possible exceptions of Hong Kong and Singapore, without elevating new countries into the ranks of the developed economies.

However, optimistic generalizations, such as those presented earlier (Belassa, Warren), and those made from a superficial look at selected facts, mask two aspects of the industrialization process – the tendency for variation across time and space, and the tendency for contradictory processes to destroy the conditions of their own further development. Using categories similar to those proposed by the regulation school, what does a Marxian analysis of the data have to say about the continuing potential for socio-economic transformation through industrialization? Table 9.1 gives data for all Third World countries (for which data are available) with significant industrial production in the late 1980s. The countries are divided into three groups. *Group 1* corresponds roughly with the *older 'peripheral Fordist'* countries – large in size and with a history of sophisticated industrial production. This group actually has two subgroups. India and China are low-income countries whose significant industrial base mainly reflects their huge populations. Their growth trajectories are somewhat different, in terms for example of state direction and external debt, from those of the other countries in the group, which are the larger and richer countries of the Third World – with conditions of production (such as the size of the internal market) not frequently replicated elsewhere. Through a combination of import substitution/ state planning and, later, export-orientation, most have been able to achieve rapid industrial growth since 1965. All are now major industrial powers. Excepting India and China, growth was financed by external borrowing, with the result that one-third to one-half of export earnings must now be devoted to servicing long-term debts which show little sign of diminishing. Debt crises intensify inequality and worsen social problems as Third World governments divert whatever paltry funds they once devoted to social services into debt servicing and budget balancing (Pollin, 1989; George, 1988; Branford and Kucinski, 1988). On the whole, rapid industrial growth has not reverberated through these economies to bring similarly rapid growth in GNP per capita. As a result, these countries are characterized by social and political instability which can be controlled only by periodic state violence or military take-overs of the government. The recent history of Argentina, a major Third World industrial power in the 1960s, shows the possibility of economic instability verging on collapse. In summary, the industrial model provided mainly by the Latin American peripheral Fordist countries is not easily replicated, has contradictions which yield severe economic, social and political problems, and has shown only a modest capability of transforming the living standards of the mass of the population.

Group 2 is composed of countries which, until the late 1960s, hardly existed as industrial producers but which have seen rapid and sustained growth, including growth in sophisticated industries such as machinery, transportation equipment and chemicals, so

Table 9.1 Manufacturing and economic development

	Value added in manufacturing (MVA) (billions of current dollars)		% MVA in machinery, transport equipment and chemicals		Average annual growth rate of manufacturing		Gross national product per capita		Total external debt (billions of dollars)	Total long-term debt service as % exports of goods and services		Manufacturing as % merchandise exports
							Dollars	Average annual rate of growth				
	1970	1986	1970	1986	1960–80	1980–7	1987	1965–87	1987	1970	1987	1987
Group 1												
China	28.8	91.5	n/a	36	9.5	12.6	290	5.2	30	n/a	7.1	70
India	6.7	38.3	34	41	4.3	8.3	300	1.8	46	23.6	24.0	69
Mexico	8.4	32.0	24	26	7.4	0.0	1,830	2.5	108	44.3	38.4	47
South Africa	3.9	12.3	27	28	n/a	−0.5	1,890	0.6	n/a	n/a	n/a	78
Brazil	10.4	69.4	32	33	9.6	1.2	2,020	4.1	124	21.8	33.2	45
Argentina	5.8	21.5	27	28	2.7	0.0	2,390	0.1	57	51.7	52.0	31
Group 2												
Malaysia	0.5	n/a	17	37	n/a	6.3	1,810	4.1	n/a	4.5	20.0	40
Korea, Republic	1.9	29.4	22	33	18.7	10.6	2,690	6.4	41	20.4	27.5	92
Singapore	0.4	4.7	32	54	13.2	3.3	7,940	7.2	5	3.9	2.4	72
Taiwan	1.6	28.3	n/a	n/a	14.6	9.6	4,630	9.1	n/a	n/a	n/a	92
Group 3												
Bangladesh	0.4	1.2	14	23	6.8	2.4	160	0.3	10	0.0	24.2	50
Pakistan	1.5	5.1	15	20	5.7	8.9	350	2.5	16	23.6	26.3	67
Nigeria	0.5	5.2	n/a	n/a	4.6	−2.1	370	1.1	29	7.1	11.7	1
Sri Lanka	0.3	0.9	21	n/a	3.2	6.2	400	3.0	5	n/a	20.2	40
Indonesia	1.0	10.6	n/a	20	12.0	7.8	450	4.5	53	13.9	33.2	27

Country												
Zimbabwe	0.3	1.4	20	19	n/a	1.8	580	0.9	3	n/a	n/a	40
Philippines	1.6	7.6	21	17	7.5	-1.1	590	1.7	30	23.0	25.7	62
Morocco	0.6	2.6	n/a	21	5.9	1.5	610	1.8	21	9.2	30.8	49
Egypt	n/a	4.4	21	23	n/a	6.1	680	3.5	40	n/a	21.5	19
Dominican Republic	0.3	0.8	7	6	8.9	0.4	730	2.3	4	15.2	n/a	22
Ivory Coast	0.1	1.2	15	n/a	9.1	8.2	740	1.0	14	7.5	40.8	9
Thailand	1.1	9.7	15	20	11.2	6.0	850	3.9	21	14.0	20.6	53
Cameroon	0.1	1.3	9	13	7.0	8.5	970	3.8	4	4.0	27.9	9
Ecuador	0.3	2.2	11	17	11.5	0.2	1,040	3.2	10	14.0	21.9	4
Tunisia	0.1	1.2	17	20	9.9	6.1	1,180	3.6	7	n/a	29.4	61
Turkey	1.9	13.3	15	23	7.5	8.2			41	22.6	34.0	67
Columbia	1.2	5.8	19	21	6.2	3.2	1,240	2.7	17	19.0	36.3	21
Chile	2.1	n/a	16	12	0.6	0.9	1,310	0.2	21	24.5	26.4	7
Peru	1.4	6.7	14	21	3.8	-1.5	1,470	0.2	18	40.0	12.9	19
Uruguay	n/a	1.4	13	18	n/a	-1.6	2,190	1.4	4	23.6	25.7	44
Algeria	0.7	7.4	13	12	9.5	8.5	2,680	3.2	23	3.9	49.0	1
Venezuela	2.1	14.1	17	20	5.8	3.0	3,230	-0.9	37	4.3	32.4	8
Hong Kong	1.0	8.0	18	22	n/a	n/a	8,070	6.2	n/a	n/a	n/a	92

Statistical sources: World Bank, *World Development Report 1989*; Republic of China, *Statistical Yearbook 1988*

Notes

Group 1 Countries with over 3.5 billion dollars MVA in 1970, over 20% MVA in machinery, transport equipment and chemicals in 1970 and over 25% in 1986

Group 2 Countries with over 4.0 billion dollars MVA in 1987 and over 25% MVA in machinery, transport equipment and chemicals in 1986

Group 3 Countries with over 0.8 billion dollars MVA in 1986 that they are now *'peripheral Fordist'* in character. In all these countries, manufacturing wages have increased and, more generally, GNP per capita has risen more than 4 per cent anually. On the whole, these are not countries saddled with unmanageable debt burdens. Free enterprise and state repression coexist and, with the exception of Korea in the post-1987 period, governmental control is not seriously challenged. These countries have seen sharply lower growth rates in industrial output in the 1980s. Yet they do provide the most successful capitalist model for Third World transformation, or rather they did provide such a model – a point taken up shortly.

Group 3 is composed of all Third World countries with more than $0.8 billion of manufactured value added in 1986. This is a *diverse group* following several models of growth. Generally, manufacturing remains an activity associated with food or raw material processing, textiles or other relatively simple forms of production, and only rarely does manufacturing account for more than 20 per cent of GDP: these are not industrial countries. Given the low growth rates in manufacturing output in the 1980s, the indicators are that few will enter the ranks of the industrial countries in the foreseeable future. Also, with few exceptions, even manufacturing growth rates of 7–15 per cent a year, rates which have proven impossible to sustain in the 1980s, were insufficient to increase GNP per capita substantially. The diverse experiences of Pakistan, Indonesia, Thailand, Cameroon, Tunisia and Algeria might inconsistently indicate some aspects of a development model deserving emulation, but in general there is little evidence here of industry growing rapidly and transforming material conditions for the mass of the people.

We now take up the case of *Group 2* countries (the 'miracle economies') in more detail, asking the questions: under what conditions was rapid industrial growth possible and will these conditions be widely replicated in the future? The common characteristic in the experience of the Group 2 countries is very rapid growth in the period 1965–80 – that is, in regulationist terms, during the crisis of Fordism and transition to post-Fordism. As we have seen, the Fordist model of capital accumulation counterposes assembly line mass production with mass demand from unionized workers concentrated in a limited space at the industrial centre of the global capitalist system. The central regulatory device of ensuring the reproduction of this relation is collective bargaining, whereby wage increases are linked to rising productivity. The contradiction inherent in the relation is the possibility of relocating production in space to use low-waged, non-unionized labour while relying on the

Table 9.2   Global employment in manufacturing, 1974–87

Region	Employment in manufacturing (millions)		
	1974	*1980*	*1986–7*
North America	22.0	22.4	21.1
Western Europe	37.5	34.0	30.5
Japan	12.0	11.4	12.2
Latin America[1]	8.4	10.3	12.1
South Asia[2]	5.3	6.0	6.5
East Asia[3]	6.3	8.9	10.6
Africa[4]	3.1	3.5	3.9
Capitalist world	94.6	96.5	96.9
China	40.0 (est)	46.7	59.7
USSR	33.4	36.4	38.2
Eastern Europe	16.7	18.1	18.2
Non-capitalist world	90.1	101.1	116.1

Source: ILO, *Yearbook of Labour Statistics* (various issues)

Notes:

1 Bolivia, Brazil, Mexico, Venezuela

2 India, Sri Lanka

3 Hong Kong, Korea (Republic), Malaysia, Philippines, Singapore, Taiwan, Thailand

4 Cameroon, Egypt, Ethiopia, Kenya, Malawi, Mauritius, South Africa, Tanzania, Zimbabwe

continued growth of mass demand from high-waged workers at the centre. As part of the crisis of Fordism and transition to a post-Fordist regime which is more flexible in its use of space, 8 million jobs were lost in the centre industrial countries and a similar number gained in Latin America and East Asia (Table 9.2). The crucial characteristic of the centre countries where jobs were lost jobs was their degree of unionization and high wages relative to the conditions of employment prevailing in the periphery (Table 9.3). As a consequence of employment migration unemployment rates in the old industrial regions of the centre, which typically under Fordism were considered high if they reached 5 per cent of the labour force, have remained around the 10 per cent level since the early 1980s (Peet, 1987). Labour unions in the centre countries are declining in terms of number of members, solidarity and bargaining power – hence the incidence of strikes has decreased dramatically in the 1980s (Table 9.3). Economies have restructured towards service

Table 9.3 Labour conditions in global manufacturing

Country	Average hourly earnings in manufacturing		Industrial disputes*	
	Early 1980s (US $)	Mid–late 1980s (US $)	1977–81	1982–7
USA	8.83	9.91	220	97
UK	5.25	6.93	579	381
Germany, Federal Republic	5.94	9.74	42	41
Japan	6.91	11.70	22	7
Venezuela	3.63	2.78	41	57
Mexico	1.59	1.07	n/a	89
Hong Kong	1.26	1.70	13	3
Korea, Republic	1.35	2.16	3	93
Singapore	1.43	1.98	0	0
Taiwan	1.67	2.89	n/a	n/a
China, People's Republic	—	0.17	n/a	n/a
India	0.40	0.38	1,518	1,882
Sri Lanka	0.17	0.20	582	482

Source: ILO, *Yearbook of Labour Statistics*; exchange rates from IMF

* Average annual number of days lost from disputes per 1,000 non-agricultural workers

employment with lower wage standards and lower union membership. Collective bargaining no longer automatically produces an increase in worker incomes, and without this incessant push, and because of the persistence of high unemployment rates, global capitalism experiences an underconsumption crisis. Certainly the growth of world output, which was 5 per cent a year in the period 1963–72 was reduced to 3 per cent in 1978–90 (IMF, 1985: 1989). The post-Fordist world of reduced demand and lower growth rates provides an entirely different environment for peripheral industrialization oriented towards exports. It makes unlikely the repetition of the development of manufacturing at 13–18 per cent a year for fifteen years. We conclude that the industrialization of Korea, Taiwan and Singapore was one component of the transition from Fordist to post-Fordist regimes of accumulation and therefore is not generalizable to the rest of the Third World in the foreseeable future. Industrialization shows the potential for transforming the world but, under the existing social and spatial relations, this potential is only partly, inconsistently, and sporadically realized. Do alternative models of industrialization exist?

An alternative strategy

Industrialization has brought high economic growth rates to some Third World countries proving that rapid development is possible. Industrialization under the existing social and spatial relations has also meant the continuation of historical forms of exploitation: the use of peripheral cheap labour to produce low-cost commodities for centre markets; restructuring of peripheral economies to match the demands of centre peoples; the incursion of a mountain of debts and loss of surplus through interest payments; and the precariousness of regional economies in the face of change occurring elsewhere. Most significant, however, is the limited nature of the recent industrialization – industry now employs some 30 million people in the capitalist Third World and, given the slowing down in the rate of global economic growth, this number cannot be expected to increase rapidly in the next several decades. Yet the population of the capitalist Third World crying out for development is 3 billion. It is difficult to support the optimistic conclusion that capitalist industrialization, now employing 1 per cent of the Third World's people after a quarter of a century of rapid growth, can transform the world's underdeveloped economies. It is also difficult to see how the industrialization that has occurred challenges Marxist and neo-Marxist underdevelopment theory – rather it confirms the scepticism which comes from their analysis of global history.

The constructive side of critical theory is to point to those conditions which must be transformed before development can occur. Radical theory proposes that the social relations and socio-economic objectives prevailing in the past must be reversed before underdevelopment can be transformed into development: thus class and gender relations must be egalitarian rather than unequal, productive resources must serve local people rather than distant demands, and decisions must be democratically made rather than the prerogative of the elites. The objective of developing an economy is directly to satisfy needs, especially urgent necessities not presently met. This can only be achieved if the productive effort of a Third World society is geared directly towards this single objective. Needs cannot be satisfied via the trickling down of benefits from an economy directed at satiating demands in the centre.

Critical theory must also select means of development which

have shown a potential for promoting development – here the principles and techniques of industrialization are obvious cases. A model which captures these sentiments has been developed by Clive Thomas (1974), a student of Walter Rodney. Thomas argues that both neo-classical (conservative) and classical-socialist economic theories have ignored the typically small, underdeveloped social formations of the Third World. As a result of the last several hundred years of capitalist underdevelopment, these economies are characterized by: foreign dominance over the local means of production, with all the forms of dependence arising from this, especially in cultural attitudes; and a specialization on agriculture with a low productivity of labour. The crucial features are dynamic divergence between domestic resources and domestic demand and between demand and mass needs. Material development, he says, means initiating economic processes which overcome these divergences: as they are rooted in basic structures a revolutionary break with the past has to occur. His model assumes a situation in which a political revolution has transferred state power to a worker–peasant alliance. The objectives are to disengage from international capitalism, bring the productive forces under collective control, and improve material welfare for the masses.

In terms of agriculture, there is a need to reorient production away from tropical and subtropical staple exports and towards crops which immediately meet the needs of the people – Thomas compares this with the conventional view that the key to agricultural development lies in improving the efficiency of export production, despite the fact that this solution has already been tried for a hundred years with little developmental result. Immediately production should be reoriented to achieve self-sufficiency in food and provide crucial industrial raw materials, with exports as a subordinate objective. As incomes rise, demand rapidly increases for nutritional foods like dairy products, meat, fruit and vegetables – emphasizing these gives dynamism to the agricultural sector. As to productive means, Thomas finds peasant farmers to be rational and efficient in their use of resources. The transformation of agriculture, however, entails: increasing the size of farming and marketing units; using production techniques which are capital- and skill-intensive; using other modernized inputs to transform productivity; eventually transferring labour from agriculture to other rural and urban activities; and, most significantly, building political and social relations which eliminate exploitation in the rural economy but preserve voluntarism and are based in democratic decision making. Thomas has in mind not forced collectivization, which (merely in practical terms) the recent history of Eastern Europe shows to be counter-productive, but a diversity of co-operative institutions matched with local situations, the basic organizing principle being democracy and mass participation. And while his principles might appear similar to Tanzania's experiment with rural socialism, the Ujamaa village programme actually devoted resources to becoming more competitive in a non-dynamic export market while Tanzania was importing meat and milk to fill its rapidly increasing demand. Tanzania, he claims, is not much different from conventional models stressing export-oriented agriculture.

However, structural development implies industrialization as its most logical outcome. Industrialization is to be valued because of its role in increasing productivity in all parts of an economy and the change in attitudes it promotes towards the material world. At present underdeveloped countries such as Tanzania have not realized the potential for poor people to transform their environments through industrial means. Existing models, such as the Soviet concentration on heavy industries, or import substitution, have also not helped. Instead, Thomas's basic industrial strategy involves planning the convergence between domestic resource use and domestic needs via the development of an indigenous technology matched with local conditions. Also crucial is the resource content of industrial goods. Thomas finds that a large number of final products derive from a narow range of basic materials two of which, iron/steel and textiles, form the backbone of modern industrial consumption. Add paper, plastics, rubber, glass and a few others and we have the range of strategic materials linked with most of the value added by industry. These materials should form the cornerstone of an industrialization programme for, if they are not produced locally, the organic linkages between domestic demand and domestic production will forever lie outside the country, with the growth of demand merely transferring value added elsewhere. Income elasticity for basic materials is high and they have many forward and backward linkages with other activities. A convergence strategy therefore entails focusing on '*basic industries*', the production of the materials which enter into the production of all other goods.

The further implication is that the basic materials substantially be derived from domestic natural resources. This means inventorying a country's resources, something which often has not yet been carried out, for the colonial powers were solely concerned with developing resources of interest to the metropolis – for example Africa, with the world's best hydropower endowment, has only 0.6 per cent of the world's hydroelectric facilities. Where resources are not available, substitutions can be made, or input mixes varied, and in the last resort materials can be imported in a raw or semi-finished state. This raises two issues of significance. First an indigenous technology must be developed to match the available resources to local needs. And second, economies of scale are such that a critical minimum size can be reached at a fairly low level of output, beyond which the cheapness of local materials, or advantages of location, can be substituted for further production cost descreases. A range of complementary activities forms the rest of the comprehensive industrialization programme. Machine tool production is indispensable for industrial transformation, as are rapid growth in power production and the improvement of transportation. Small-scale industries and agriculturally oriented industries can offset the tendency for rural−urban differences to widen. Hence for Thomas the solution in the Third World has to be found not in trade but in the structures which determine a country's trading capacity. For Thomas, a country incapable of using its own resources to meet its basic requirements remains forever undeveloped (Thomas, 1974: 225).

Let us make clear the further social and political implications of Thomas's model. It entails popular control of the production process, but also the planning of consumption to match the possibilities of local production. It involves a transformation in class and gender and in spatial relations towards complete equality. It means excruciatingly hard work for at least a generation before material needs can be fully met. But most importantly it means democracy in all aspects of social and economic life. It is a process not to be supported lightly but only to be undertaken by a people united in their opposition to the stuctures that now prevail and determined to make entirely new forms of life in the future.

Conclusion

In both the conventional and some of the Marxist literatures, industrialization is proposed as the main way of transforming the structure of global inequality. Evidence that this process is already underway is found in the recent experience of the NICs − several Third World (and peripheral First World) countries have seen rapid industrial and economic growth and an increase in material standards of living. Conventional (neo-classical) economic theory, modernization theory and some Marxist theories of the progressive (if flawed) nature of capitalism, see this process of export-oriented industrialization as unproblematic, and the whole argument made obvious by the empirical data. Radical theory shares the belief that industry and progress are essentially connected, but argues that the social and spatial relations which control the industrialization process have also to be considered. Under the existing relations. Marxist theory argues, industrialization has negative consequences for the workers involved, especially for women, is limited in its transformative effects on the rest of the economy, and because of contradictions (like decreasing global demand through reducing aggregate worker incomes) is restricted in its rate of growth and geographic area of influence. From this point of view, therefore, the existing industrialization does *not* afford the potential for global transformation.

This chapter is underlain by a second theme, one which will be made more apparent in the following, final chapter. Critics of neo-Marxist dependency theory (Corbridge, 1986; Booth, 1985) argue that the industrial transformation of the Third World contradicts the thesis of the development of underdevelopment – even Lipietz (1987) finds the temporary success of peripheral Fordism 'completely discrediting' the underdevelopment thesis. The assumptions of these critics are that industrialization is automatically progressive, inherently constituting development, and that dependency theory cannot encompass Third World industrial development. Both assumptions are erroneous. Capitalist industrialization does not *necessarily* promote economic and social development – it can, and often does, amount to little more than a new way of exploiting unprotected and unorganized Third World labour. Industrialization can be just one more way of extracting surplus from Third World peoples, this time through eternal debt repayments. The opportunity to move from cheap labour production to a broader range of more sophisticated industries is limited in time, geographic scope, and numbers of workers involved. The recent experience can thus be interpreted as dependent and partial industrialization. Rather than contradicting the underdevelopment thesis, this confirms it. Dependency theory may have its problems. But jettisoning the entire approach on the basis of the limited achievements of Korea and Brazil over the last twenty years goes too far.

Finally, the chapter poses an alternative to the export-oriented agriculture and manufacturing proposed by the World Bank and similar development agencies. Drawing on neo-Marxist dependency theory (the idea of partial withdrawal from the global capitalist economy) but restating the analysis in structural and class terms (industrial transformation, worker/peasant ownership of productive resources), the Thomas model proposes that industrialization be used directly to transform the material conditions of the masses rather than as a new way of inserting a Third World country into the international division of labour. Industry has this potential because it bridges the gap between natural resources and material consumption, a link subject to rapid change in productivity. This potential has to be captured by the peoples of the underdeveloped countries themselves via an indigenous technology, and the industrialization process has to be collectively owned and democratically organized by the workers involved before it can transform their conditions of existence. Thus the initial proposition of the chapter is supported – industry does afford the potential for global transformation, but only as part of a democratic socialist revolution.

Chapter ten

Conclusion: the critique of Marxist development theory (and a reply)

Marxist and neo-Marxist theories counter the prevailing notions of development provided by environmental determinism, modernization theory, neo-classical economics and the like. Indeed Marxism argues that conventional science has been hopelessly biased by its underlying social purpose of legitimizing the dominant capitalist social order. Yet in the case of development theory, the obvious success of capitalist social relations in yielding high material standards of living obliterates the criticism that high incomes for some have been achieved at the expense of the poverty of many. Likewise, in the present intellectual climate ('post-history') the very idea that alternative modes of development are possible has almost disappeared from mention. Given the problems still faced by humankind this type of scientific amnesia is a tragedy of intellect and a travesty of justice.

We cannot survey the entire range of criticisms of Marxism, or even of Marxist development theory, in this concluding chapter. Instead we take a couple of leading critiques, one dealing with development theory (Booth, 1985), the other focusing a little more broadly on radical geography (Corbridge, 1986), as illustrative of more general critical tendencies. We reply at the theoretical-philosophical level and by reviewing development theories to see what validity the criticisms may have. We then return to the more effective feminist criticism outlined earlier in Chapter 5 and suggest an extension of the concept mode of production which would enable a more complete explanation of the development process.

The critique of Marxist development theory

The progress of Marxist development theory has hardly gone uncontested. Booth (1985) argues that after a vigorous growth, the Marxist sociology of development reached an impasse, related to generic difficulties in its underlying social theory. For him, the

171

basic problem with Marxist theory is a metatheoretical commitment to demonstrating that what happens in capitalist societies is not only explicable, but necessary. This commitment to necessity is expressed in development theory in two main forms:

> The first operates through the way in which it is usual to conceive of the relation between the theoretical concept of the capitalist mode of production and the national or international economies, politics and social formations under analysis. The other – if anything more persistent and fundamental – involves a form of system teleology or functionalism.
>
> (Booth, 1985: 773)

Both of these faults, Booth continues, have been discussed by Hindess and Hirst (1977; Cutler, *et al*. 1977–8). These writers argue that in *Capital* Marx reads the characteristics of social formations from the laws of motion of the capitalist mode of production; they object specifically to the idea that social totalities have necessary effects inscribed in their structures. Booth finds their criticism an accurate appreciation of the trouble with Marxist development theory. Either development problems are explained by their particular insertion into international capitalism, or socio-economic processes in the Third World take a form which contributes to the wider process of capitalist accumulation. The persistence of such ideas is explained by the seductive appeals of functionalism and system teleology to the social sciences, where interest lies in discovering deeper, effectively more teleological, reasons for development problems. In common with Giddens (1981) and Hindess and Hirst, Booth finds this damaging to Marxism's intellectual standing. It is wrong to pretend that functional claims are explanatory in sociology – for example he doubts the existence of feedback mechanisms of the type claimed by functionalism, whether Parsonian or Marxist. And functionalism reifies certain social institutions, placing them by metatheoretical fiat further beyond human control than they can empirically be shown to be – this is socially and politically corrupting. All this accounts for the repetitive, non-cumulative character of the dependency literature, the forcing of Marxist theory along restricted lines, and its failure to explore urgent empirical issues systematically.

A similar, and to some extent parallel, critique comes from the geographer Stuart Corbridge (1986). This critique, however, places more emphasis on the Althusserian version of the concept of modes of production and its application to development issues. Corbridge objects to this analysis as rationalist, in the sense that abstract theory is made the guarantor of concrete events, and structural-functionalist in that, for example, peripheral pre-capitalist modes of production serve the reproductive needs of the central capitalist mode of production. And finally it is economistic in that while the economy is subject to feedback, it remains determinant in the last instance. For support, Corbridge also turns to Hindess and Hirst, who argue that modes of production can only be theorized in the rationalist format which Corbridge is trying to reject. Furthermore, Hindess and Hirst argue that while specific relations of production always presuppose definite social conditions of existence, they neither secure these conditions through their own action, nor determine the form in which they will be secured. This last point establishes in Corbridge's (1986: 67) mind that 'there is nothing in the concept of capitalism itself which should lead us to expect that it must have X, Y, or Z development (or underdevelopment) effects. Such contingencies are not forged at this macro-theoretical scale.' Hence, the thrust of Corbridge's alternative theorization is to the empirical and the particular.

Theoretical reply

Where do Booth, Corbridge and others get their notions of structural Marxism? One piece of evidence is provided by their common reference to Hindess and Hirst. Unfortunately therefore we also must return to this version of structural theory − 'unfortunately' because these particular writers take abstract abstruseness far beyond the point of absurdity. In the mid-1970s, Hindess and Hirst were Althusserian Marxists of an excessively rationalist persuasion. Their book *Pre-Capitalist Modes of Production*, they said, was a work of theory, aimed at raising Marx's concept of modes of production to a more rigorous level. For Hindess and Hirst, concepts were formed within knowledge, and were not reducible to, or even derivable from, a set of given, real conditions. Hence a specific mode of production was a theoretically valid concept only if it had been constructed according to (their version of) the Marxist theory of modes of production! Such a theory had the distinct advantage of not being refutable by 'any empirical recourse to the supposed "facts" of history' (Hindess and Hirst, 1975: 3). They thus rejected the 'notion of history as a coherent and worthwhile object of study' in favour of the development of concepts exclusively for elaborating the theory of modes of production (Hindess and Hirst, 1975: 321).

It was clear to all Marxists outside an ever-decreasing circle of Hindess and Hirst's followers, that such a theoretical project was doomed from the start. (Marxist theory must be used to interpret and change reality; the very process of theory building involves generalizing from historical experience.) Hence, soon after penning the above words, Hindess and Hirst realized that something was fundamentally wrong. One moment of this realization, referred to by Corbridge, was that while the 'relations of production pre-suppose that other social relations and practices satisfy certain abstract and general conditions,' – for example that the legal system be of a certain kind – 'the concept of determinate [specific] relations of production does not tell us in what precise form these effects will be secured nor does it tell us the precise character of the relations which secure them' (Cutler *et al.*, 1977–8: 209). In other words, the limits to theory-making exclusively through the elabora-tion of concepts is reached well before all conditions are explained – this, by the way, is a conclusion reached earlier by Marx (see the quotation in Chapter 5, p. 62). One reaction to this limitation to purely rationally-derived theory might be to go as far as possible with a structural interpretation of the influences and limits imposed by the social relations of production on the legal system, politics, the state, etc., and then use the theoretical results to interpret history, or, given Hindess and Hirst's aversion to history, to look at the contemporary world. After such a practical confrontation, it would be necessary to modify or reject the conceptual results of abstract theory building. The limits to rationally-derived theory would thus be found by empirical practice. But Hindess and Hirst are typical of their time in this respect at least that the nearest they get to the real world is in the deconstruction of texts about it, or rather their own earlier text which was not about it. This decon-struction (Hindess and Hirst, 1977) reaches the following bizarre conclusions:

1 It is necessary to reject the pertinence of the concept of mode of production altogether. The social formation is not a totality governed by an organizing principle. The great part of Marxist analysis of politics, the state, ideology etc. must be abandoned. Socialist politics are no longer necessarily oriented towards revolution. And the pertinence of class analysis for socialist 'political calculation' must be questioned.
2 The whole epistemological enterprise is arbitrary and dogmatic. The idea that there are separable realms of objects and theoretical discourse has to be rejected. In fact there is no question of whether objects of discourse exist independently: 'Objects of dis-course do not exist at all in that sense: they are constituted in and through the discourses which refer to them' (Cutler *et al.*, 1977–8: chs. 8, 9, 13).

174

It might be added that this jettisoning of structural theory and revolutionary politics (Wood, 1986: 79) was accompanied by a Byzantine process of squabbles, resignations, and ever-smaller group formation in the alphabet soup of British radical politics (Elliott, 1986).

The problem here lies in Hindess and Hirst's initial supposition that the rational development of structural concepts was able to replicate completely the myriad possibilities of reality. All individual and group actions would thus be forecastable by rationally derived theory. We could act perfectly in history. The necessary corollary has to be that such theory cannot be challenged by the empirical! This is surely a case of new adherents to structural theory taking it to ridiculous excess. Such an extreme rationalist position is not inherent in the structural view.

As to Hindess and Hirst's second position we can agree that the question of the accuracy of concepts in describing and explaining reality is extraordinarily difficult. But to imply from this that reality cannot be independent of the discourse about it is merely to extend the earlier confusion about the power of rational thought into a later one about the constitutive powers of theory. Ideas may not exactly replicate real events, yet they are derivable from them, and they are continually tested by reapplication to the material world.

Further, Hindess and Hirst use their rejection of an earlier position which few others shared, for the jettisoning of structural Marxism *in toto*, its carefully elaborated concepts, and its political vision of a far better world. What was literally Hindess and Hirst's autocritique is then expanded out of proportion by Booth, Corbridge and others into a critique of structuralist Marxism in general and Marxist development theory in particular. Why is it that this convoluted process of self-criticism overwhelms in the critics' minds all the other ideas and work by structuralists, especially the many empirical studies using the structural concept of articulation of modes of production (Long, 1975; Post, 1978; Rey, 1973; Watts, 1983a)? The answer can lie only in the political mood of the times and the academic purpose of the critics (Peet, 1988). We live in conservative times.

The broader critique emerging from Booth and Corbridge, one declared rather than argued (except by recourse to Hindess and Hirst), is that Marxism is economistic functionalism of a teleological variety. Marxism describes systems as having needs, sees effects being inscribed in structures, and find events predetermined. This set of criticisms should ring familiar; they are almost identical to the critique of structural functionalism and modernization theory

(Chapter 3). Indeed structural functionalism and structural Marxism are often equated. Conceding certain similarities, it is the case that Marxism begins with the naturalness of life, is 'economistic' in that it privileges social practices and relations which enable the reproduction of existence, and employs functional arguments in the sense of emphasizing necessary activities, things which must be done for societies to continue in existence – even to the point of seeing people collectively (i.e. in society) as having 'needs'. Such necessary functions provide food for children and occupy a large part of lifetime; a totality of such functions reproduces social existence. But Marxism also differs in fundamental ways so that criticisms of structural functionalism do not automatically apply to structural Marxism. We saw earlier, in Chapter 3, that Parsons did not manage a successful synthesis of structural imperative and human behaviour in the theory of social action. This is because there is no real conception of human nature or class behaviour in Parsons, which could form the focal point around which synthesis could emerge. This is hardly the case with Marxism, which has strongly developed theories of human nature, from Ollman's (1976) elaboration of Marx's thesis on alienation to Jagger's (1981) socialist feminist ideas on woman's nature, and which emphasizes class and class struggle in the making of history. In addition, structural functionalism has a non-dialectical conception of societal change, whereas Marxism stresses the contradictory nature of the social performance of functions, so that struggle occurs in the very productive acts which make life possible. Such struggle is deeply felt exactly because it occurs in fundamental, essential activities – people's acts of collective self-creation. If multiple social contradictions become fused in common experience, revolutionary acts take place and society may change. As opposed to structural functionalism, structural Marxism thus encompasses individual volition, system-changing activities, and the sense of imminent transformation. Exactly for reasons like this, structural functionalism and Marxism are on opposite sides of the political fence, the one being a leading instance of legitimation theory, the other a leading revolutionary theory. Equating the two is a cruel hoax played on the unsuspecting and the ignorant.

The validity of criticism

We now turn to the related criticisms that in Marxism historical events are inscribed in theoretical structures and that the 'needs' of central capitalism have developmental effects in the periphery. This book has presented many of the theories which are the objects of such criticism. How valid are these criticisms?

Chapter 5 outlined mode of production as an abstract analytical category organizing generalizations derived from historical instances showing similarity of form and dynamic. Similarities between societies derive from the necessary features of human existence, like the need to eat and the urge to reproduce. Mode of production theory marshals the theoretical components replicating common aspects of existence into structural wholes called modes of production. These are then reapplied in the interpretation of reality – in practice we find structural necessity confronting myriad circumstances. The outcomes of such encounters are poorly described as contingencies, in the sense of chance occurrences. Human beings do not reproduce themselves by chance but through deliberate effort. The challenge is to discover the variety of ways in which structured 'types of effort' (forces expended on nature, relations organizing these forces) occur in empirical practice.

Thus Chapter 6 surveyed three pre-capitalist modes of production in terms of their constituent social formations. Primitive communism, in Sanday's (1981) view, took the form of 'cultural configurations' which, when subjected to stress, developed gender relations varying from male dominance, through relative gender equality, to female-centred societies. Lineage societies were shown by Friedman and Rowlands (1977) to take an extraordinary profusion of forms depending on circumstance, with tendencies towards the conical clan system and the state, the 'big man' system, or the retention of elements of primitive communism in kin-ordered systems. The work of Wittfogel (1985) and Amin (1989) shows the tributary mode of production to include societies as different as the state-centred system of classical China and the various decentralized feudal orders of Europe. The dynamics of centralized and decentralized tributary formations are so different that the one type could give rise to capitalism, the other could not. Brenner's (1985) argument, reproduced in Chapter 7, is that even the different *regional* versions of feudalism had varying potentials for transformation into capitalism. Similarly we found theorists elaborating Marxian concepts, like Wolpe (1980), Bettelheim (1972), Bradby (1980) and Taylor (1979), agreeing with more empirically oriented Marxist work by Frank (1969b; 1979), Stavrianos (1981), Rodney (1974) and Mukherjee (1974) that a variety of societal outcomes emerged from capitalism's expansion after 1500 and its articulation with pre-capitalist modes of production (for details see Chapters 5 and 8). All however stress the destructive (underdeveloping) influences wrought on pre-capitalist societies. And finally neo-structuralist explanations of regimes of accumulation (Aglietta, 1979; Lipietz, 1986, 1987) and the global space economies of twentieth-century capitalism (Harvey, 1989; Scott, 1988), outlined in Chapter 9, show formations with differing types and potentials of industrialization. Thus, far from seeing modes of production as monoliths inscribing given effects in history, Marxist and neo-Marxist theories have explored the multiple social formations which make up a given mode and, instead of saying that capitalism automatically creates given developmental effects, these theories emphasize variety of articulations, multiplicity of processes and yet common themes in outcomes. If modes of production have effects inscribed in their structures, these are many and contradictory. If Marxism is teleological, it is a logic which may or may not unfold. If Marxism is rationalist, it finds a constant need to explore the empirical validity of its logic. In brief we find much of the criticism simply does not ring true for the wide range of development theories we surveyed. We conclude further that rather than being at an impasse, Marxist thought suffers instead from a loss of nerve – especially structural Marxism. It is time to recover that nerve.

Rumours of the death of structural Marxism have therefore been greatly exaggerated. Gross forms of structural rationalism indeed have to be rejected (if indeed they were ever widely accepted). Structuralism may need a more coherent theory of the relations between events, experience, consciousness and action. Certainly the conditions under which system-reproducing probabilities are transformed into system-changing possibilities need exploring. But this can be done by adding to structural ideas rather than denying them. The idea of structured totalities characterized by inherent contradictions and therefore multiple reactions, with human activity making and sometimes breaking reproductive patterns, captures society better than its theoretical alternatives. It is to be preferred over contingent theories of an open-ended history, certainly in terms of a philosophical base for theories which purport to explain the long-lasting reality of Third World poverty. (Try telling a peasant there is no such thing as necessity!) We can learn something, but not very much, from the anti-structuralist argument.

Reproduction and development

More convincing is the feminist critique that in isolating those key relations which form the basis of society, Marxism focuses too readily on production relations and virtually ignores gender relations. We could add to this the geographer's complaint that Marxism has little to say about relations with nature and sees events occurring on top of a pin rather than in space. Responding to these valid criticisms, there is a need for a broader conception of *mode of reproduction* which can be applied to the question of development.

There are, of course, many aspects or dimensions to social existence – environmental relations, material production, sexual reproduction, racial relations, regional characteristics, consciousness and styles of behaviour to name but a few. A reasonable case can be made for environment, production and reproduction as essential to something inherently desirable, continued existence. The argument for production as the social transformation of nature was made earlier. Production most distinguishes human beings from the rest of nature – it is the material practice through which human evolution becomes self-directed. *R*eproduction is a more general set of practices, more organically linked with natural necessity than production. Reproduction is the total set of practices and relations through which humans make and remake their existence. In this totality, certain practices distinguishable by their essential nature give transhistorical coherence to the way all human beings live:

1 The territorial base, location of a society in earth-space, natural environment from which a living is made and which bears the mark of human activity.
2 The forces of production used for gaining a livelihood from nature, including human labour power, and socially reconstructed means of production.
3 Social relations between groups, especially production relations in the making of products and gender relations in the making of people.
4 Necessary activities, of a material-practical kind like production and consumption, surplus generation and distribution, and procreation and of a thoughtful kind (consciousness).
5 Social regulation by which the cohesion of the whole order is maintained, especially the organization of collective force in the state, the unification of understanding through ideology, the socialization of new members of society, and in general the way of life or culture.
6 Geographical articulation or external spatial relations between one localized social group and another, these relations being characterized by partial and total interactions between individuals, groups and whole social orders.

Beginning where humans did, in the natural world, a specific kind of reproductive practice grows out of a certain environment: all social activity occurs in a place and is influenced by the frictions of distance. Life is earned by transforming a limited array of natural resources. Likewise, means of production are originally natural forces and materials reconstituted by human labour. As in the natural world, the human individual must enter into relations with others to achieve continued existence: gender relations, which take social forms like the family in which procreation and socialization occur; and production relations, defined most clearly by control over the means of production, which materialize in a specific labour process, a certain combination of labour power, technology and means of production. This yields products for mass consumption, which it should be remembered are pieces of nature and therefore take regional forms; renewed means of production; and surplus, consumed in part as luxury but in part saved or reinvested, most importantly as improved means of production. Humans are natural beings also in terms of their sexual relations, which have an essential similarity with those of the organic world. They are particular kinds of natural beings with specific social objectives in the making, support and socialization of children. Consciousness develops in this socil context. As people make their lives they think and speak about events – language being the means of communication between individuals joined by social relations. Consciousness in applied and theoretical forms is the medium through which human beings achieve partial liberation from natural constraint. For consciousness reflects reality in a dual sense – mirroring it in terms of structure and content, but also contemplating on it and achieving innovative distance. The partial character of its liberation forces consciousness to take ideological forms typified best by religion. All aspects of culture have dual characteristics of necessity, so that children have to be disciplined into being certain kinds of people, and of freedom, so that people discover new kinds of being. The state also co-ordinates social activity, enforcing the prevailing class and gender relations, and protecting the society's use of a given territory. State and culture permeate all aspects of life, directing, compelling and persuading people to act in prescribed ways while proving organized means through which new forms of activity are also possible. Each society has interrelations over longer distances with others occupying different places – these external relations occur between single individuals and activities (as when ideologies spread from their society of origin) and between whole regional formations (when war marshals all against the common enemy). There is a connection between the structure of inner relations tying regional society together and the form taken by outer relations connecting one society to all others. In the total set of relations which connect the parts of the whole life process, two kinds of feedback are especially important. Directly through the labour process and consumption, but supported by ideology and the state, societies transform nature into progressively socialized environments; through their development of consciousness and distinct socialization practices, humans make themselves into new kinds of being. Finally, and most importantly, the relations which organize social existence are complementary in terms of co-operative effort but also may be contradictory in terms of the exploitation and unequal power and material benefits which stem from class and gender domination of reproductive institutions.

Returning to the previous discussion of limitations on the development of consciousness, natural necessity is partially overcome by human activity organized by exploitative relations. Limited consciousness takes ideological forms which support the dominating social order. Oppositional ideologies also emerge from struggle relations at home and at work. More generally, cultures and states are driven by the dialectic between supportive and oppositional beliefs – even religion has its liberating moments. Thus change within and between modes occurs through the struggle between social opposites. Modes vary in the permanence of their structures. Rapid development is concentrated in volatile social orders.

In this conception, development is the dynamic of social reproduction. Marxism finds the source of societal dynamics in the relations which people enter in the reproduction of their existence. In a reproductionist sense, these include relations between societies and environments, between different societies over space, between gender groups, as well as class relations. All these relations are part of the surplus generation process. Thus gender relations may involve the free use of female labour in producing and socializing children, environmental relations may mean the destruction of natural ecosystems for quick profit, spatial relations may mean the draining of surplus from dominated societies, while class relations involve the exploitation of labour directly in production. Development has been underlain by massive interlocking systems of the extraction of surplus and its concentration in a limited global space. Social relations between the 'owners' of global surplus direct its use in terms of luxury consumption or investment and the kinds of investment – whether in improved means of production, the development of science, technology, education or infrastructure. The social relations of reproduction thus direct the kind and level of development – shape its dynamic – while struggles of various kinds determine the distribution of the material benefits flowing from development. As in structural Marxism this process is legitimated in ideology and protected by the state, although a reproductive analysis sees such 'super-structural' characteristics as multiply determined.

Developed societies are therefore organized by dynamic modes of reproduction and characterized by the concentration and reinvestment of surplus, rationality and technical progress, forms of ideology and socialization in accord with productive effort, empowerment of the state, and expansion in geographical scale of their control over productive resources and flows of surplus.

An alternative development?

The challenge for those critical of a development process founded on class and patriarchy, which destroys or damages natural environments, and relies on intersocietal domination, is to retain the dynamism of capitalism while changing the exploitative form of its dynamic. Yet this entire book has exemplified how developmental dynamics are rooted in social relations which last for centuries, if not millennia. This makes the search for a new form of social relations particularly difficult and its materialization seemingly impossible. Indeed an argument can be made that capitalist social relations are so productive that they must persist until contradictions (with the environment most obviously) force their abandonment; the fearful aspect of this is that mass realization of the destructive nature of capitalist development will come too late.

But it is also the case that the maturation of contradiction makes the impossible progressively more realistic. And the analysis presented in Chapter 9 of the plausibility of widespread transformation through an expanded industrialization of the Third World, together with other aspects of the contemporary global capitalist system (the debt problem, low prices for agricultural and raw material exports etc.), indicate a growing contradiction between the have-too-much and the have-nots. One half of Third World societies have active (revolutionary) resistance forces. Likewise the tendency evident in the last two decades for Third World peoples to support socialist forms of development indicates that 'another way' is not just another utopian fantasy. There are billions of peasants, workers, students and intellectuals who want, expect and are prepared to struggle for a form of development organized to transform the life of the masses.

A model for this kind of development essentially involves combining two lessons derived from a critical appreciation of past events, especially those of the last several hundred years of capitalism. The first (positive lesson) is that for development to occur and material standards of living to be raised, a society must invest its surplus product in science, technology and the improvement of productivity through superior means of production. The second (negative lesson) is that to minimize the growth of destructive contradictions and to ensure the spread of material gains, relations with nature have to be sustainable, social and spatial relations egalitarian, and decisions democratically made by those affected by them. This means that the productive forces are developed under collective control. We have learned from the experience of the Soviet Union and China that 'collective control' cannot mean commands from a non-elected bureaucratic state. It means instead direct worker ownership, co-operatives and partnerships, and it entails planning rather than market mechanisms in articulating democratically-reached social goals. It means recognizing and valuing all efforts in the reproduction of existence, especially in the making and raising of the society's new subjects – here we can learn much from the millennia of primitive communism. It means developing new attitudes towards other societies, in which exchange is based on equitable principles, like the productive effort invested in goods, or a society's needs. And it means new relations with the natural world, so that the development is environmentally sustainable. Principles like these are worth the finest of intellectual and practical effort.

Epilogue

Is there a better way? Can development occur outside capitalism? How do we know that people are capable of co-operativeness? The answer has to be that we do not know for certain. This is very much because socialism, the leading contender with capitalism, has so far been practised in societies long characterized by centralized tributary modes of production which still remain structurally intact – hence the absence of democracy, the authoritarian, ideologically-laden ways of motivating effort, the problems of central authority and regional autonomy, the recent desperate openings to the outside, all continue the age-old tendencies of this kind of absolutist social formation. In the absence of proven models of democratic socialist development, we can only suggest some alternative principles which might underlie this, an ethic of development rather than a blueprint for it.

Ethics are principles of right and wrong, good and bad, which human beings following their best intentions try to exercise in their relations with others and towards the world in general. Humans differ from animals in the fundamental sense of having consciousness of their existence, but also in having conscience about their actions. That is, we have the sense that our actions should be judged relative to some broader context, something greater than the particular, something long-lasting, perhaps even eternal. For religious people this something is God, originator of life and guardian of life's purposes. And for religious people, the source of the ethical principles by which to live is easy to find – the principles were set down once and for all by the prophets who established a direct connection between themselves and the heavens. For non-religious people, the source of an ethical sensibility is more difficult to find, in part because we too have had our search turned down what are quite literally blind alleys by religious ways of thinking – hence ethics and spirituality seem to come along together. Socialists, however, find the sources of ethical principles in the material conditions of existence and the social relations people enter. In other words, when we ask the question, 'How should we live and why should we do things a certain way?', the only sure guide is what we have done and what we can learn from practice to guide future behaviour. This may seem a functional approach which limits the imagination. It is meant as practical and yet liberative thinking.

Now, a basic problem with this position is that it places a heavy burden on the mode of analysis of the human experience. We have not only to feel our emotional reactions to the human experience, but we have also to subject both experience and emotional reactions to analysis if we are to find some principles of ethical behaviour and then extend this into a just society and an equitable form of development. That is why Marxism is so important for socialists – it is the summary of the best analytical thoughts of several generations of people committed to a better life for the world's masses of exploited people. Marxism emphasizes the collective character of human reproduction, asks of any society how is reproduction organized and what relations people engage in for the reproduction of their kind? Anarchism, as a second type of radical thinking, focuses on the relations between the individual and the collective, especially the freedom of individual thought and actions in relation to society organized through the state. A third line of radical thinking which has its origin in the organicism of the nineteenth century, but is expressed today in the ecology movement, inquires into human relations with the natural world. Socialist feminists want to know about the position of women in societies, and the relations between men and women. Blacks and other minorities in white-dominated societies and members of minority ethnic and tribal groups inquire about the position of such minorities. All of these lines of radical thought conclude in proposals for changing the structure of society in a fundamental way. In doing so, they make ethical judgements and propose ethical solutions: i.e. they make social statements about what is good and bad. So radical politics is a series of ethical statements about what exists, what needs to be changed, and what should come into existence in the future – it is a statement about the good society.

From such analyses, radical people derive their conceptions of the good life and their principles of ethical behaviour. The kinds of conclusions reached are as follows. We too share and value capitalism's great discovery, that people freed of servile relations are creative and innovative, capable of doing almost anything. But we want this sense of freedom to be felt by everyone and not just a small minority. In addition, we have the strong sense that one person's, one class's or one society's freedom cannot be gained by depriving others. In the past, at low levels of economic development, arguments that one person's livelihood had necessarily to be gained at the expense of another's may have had some harsh validity. It would now be difficult to justify such reasons for depriving others, although of course non-economic motives for such deprivation exist in the lust for power. The argument often made here is that depriving others means, in the end, depriving oneself. That is, we should want all other people to be fully developed to make the world a more interesting and satisfying place in which to spend one's own life. This argument certainly has appeal. But it also has its limitations. Is it possible that we could want the best life for everyone, just for its own sake, for their sake, or our sakes collectively? And that we would want the kind of society which would enable all human potential to be realized just because we believe in this, in and of itself? And, most difficult of all, could we ourselves act in ways which are consistent with such an ideal? If we are realistic about our present limitations, if we can see how much behaviour would have to change, then we must also realize that the best we can accomplish is flashes of the second ethic but mainly an everyday ethic at the first level – the wanting of freedom for others for egoistic or quasi-egoistic reasons. But other humans of the future, raised in an environment in which people are striving to exercise their freedom without greatly diminishing the freedom of others, people raised with a deep sense of responsibility for others, might be able to break through egoism and want the good of everyone just for its own sake or rather for the sake of humanity. In such a just society the ethical principle guiding behaviour would therefore consist in exercising one's individuality within a sense of responsibility for the happiness of all. Some of the ways this might work its way out would include direct democracy, worker self-management, the equal sharing of obnoxious tasks, the making of work into a creative act and the distribution of products according to need.

These sentiments particularly apply to the relations between men and women. In patriarchal societies men derive personal power and pleasure by dominating women – a woman's deprivation is a man's enhancement. Why have men been able to get away with this? The basic answer has to be through monopolizing economic power. In turn, this rests in part on man's continuous availability for work and woman's particular role in reproducing the species. A basic question is why the economic, productive role has been valued higher than the social and species reproductive role? More bluntly, why is it deemed more important to make material objects than human subjects? The answer can only lie in an ethical system thrown out of balance by the urgency of material development. We could suggest that social roles be evened out, so that men and women as far as possible do the same things. But the real lesson from the experience of women's oppression has to involve the revaluing rather than the redistribution of people's efforts and contributions. Anyone who makes a significant contribution to society, and especially to making good people possible, deserves the appreciation of her fellow human beings. This is the material basis of the ethic of gender equality and many other forms of equality between the various kinds of people.

Likewise, the present environmental 'ethic' forms under conditions of alienation from the natural world, the cushioning of the city where even the weather seems 'outside', the feeling high technology gives of being 'post-natural' – i.e. that humans are superbeings who only realize their naturalness when they bump hard against the imminence of death. The idea of the human conquest of nature is both fallacious (because we haven't) and arrogant (because we may want to). Instead, it is clear from the experience of history that a people wanting to live in harmony with nature have to see themselves as natural beings. This seems to imply that we live in nature, make encounters with natural processes an everyday occurrence, even feel the soil run through our fingers, grow plants, etc. If society does not relax back into nature, then nature is encountered only as a natural museum, maybe indeed a natural mausoleum, and we value environmental preservation only because we feel sorry for creatures less powerful than ourselves. In other words, an environmental ethic can only come about with the realization of the naturalness of being.

This does not take us very far into the ethics of development. It avoids saying what makes some actions good and others bad in an abstract, philosophical way, because the answers to this are not convincing. We merely conclude that an alternative ethic is derived from critically examining the human experience, talking about how we feel about it, and that it consists in exercising one's own freedom in a manner consistent with maximizing the freedom of others, valuing a variety of contributions to society and relating to nature as a natural being. Socialism is a form of politics in which such ethical principles can be realized, where development can be guided by ethics like these and a society achieved which regenerates such ethics in ever purer forms.

Bibliography

Aglietta, M. (1979) *A Theory of Capitalist Regulation*, London: New Left Books.

Althusser, L. and Balibar, E. (1970) *Reading Capital*, London: New Left Books.

Amin, S. (1972) 'Underdevelopment and Dependence in Black Africa', *Journal of Modern African Studies* 10: 503–24.

Amin, S. (1973) *Neo-Colonialism in West Africa*, New York: Monthly Review Press.

Amin, S. (1976) *Unequal Development*, New York: Monthly Review Press.

Amin, S. (1981) 'Underdevelopment and Dependence in Black Africa – Origins and Contemporary Forms', in D.L. Cohen and J. Daniel (eds) *Political Economy of Africa*, London: Longman, pp. 28–44.

Amin, S. (1989) *Eurocentrism*, New York: Monthly Review Press.

Anderson, P. (1979) *Lineages of the Absolutist State*, London: Verso.

Ardrey, R. (1970) *The Territorial Imperative*, New York: Atheneum.

Austen, R.A. (1987) *African Economic History: Internal Diplomacy and External Dependence*, Portsmouth, NH: Heinemann.

Balibar, E. (1970) 'The Basic Concepts of Historical Materialism' in L. Althusser and E. Balibar, *Reading Capital*, London: New Left Books.

Banaji, J. (1977) 'Modes of Production in a Materialist Conception of History', *Capital and Class* 3: 1–44.

Baran, P. (1977) *The Political Economy of Growth*, New York: Monthly Review Press.

Barnett, T. (1989) *Social and Economic Development*, New York: The Guilford Press.

Barone, C. (1983) 'Dependency, Marxist Theory, and Salvaging the Idea of Capitalism in South Korea', *Review of Radical Political Economics* 15(1): 41–67.

Beaud, M. (1983) *A History of Capitalism: 1500–1980*, New York: Monthly Review Press.

Belassa, B. (1981) *The Newly Industrializing Countries in the World Economy*, New York: Pergamon Press.

Benston, M. (1969) 'The Political Economy of Womens Liberation', *Monthly Review* 21(4) (September): 13–27.

Benton, T. (1986) *The Rise and Fall of Structural Marxism*, New York: St Martin's Press.

Bergquist, C. (ed.) (1984) *Labor in the Capitalist World Economy*, Beverly Hills: Sage Publications.

Bernal, M. (1987) *Black Athena: The Afroasiatic Roots of Classical Civilization*, Vol. 1: *The Fabrication of Ancient Greece 1785–1985*, New Brunswick, NJ: Rutgers University Press.

Bettelheim, C. (1972) 'Theoretical Comments', in A. Emmanuel (ed.) *Unequal Exchange: A Study of the Imperialism of Trade*, New York: Monthly Review Press, pp. 271–322.

Bhattucharya, S. (1954) *The East India Company and the Economy of Bengal from 1704 to 1740*, London: Luzac & Co.

Bienefeld, M. (1981) 'Dependence and the Newly Industrializing Countries (NICs): Towards a Reappraisal', in D. Seers (ed.) *Dependency Theory: A Critical Assessment*, London: Frances Pinter, pp. 79–96.

Blaut, J. (1977) 'Where Was Capitalism Born?' in R. Peet (ed.) *Radical Geography*, Chicago: Maaroufa Press, pp. 95–110.

Blaut, J.M. (1989) 'Colonialism and the Rise of Capitalism', *Science and Society* 53(3): 260–96.

Blomstrom, M. and Hettne, B. (1984) *Development Theory in Transition*, London: Zed Books.

Boeke, J.H. (1953) *Economics and Economic Policy of Dual Societies*, New York: Institute of Pacific Relations.

Booth, D. (1985) 'Marxism and Development Sociology: Interpreting the Impasse', *World Development* 13(7): 761–87.

Boserup, E. (1970) *Woman's Role in Economic Development*, New York: St Martin's Press.

Bradby, B. (1980) 'The Destruction of Natural Economy', in H. Wolpe (ed.) *The Articulation of Modes of Production*, London: Routledge & Kegan Paul, pp. 93–127.

Branford, S. and Kucinski, B. (1988) *The Debt Squads, the U.S., the Banks and Latin America*, Atlantic Highlands, NJ: Zed Books.

Braudel, F. (1972) *The Mediterranean and the Mediterranean World in the Age of Phillip II*, New York: Harper & Row.

Braudel, F. (1973) *Capitalism and Material Life, 1400–1800*, New York: Harper & Row.

Breitbart, M.M. (1981) 'Peter Kropotkin, the Anarchist Geographer', in D.R. Stoddart (ed.) *Geography, Ideology and Social Concern*, Oxford: Basil Blackwell, pp. 134–53.

Brenner, R. (1977) 'The Origins of Capitalist Development: A Critique of Neo-Smithian Marxism', *New Left Review* 104: 25–92.

Brenner, R. (1985) 'Agrarian Class Structure and Economic Development in Pre-Industrial Europe', in T.H. Aston and C.H.E. Philpin (eds) *The Brenner Debate*, Cambridge: Cambridge University Press, pp. 10–63.

Brewer, A. (1980) *Marxist Theories of Imperialism: A Critical Survey*, London: Routledge & Kegan Paul.

Browett, J.G. (1986) 'Industrialisation in the Global Periphery: The Significance of the Newly Industrialising Countries of East and South-east Asia', *Society and Space* 4: 401–18.

Buchanon, K. (1980) 'Delineation of the Third World', in I. Vogeler and A.R. deSouza (eds) *Dialectics of Third World Development*, Montclair, NJ: Allanheld, Osmun, pp. 28−51.

Caldwell, M. (1977) *The Wealth of Some Nations*, London: Zed Books.

Cardoso, F. and Faletto, R. (1979) *Dependency and Development*, Berkeley: University of California Press.

Cheng, N. (1976) 'Underdevelopment and the World Capitalist Structure: An Evaluation of Some Recent Studies', M.Sc. thesis, University of Salford, Department of Sociological and Political Studies.

Chilcote, R.H. (1984) *Theories of Development and Underdevelopment*, Boulder, Colo.: Westview Press.

Childe, V.C. (1951) *Man Makes Himself*, New York: Mentor Books.

Childe, V.G. (1954) *New Light on the Most Ancient East*, New York: Norton.

Cohen, B.J. (1973) *The Question of Imperialism*, New York: Basic Books.

Coontz, S. and Henderson, P. (1986) 'Property Forms, Political Power, and Female Labour in the Origins of Class and State Societies', in S. Coontz and P. Henderson (eds) *Women's Work, Men's Property*, London: Verso.

Corbridge, S. (1986) *Capitalist World Development: A Critique of Radical Development Geography*, Totowa, NJ: Rowan & Littlefield.

Corbridge, S. (1989) 'Marxism, Post-Marxism and the Geography of Development', in R. Peet and N. Thrift (eds) *New Models in Geography*, London: Unwin-Hyman, pp. 224−54.

Cornforth, M. (1953) *Materialism and the Dialetical Method*, New York: International Publishers.

Cutler, A., Hindess, B., Hirst, P. and Hussain, A. (1977−8) *Marx's Capital and Capitalism Today*, Vol. 2, London: Routledge & Kegan Paul.

Darwin, C. (1859) *The Origins of Species by Means of Natural Selection*, New York: Modern Library.

Davey, B. (1975) *The Economic Development of India*, Nottingham: Spokesman.

deJanvry, A. (1981) *The Agrarian Question and Reformism in Latin America*, Baltimore: Johns Hopkins University Press.

Della Costa, M. (1973) 'Women and the Subversion of the Community', in *The Power of Women and the Subversion of the Community*, Bristol: Falling Wall Press, pp. 19−54.

Deutsch, K. (1961) 'Social Mobilization and Political Development', *American Political Science Review* 60 (September): 463−515.

Dobb, M. (1963) *Studies in the Development of Capitalism*, London: Routledge & Kegan Paul.

Dobb, M. (1978) 'A Reply', in R. Hilton (ed.) *The Transition from Feudalism to Capitalism*, London: Verso, pp. 57−67.

Dodgshon, R.A. (1987) *The European Past: Social Evolution and Spatial Order*, London: Macmillan.

Dos Santos, T. (1969) 'The Crisis of Development Theory and the Problem of Dependency in Latin America', in H. Berstein (ed.) *Underdevelopment and Development*, Harmondsworth: Penguin.

Dos Santos, T. (1970) 'The Structure of Dependence', *American Economic Review* 60 (May): 231–6.

Dunford, M. and Perrons, D. (1983) *The Arena of Capital*, New York: St Martin's Press.

Eisenstadt, S.N. (1973a) *Tradition, Change and Modernity*, New York: John Wiley.

Eisenstadt, S.N. (1973b) 'Social Change and Development', in S.N. Eisenstadt (ed.) *Readings in Social Evolution and Development*, Oxford: Pergamon Press, pp. 3–33.

Eisenstadt, S.N. (1986) *The Origins and Diversity of Axial Age Civilizations*, Albany: State University of New York Press.

Eisenstadt, S.N. (1987) *European Civilization in a Comparative Perspective*, Oslo: Norwegian University Press.

Elliott, G. (1986) 'The Odyssey of Paul Hirst', *New Left Review* 159 (September): 81–105.

Emmanuel, A. (1972) *Unequal Exchange: A Study of the Imperialism of Trade*, New York: Monthly Review Press.

Engels, F. (1972) *The Origin of the Family, Private Property and the State*, New York: International Publishers.

Etienne, M. and Leacock, E. (eds) (1980) *Women and Colonization*, New York: Praeger.

Evans, P. (1984) *Dependent Development: The Alliance of Multinational, State and Local Capital in Brazil*, Princeton: Princeton University Press.

Fairbank, J.K. (1964) *Trade and Diplomacy on the China Coast*, Cambridge, Mass.: Harvard University Press.

Fairbank, J.K., Reischauer, E.O. and Craig, A.M. (1973) *East Asia: Tradition and Transformation*, London: George Allen & Unwin.

Fieldhouse, D.K. (1973) *Economics and Empire*, London: Weidenfeld & Nicolson.

Frank, A.G. (1969a) *Latin America: Underdevelopment or Revolution?*, New York: Monthly Review Press.

Frank, A.G. (1969b) *Capitalism and Underdevelopment in Latin America*, New York: Monthly Review Press.

Frank, A.G. (1979) *Dependent Accumulation and Underdevelopment*, New York: Monthly Review Press.

Frank, A.G. (1989) 'The Development of Underdevelopment', *Monthly Review* 41(2) (July): 37–51.

Franke, R.W. and Chasin, B. (1980) *Seeds of Famine*, Montclair, NJ: Allanheld, Osmun.

Friedman, J. and Rowlands, M.J. (1977) 'Notes Towards an Epigenetic Model of the Evolution of Civilization', in J. Friedman and M.I. Rowlands (eds) *The Evolution of Social Systems*, London: Duckworth 201–76.

Fuentes, A. and Ehrenreich, B. (1987) 'Women in the Global Factory', in R. Peet (ed.) *International Capitalism and Industrial Restructuring*, Boston: Allen Unwin: 201–15.

Furtado, C. (1963) *The Economic Growth of Brazil*, Berkeley: University of California Press.

Gakou, M.L. (1987) *The Crisis in African Agriculture*, Atlantic Highlands, NJ: Zed Books.

Galeano, E. (1973) *Open Veins of Latin America: Five Centuries of the Pillage of a Continent*, New York: Monthly Review Press.

Galtung, J. (1971) 'A Structural Theory of Imperialism', *Journal of Peace Research* 2: 81–116

George, S. (1988) *A Fate Worse Than Debt: The World Financial Crisis and the Poor*, New York: Grove Press.

Giddens, A. (1977) *Studies in Social and Political Theory*, New York: Basic Books.

Giddens, A. (1981) *A Contemporary Critique of Historical Materialism*, Berkeley: University of California Press.

Goldfrank, W.L. (1979) *The World-System of Capitalism: Past and Present*, London: Sage Publications.

Gould, M. (1987) *Revolution in the Development of Capitalism*, Berkeley: University of California Press.

Gould, P. (1964) 'A Note on Research into the Diffusion of Development', *Journal of Modern African Studies* 2: 123–5.

Gouldner, A. (1970) *Coming Crisis of Western Sociology*, New York: Basic Books.

Gramsci, A. (1971) 'Americanism and Fordism', in Q. Hoare and G.N. Smith (eds) *Selections from the Prison Notebooks of Antonio Gramsci*, New York: International Publishers, pp. 277–322.

Greenberg, M. (1951) *British Trade and the Opening of China: 1800–1842*, Cambridge: Cambridge University Press.

Hagen, E. (1962) *On the Theory of Social Change*, Homewood, Ill.: The Dorsey Press.

Hagerstrand, T. (1952) 'The Propagation of Innovation Waves', *Lund Studies in Geography*, Series B, No. 4.

Harris, N. (1986) *The End of the Third World*, Harmondsworth: Penguin.

Harrison, D. (1988) *The Sociology of Modernization and Development*, London: Unwin Hyman.

Hart-Landsberg, M. (1984) 'Capitalism and Third World Economic Development: A Critical Look at the South Korean "Miracle" ', *Review of Radical Political Economics* 16(2/3): 181–93.

Hart-Landsberg, M. (1987) 'South Korea: The Fraudulent Miracle', *Monthly Review* 39.

Hartmann, H. (n.d.) 'The Unhappy Marriage of Marxism and Feminism: Towards a More Progressive Union', in L. Sargent (ed.) *Women and Revolution*, Boston: South End Press.

Harvey, D. (1989) *The Condition of Post-Modernity*, Oxford: Basil Blackwell.

Hayter, T. (1981) *The Creation of World Poverty*, London: Pluto Press.

Hecksher, E.F. (1935) *Mercantilism*, 2 vols, London: Allen & Unwin.

Hegel, G.W.F. (1967) *The Phenomenology of Mind*, New York: Harper.

Heiser, C.B. (1981) *Seed to Civilization*, San Francisco: W.H. Freeman.

Henn, J. (1978) 'Peasants, Workers and Capital: The Political Economy of Labor and Incomes in Cameroon', Ph.D. thesis, Harvard University.

Henn, J. (1984) 'Women in the Rural Economy: Past, Present and Future', in J. Henn and S. Sticher (eds) *African Women South of the Sahara*, London: Longman, pp. 1–18.

Hindess, B. and Hirst, P. (1975) *Pre-capitalist Modes of Production*, London: Routledge & Kegan Paul.

Hindess, B. and Hirst, P. (1977) *Mode of Production and Social Formation: An Autocritique of Pre-Capitalist Modes of Production*, London: Macmillan.

Hirsch, J. (1978) 'The State Aparatus and Social Reproduction: Elements of a Theory of the Bourgeois State', in J. Holloway and S. Picciotto (eds) *State and Capital: A Marxist Debate*, London: Edward Arnold, pp. 57–107.

Hobsbawm, E. (1968) *Industry and Empire*, New York: Pantheon Books.

Hobson, J.A. (1902) *Imperialism: A Study*, London: Allen & Unwin.

Hofstadter, R. (1955) *Social Darwinism in American Thought*, Boston: Beacon Press.

Hoselitz, B. (1960) *Sociological Aspects of Economic Growth*, Glencoe: Free Press.

Huntington, E. (1915) *Civilization and Climate*, New Haven: Yale University Press.

Huntington, E. (1965) *Mainsprings of Civilization*, New York: John Wiley.

Huntington, S. (1975) 'Issues in Woman's Role in Economic Development Critique and Alternatives', *Journal of Marriage and the Family* 37: 1,001–12.

ILO (1984) *Statistical Yearbook*, Geneva: International Labour Organization.

ILO (1988) *Statistical Yearbook*, Geneva: International Labour Organization.

IMF (1985) *Survey* 21 January and 4 February.

IMF (1989) *World Economic Outlook*, Washington: International Monetary Fund.

Jackman, R.W. (1984) 'Dependence on Foreign Investment and Economic Growth in the Third World', in M.A. Seligson (ed.) *The Gap Between Rich and Poor: Contending Perspectives on the Political Economy of Development*, Boulder, Colo.: Westview Press, pp. 211–23.

Jaffe, H. (1985) *A History of Africa*, London: Zed Books.

Jagger, A.M. (1981) *Feminist Politics and Human Nature*, Sussex: Harvester Press.

Kaplan, G.H. (ed.) (1978) *Social Change in the Capitalist World Economy*, London: Sage Publications.

Kasaba, R. (1988) *The Ottoman Empire and the World Economy*, Albany: State University of New York.

Koning, H. (1976) *Columbus: His Enterprise*, New York: Monthly Review Press.

Laclau, E. (1971) 'Feudalism and Capitalism in Latin America', *New Left Review* 67 (May–June): 19–38.

Landsberg, M. (1979) 'Export-Led Industrialization in the Third World:

Manufacturing Imperialism', *Review of Radical Political Economics* 11(4): 50–63; reprinted in R. Peet (ed.) *International Capitalism and Industrial Restructuring*, Boston: Allen & Unwin, 1987: 216–39.

Leacock, E. (1972) 'Introduction' to F. Engels *The Origin of the Family, Private Property and the State*, New York: International Publishers, pp. 7–67.

Leacock, E. (1982) 'Relations of Production in Band Society', in E. Leacock and R. Lee (eds) *Politics and History in Band Societies*, Cambridge: Cambridge University Press, pp. 159–70.

Leacock, E. and Lee, R. (1982) *Politics and History in Band Societies*, Cambridge: Cambridge University Press.

Lee, R. (1982) 'Politics, Sexual and Non-Sexual, in an Egalitarian Society', in E. Leacock and R. Lee (eds) *Politics and History in Band Societies*, Cambridge: University Press, pp. 37–59.

Lenin, V.I. (1975) *Imperialism, the Highest Stage of Capitalism*, Peking: Foreign Language Press.

Lerner, G. (1986) *The Creation of Patriarchy*, New York: Oxford University Press.

Lipietz, A. (1985) *The Enchanted World*, London: Verso.

Lipietz, A. (1986) 'New Tendencies in the International Division of Labor: Regimes of Accumulation and Modes of Regulation', in A. Scott and M. Storper (eds) *Production, Work, Territory*, Boston: Allen & Unwin, pp. 16–40.

Lipietz, A. (1987) *Mirages and Miracles*, London: Verso.

Liss, S. (1984) *Marxist Thought in Latin America*, Berkeley: Univeristy of California Press.

Long, N. (1975) 'Structural Dependency, Modes of Production and Economic Brokerage in Peru', in I. Oxaal, A. Barnett and D. Booth (eds) *Beyond the Sociology of Development*, London: Routledge & Kegan Paul.

Luxemburg, R. (1951) *The Accumulation of Capital*, London: Routledge & Kegan Paul.

McClelland, D.C. (1961) *The Achieving Society*, Princeton, NJ: D. Van Nostrand.

McClelland, D.C. and Winter, D.G. (1971) *Motivating Economic Achievement*, New York: The Free Press.

Magdoff, H. (1982) 'Imperialism: A Historical Survey', in H. Alavi and T. Shanin (eds) *Introduction to the Sociology of 'Developing Societies'*, New York: Monthly Review Press, pp. 11–28.

Mandel, E. (1969) *Marxist Economic Theory*, New York: Monthly Review Press.

Marx, K. (1970) 'Preface' in *A Contribution to the Critique of Political Economy*, Moscow: Progress Publishers, pp. 19–23.

Marx, K. (1973) *Grundrisse*, Harmondsworth: Penguin.

Marx, K. (1976) *Capital*, Vol. 1, Harmondsworth: Penguin.

Marx, K. (1981) *Capital*, Vol. 2, Harmondsworth: Penguin.

Marx, K. (1983) *Capital*, Vol. 3, Harmondsworth: Penguin.

Marx, K. and Engels, F. (1981) *The German Ideology*, New York: International Publishers.

Meier, G. (1970) *Leading Issues in Economic Development*, London: Oxford University Press.

Meillasoux, C. (1972) 'From Reproduction to Production', *Economy and Society* 1(1): 93–105.

Melotti, U. (1977) *Marx and the Third World*, London: Macmillan.

Mies, M. (1986) *Patriarchy and Accumulation on a World Scale*, London: Zed Books.

Mitchell, B.R. (1988) *British Historical Statistics*, Cambridge: Cambridge University Press.

Mitchell, J. (1966) 'Women: The Longest Revolution', *New Left Review* 40 (November–December): 11–37.

Moghadem, F.L. (1988) 'Nomadic Invasions and the Development of Productive Forces: An Historical Study of Iran (1000–1800)', *Science and Society* 52(4): 389–412.

Mommsen, W.J. (1980) *Theories of Imperialism*, Chicago: University of Chicago Press.

Morten, P. (1971) 'A Woman's Work is Never Done', in E. Altbach (ed.) *From Feminism to Liberation*, Cambridge Mass.: Schenkman, pp. 211–27.

Mukherjee, R. (1974) *The Rise and Fall of the East India Company*, New York: Monthly Review Press.

Munch, R; (1987) 'Parsonian Theory Today: In Search of a New Synthesis', in A. Giddens and J.H. Turner (eds) *Social Theory Today*, Cambridge: Polity Press, pp. 116–55.

Nash, J. and Fernandez-Kelly, M.P. (eds) (1983) *Women, Men, and the International Division of Labor*, Albany: State University Press.

Newman, P.C. (1952) *The Development of Economic Thought*, New York: Prentice Hall.

Ollman, B. (1976) *Alienation: Marx's Conception of Man in Capitalist Society*, Cambridge: Cambridge University Press.

Palma, G. (1978) 'Dependency: A Formal Theory of Underdevelopment or a Methodology for the Analysis of Concrete Situations of Underdevelopment?', *World Development* 6: 881–924.

Palma, G. (1981) 'Dependency and Development: A Critical Overview', in D. Seers (ed.) *Dependency Theory: A Critical Assessment*, London: Frances Pinter, pp. 20–78.

Parsons, T. (1948) *The Structure of Social Action*, New York: McGraw-Hill.

Parsons, T. (1951) *The Social System*, Glencoe: The Free Press.

Parsons, T. (1960) *Structure and Process in Modern Societies*, Glencoe: The Free Press.

Parsons, T. (1961) 'Some Considerations on the Theory of Social Change', *Rural Sociology* 26(3): 219–39.

Parsons, T. (1966) *Societies: Evolutionary and Comparative Perspectives*, Englewood Cliffs, NJ: Prentice Hall.

Parsons, T. (1971) *The System of Modern Societies*, Englewood Cliffs, NJ: Prentice-Hall.

Parsons, T. and Shils, E. (1951) *Towards a General Theory of Action*, Cambridge, Mass.: Harvard University Press.

Parsons, T. and Smelser, N.J. (1956) *Economy and Society*, London: Routledge & Kegan Paul.

Pearse, A. (1975) *The Latin American Peasant*, London: Frank Cass.

Peet, R. (1985a) 'The Social Origins of Environmental Determinism', *Annals Association of American Geographers* 75(3): 309–33.

Peet, R. (1985b) 'Introduction to the Life and Thought of Karl Wittfogel', *Antipode* 17(1): 3–20.

Peet, R. (1987) *International Capitalism and Industrial Restructuring*, Boston: Allen & Unwin.

Peet, R. (1988) 'Review of *Capitalist World Development* by Stuart Corbridge', *Economic Geography* 64(2) (April): 190–2.

Peet, R. (1989a) 'The Destruction of Regional Culture', in R.J. Johnston and Peter Taylor (eds) *The World in Crisis?* 2nd edn, Oxford: Basil Blackwell.

Peet, R. (1989b) 'Conceptual Problems in Neo-Marxist Industrial Geography', *Antipode* 21(1): 35–50.

Piore, M. and Sabel, C. (1984) *The Second Industrial Divide*, New York: Basic Books.

Pirenne, H. (1936) *Economic and Social History of Medieval Europe*, London: K. Paul, Trench, Trubner.

Pollin, R. (1989) 'The Abyss of Third World Debt', *Monthly Review* 40(10): 54–60.

Post, K. (1978) *Arise Ye Starvlings*, The Hague: Martin Nijhoff.

Quani, M. (1982) *Geography and Marxism*, Oxford: Basil Blackwell.

Republic of China (1988) *Statistical Yearbook*, Taipai: Republic of China.

Rey, P.-P. (1973) *Les Alliances de Classes*, Paris: Maspero.

Rhodes, R.I. (ed.) (1970) *Imperialism and Underdevelopment*, New York: Monthly Review Press.

Riddell, J.B. (1970) *The Spatial Dynamics of Modernization in Sierra Leone: Structure, Diffusion and Response*, Evanston, Ill.: Northwestern University Press.

Roches, G. (1975) *Talcott Parsons and American Sociology*, New York: Barnes & Noble.

Rodney, W. (1974) *How Europe Underdeveloped Africa*, Washington, DC: Howard University Press.

Rogers, B. (1980) *The Domestication of Women: Discrimination in Developing Societies*, London: Tavistock Publications.

Rostow, W.W. (1960) *The Stages of Economic Growth: A Non-Communist Manifesto*, Cambridge: Cambridge University Press.

Ruyle, E. (1988) 'Anthropology for Marxists: Prehistoric Revolutions', *Nature, Society and Thought* 1(4): 469–99.

Saffioti, H. (1978) *Women in Class Society*, New York: Monthly Review Press.

Sanday, P. (1981) *Female Power and Male Dominance*, Cambridge: Cambridge University Press.

Sauer, C. (1952) *Agricultural Origins and Dispersals*, New York: American Geographical Society.

Schumpeter, J. (1952) *The Sociology of Imperialism*, New York: Kelly.

Scott, A. (1988) 'Flexible Production Systems and Regional Development: The Rise of New Industrial Spaces in North America and Western Europe', *International Journal of Urban and Regional Research* 12: 171–86.

Scott, A. and Storper, M. (eds) (1986) *Production, Work, Territory*, Boston: Allen & Unwin.

Scott, J. (1976) *The Moral Economy of the Peasant*, New Haven: Yale University Press.

Seccombe, W. (1983) 'Marxism and Demography', *New Left Review* 137: 22–47.

Semple, E.C. (1903) *American History and its Geographic Conditions*, Boston: Houghton-Mifflin.

Semple, E.C. (1911) *Influences of Geographic Environment on the Basis of Ratzel's System of Anthropo-Geography*, New York: Russell & Russell.

Simmons, I.G. (1989) *Changing the Face of the Earth: Culture, Environment, History*, Oxford: Basil Blackwell.

Slater, D. (1973) 'Geography and Underdevelopment-1', *Antipode*, 5(3): 21–32.

Soja, E.W. (1968) *The Geography of Modernization in Kenya: A Spatial Analysis of Social, Economic and Political Change*, Syracuse: Syracuse University Press.

Spencer, H. (1882) *The Principles of Sociology*, New York: D. Appleton.

Spriggs, M. (ed.) (1984) *Marxist Perspectives in Archaeology*, Cambridge: Cambridge University Press.

Stavrianos, L.S. (1981) *Global Rift: The Third World Comes of Age*, New York: William Morrow.

Storper, M. and Scott, A. (1989) 'The Geographical Foundations and Social Regulation of Flexible Production Complexes', in J. Wolch and M. Dear (eds) *The Power of Geography*, Boston: Unwin Hyman, pp. 19–40.

Sunkel, D. (1972) 'Big Business and "Dependencia"', *Foreign Affairs* 50 (April): 517–31.

Sutcliffe, R.B. (1971) *Industry and Underdevelopment*, Reading, Mass.: Addison Wesley.

Sweezy, P. (1978) 'A Critique', in R. Hilton (ed.) *The Transition from Feudalism to Capitalism*, London: Verso, pp. 33–56.

Szentes, T. (1976) *The Political Economy of Underdevelopment*, 3rd edn, Budapest: Akademia Kiado.

Szymanski, A. (1981) *The Logic of Imperialism*, New York: Praeger.

Taylor, J.G. (1979) *From Modernization to Modes of Production*, London: Macmillan.

Taylor, P.J. (1985) *Political Geography: World Economy, Nation-State and Locality*, London: Longman.

Thomas, C. (1974) *Dependence and Transformation: The Economics of the Transition to Socialism*, New York: Monthly Review Press.

Thompson, E.P. (1978) *The Poverty of Theory and other Essays*, New York: Monthly Review Press.

Timpanaro, S. (1975) *On Materialism*, London: New Left Books.

Toynbee, A. (1976) *Mankind and Mother Earth*, New York: Oxford University Press.

UNIDO (1975) *Lima Declaration of Plan and Action*, New York: United Nations.

UNIDO (1979) *World Industry Since 1960: Progress and Prospects*, New York: United Nations.

Van Allen, J. (1974) 'Memsahib, Militante, Femme Libre: Political and Apolitical Styles of Modern African Women', in J. Jaquette (ed.) *Women in Politics*, New York: Wiley, pp. 304–21.

Vogel, L. (1983) *Marxism and the Oppression of Women*, New Brunswick, NJ: Rutgers University Press.

Wallerstein, I. (1974) *The Modern World System*, Vol. 1, New York: Academic Press.

Wallerstein, I. (1979) *The Capitalist World Economy*, New York: Cambridge University Press.

Wallerstein, I. (1980) *The Modern World System*, Vol. 2, New York: Academic Press.

Wallerstein, I. (1988) *The Modern World System*, Vol. 3, New York: Academic Press.

Warren, B. (1980) *Imperialism: Pioneer of Capitalism*, London: New Left Books.

Watts, M. (1983a) *Silent Violence: Food, Famine and Peasantry in Northern Nigeria*, Berkeley: University of California Press.

Watts, M. (1983b) 'Hazards and Crisis: A Political Economy of Drought and Famine in Northern Nigeria', *Antipode* 15(1): 24–34.

Weisskopf, T.E. (1976) 'Dependence as an Explanation of Underdevelopment: A Critique', ms, University of Michigan.

Wenke, R.J. (1984) *Patterns in Pre-History*, New York: Oxford University Press.

Whyte, W.H. (1968) 'Imitation or Innovation: Reflections on the Institutional Development of Peru', *Administrative Science Quarterly* 13(3): 370–85.

Williams, E. (1944) *Capitalism and Slavery*, Chapel Hill: University of North Carolina Press.

Wittfogel, K. (1957) *Oriental Despotism*, New Haven: Yale University Press.

Wittfogel, K. (1985) 'Geopolitics, Geographical Materialism and Marxism', *Antipode* 17(1): 21–72.

Wolf, E. (1982) *Europe and the People Without History*, Berkeley: University of California Press.

Wolpe, H. (1972) 'Capitalism and Cheap Labour–Power in South Africa; From Segregation to Apartheid', *Economy and Society* 1(4): 425–56.

Wolpe, H. (ed.) (1980) *The Articulation of Modes of Production*, London: Routledge.

Wood, E.M. (1986) *The Retreat from Class*, London: Verso.

World Bank (1989) *World Development Report 1989*, New York: Oxford Univeristy Press.

Yapa, L. (1977) 'Innovation Diffusion and Economic Involution', *Antipode* 9(2) (September): 20–9.

Zeitlin, I.M. (1972) *Capitalism and Imperialism: An Introduction to Neo-Marxism Concepts*, Chicago: Markham Publishing Co.

Index

948001